P9-CFQ-965

GUNS FREEDOM ☆☆AND ☆☆ TERRORISM

Guns Freedom ☆☆and☆☆ Terrorism

Wayne LaPierre

WND BOOKS
Nashville
A Division of Thomas Nelson, Inc.
www.WNDBooks.com

Published in Nashville, Tennessee, by Thomas Nelson, Inc.

ISBN 0-7852-6221-0

Printed in the United States of America

03 04 05 06 07 BVG 6 5 4 3 2

For Charlton Heston

Who has never lost sight of what is important
in life—faith, family, and freedom.

Thank you for accepting the call and having the
courage to change history. And thank you for serving
as a daily reminder of what it truly means
to be an American.

CONTENTS

FOREWORD: INTERVIEW BY RUSH LIMBAUGH

The following is taken from an interview conducted by renowned radio talk show host Rush Limbaugh of Wayne LaPierre originally published in the July 2002 edition of *The Limbaugh Letter*:

RUSH: Let me start off by asking you a general overview question. As you look at the lay of the land today, where do you see the Second Amendment and its strength or frailty? How goes the cause?

LAPIERRE: I think the next couple years are going to be very challenging for any group of Americans that cares about maintaining individual, personal freedom. Not only the Second Amendment, but the entirety of the Bill of Rights. Due to terrorism, as our freedoms are increasingly challenged with enhanced security, with eavesdropping, it will get tougher for people to hold on to fundamental freedom and privacy.

RUSH: Are you surprised that in the latest opinion polls anywhere from 70 to 80 percent of Americans say they are willing to endure potential losses of freedoms and liberties in order to ensure security and safety against terrorist threats?

LAPIERRE: I think those figures are in the abstract. The more we get to a situation where as a nation privacy becomes a luxury and freedom is suspect, the more we find that the government distrusts us, the more we find people frisked and x-rayed and finger-printed and strip-searched, I think people will begin to mobilize and stand up for the freedoms that made this nation different from every other nation in the world. The very essence of America is our great individual freedoms that we have as citizens. American freedom is the most precious way of life the world has ever known.

What I love about working for the NRA is that we have a pact with our membership, and with a much larger nucleus of people who support the organization, to stand up for these great individual personal freedoms every day. And I have confidence that when the chips are down, the American public will rally for their freedoms. We all learned about the Bill of Rights in school. We need, as a nation, to live the Bill of Rights as adults. If you look through history, you see that societies which have been willing to trade freedom for the illusion of security, simply end up with less freedom, and not more security.

RUSH: We now have, arguably, the most sympathetic possible administration to such concerns. Is there anything about this administration that alarms you in this area?

LAPIERRE: Well, I don't know that we've crossed the line yet in terms of where we are. We all support doing everything we can to stop terrorism. We support our government's effort. The president has been placed in an incredibly difficult position. Part of this effort to fight terrorism will be driven by new technologies in the future. It's absolutely amazing when you start looking at the technology out there. For example, you can identify people by the force profiles of their feet as they're walking, the specks of their irises, the color spectrum of their skin. You've got computers programmed to recognize movement associated with criminal behavior. It's getting to the point where some think they can look at your face on a computer and decide what's in your heart. There's tremendous pressure from companies that are marketing these products, from people who don't understand that we need to preserve our freedoms, and from politicians who somehow think they can take care of us better than we can take care of ourselves, to put this stuff online. We know from history what can be lost, but no one's figured out how to get it back. If we get to the point where we've turned over our identity and our free speech to our government in the name of security, what else do we have left?

RUSH: Has it happened yet? In this particular war on terrorism, can you name any of these specific freedoms and liberties that we have lost, or are on the verge of losing, that we might not get back? We lost a lot during World War II. We had gas rationing, to mention one. But a lot of those were restored. What makes you think that future losses might not be restored?

LAPIERRE: Let's look at other societies. The United States is in many ways the last society in the world in which we have our individual freedoms intact. Look at what they're doing in England right now, where each day citizens are photographed thousands of times, over and over and over again. There's not another country with the extent of individual personal freedom that we enjoy as United States citizens. We got to where we are because Americans throughout the years have had this extraordinary commitment to personal freedom. Yet you run into politicians and others who seem to be freedom-fearing Americans rather than freedom-loving Americans. They believe that people can't be trusted, that society is better served by a diminished access to freedom. And that only the privileged—and I get back to the Second Amendment here—the rock stars, the politicians, the people with friends in high places, the Rosie O'Donnells with their body guards, have the right to personal freedoms. Everyone else is second class and does not matter. What we, the NRA, are going to emphasize is that the true patriot is someone who believes in the sanctity of American freedom as defined by the Bill of Rights, not someone who fears freedom or tries to redefine freedom.

RUSH: Let me read to you some comments you made to the CPAC [Conservative Political Action Committee] conference back in March, as excerpted in *The Washington Post.* These are your tough words about the new airport security procedures: "You see red-faced, teary-eyed, fifteen-year-old girls enduring security wands orbiting their breasts while electronic squeals detect the metal in their underwire bras. You see grandmothers shaken down and stripped of their cuticle clippers and knitting needles. You see grandfathers, men who likely fought or lost loved ones for this country, in various stages of undress. You see women cringe as security men let their wands linger between their legs. I guess it's okay to wand-rape someone's daughter in public, but no profiling. No, we don't want to risk offending an Islamic ex-con with two aliases and no job, paying cash for a one-way airline ticket with no luggage, whose shoes are packed with plastic explosives. Who're we fooling? Terrorists fit into fairly narrow categories of gender, age, nationality, and religion." You also singled out the Bush Administration for allowing the airport profiling-ban charade. What reaction did you get at CPAC?

LAPIERRE: I had a lot of people whispering to me that they agreed, but because of political correctness, they didn't want to say it publicly. Almost unanimously I had people in the military and law enforcement people telling me that they completely agreed. There's not a law enforcement person in the nation who thinks you're going to stop terrorism, or you're going to stop crime, by pulling over an eighty-year-old grandmother and frisking her and detaining her. You can't stop crime and you can't stop terrorism by harassing the people who are not committing crime, and the people who are not involved in terrorism.

RUSH: Is this being purposely done to intimidate, or is this just incompetence?

LAPIERRE: It's window dressing to pretend that we're being tougher—to pretend that we're "doing something." The fact is we know, and every law enforcement person will tell you, that terrorism is fairly narrowly defined in terms of who is committing it. If we were dealing with the Irish Republican Army, we'd be looking for a Catholic white guy. On the other hand, if we're dealing with Islamic nations, the suspects are Middle Eastern. Some people call that profiling. Law enforcement people would call it a clue. You add that clue on top of a one-way ticket with cash and similar details and you come up with a traveler profile that can be much more narrow than the useless task of pulling over General Joe Foss, 86, and confiscating his Medal of Honor, or stripping down Congressman John Dingell at Reagan National Airport. That doesn't accomplish anything. It doesn't make anybody any safer. It's simply nonsense. The law enforcement people know that; the airline people know it; and the pilots know it. That's why the pilots are so adamant about being armed right now.

RUSH: Do you think it's going to happen?

LAPIERRE: I would sure hope it would happen, Rush. I don't think there's any doubt that properly trained airline pilots will make everyone on that airplane safer if they're armed. It will give hijackers pause. It will give everyone on board a greater sense of security and give them a chance to live. The key question is: Knowing what you know now, looking back on September 11th, don't you wish those pilots were armed? How can anyone say no? Yet, for some reason Transportation Secretary Norm Mineta and Transportation Security Administration Director John Magaw are against it. I can't explain it. But the public wants this to happen. The pilots want this to happen. And it needs to happen for all of our security when we fly.

RUSH: It's not as though there's no one boarding airplanes armed today. People get on airplanes every day carrying weapons.

LAPIERRE: That's true. Yes, you have military and law enforcement people doing that every day. The pilots used to do it prior to 1986. It wasn't until '86 that we started making pilots go through metal detectors at airports. Before that, many of them, being former military, used to carry a firearm with them when they boarded that plane as the pilot.

When the airplane leaves the ground, the pilot is the law. Only a small percentage of flights have a sky marshal on board. The pilots propose never leaving the cockpit with the firearm. They simply want to use it as a last resort if a terrorist is breaking through the cockpit door, to give them a chance to save that plane and everyone on board before they're shot down by the military. Right now, we're giving them a crash axe and instructions to move the food cart crossways in the aisle.

RUSH: Senator Hollings says that the idea of a pilot being armed is simply an invitation to a terrorist to get on board that airplane, because the weapon is already there. They don't even have to carry it on.

LAPIERRE: The fact they're *not* armed is an invitation to a terrorist.

RUSH: What's the primary objection opponents are offering? Is it damage to the pressurization system? Is it the chance for accidental injury to an innocent passenger? What is it?

LAPIERRE: Rush, what I've seen so far is from two camps. One camp is the same small group that simply fears firearms, and doesn't want anybody to have a firearm or use a firearm for self-defense, whether homeowner or airline pilot. The other camp is in the corporate offices of these airline companies. It's a lot of elitism. Behind the scenes they're more than willing to whisper that they don't trust their own pilots, that they think they're cowboys and they think they're hotheads. That's the whispering campaign going on behind the pilots' backs on Capitol Hill. It's crazy—every time we board a plane we put our life in these pilots' hands. I trust the pilots a lot more than I trust some bureaucrats sitting in the Department of Transportation or some corporate executive sitting in an airline office.

RUSH: That is really silly for airline executives to be undercutting their own pilots in this way up on Capitol Hill.

LAPIERRE: That's exactly what's going on, though. I think it's ridiculous. I want the pilots to end up winning this, because as someone who flies every week, I think it's important for all of our safety. It's not a question of the firearm being a danger to the plane. There are plenty of bullets designed specifically not to penetrate the wall of an airplane. There is birdshot in a gel. In fact, now they've even proven that just a regular, normal firearm bullet would not be a problem if it went through the skin of the plane.

RUSH: All of this criticism of airline security procedures boils down to criticism of the Bush Administration. Are you taking any heat from conservatives for that?

LAPIERRE: We have been outspoken on this from the very start. We have simply viewed it as speaking the truth. That's what I love about the NRA. The NRA stands on principle for what it believes in. We're simply a large group of individuals who defend individual rights and take stands on principle, and plant our flag and say here's what we believe. We support the president on many, many things. On this particular subject I think Mr. Mineta and Mr. Magaw are wrong. And we have told the administration.

RUSH: Are you taking any heat over that, though? I ask this because I've had my own occasion to be critical and I take a ration of criticism from people who say to me, "Look, you're only helping the Democrats who want to unseat this administration. You're only helping them out. It's better than Clinton ever was, so be quiet." I just wonder if you're getting any of that. And if so, does it affect you at all?

LAPIERRE: We're prepared to take it. There are some people who say that, but I don't think that gets you anywhere in Washington, to tell you the truth. And I don't think it gets you anywhere with the American public. The public respects those who stand up for what they believe in, and who don't play this Washington game. We're not in Washington to be popular at cocktail parties. I could care less whether I'm ever on the "A-list" at Washington cocktail parties. What I care most about is whether I can look people straight in the eye, whether it's in Maine or Kansas or Texas or Wyoming or Florida, or anywhere around the country, and say, "We fought for what you believe in and what you wanted us to fight for." That's what it's about with us. I think that's why we have been pretty darn successful overall as an organization.

RUSH: Let me ask you about that, because I spoke to you soon after the so-called "Million Mom March" in the spring of 2000. At that time you said that you had gained over a million members in the previous twelve months, and you were the fastest growing association in the country at that time. Now we've got a Republican in the White House, and with that I think the threat to the Second Amendment is perceived, anyway, to be lessened. Has your membership growth kept up or has it slowed down a little bit now with a Republican in power?

LAPIERRE: Our membership is hanging right around four million members. I consider that a tremendous accomplishment. I was worried about a big drop-off because of apathy. I thank people all over the country for realizing it's important to remain vigilant. Meanwhile, the last Million Mom March missed the mark by about 999,800 marchers. They've laid off 30 of their 35 employees. But the NRA is thriving because ultimately people in this country believe they have a right to own a firearm. It should be their choice, not a politician's, not the government, not Sarah Brady or Michael Barnes or Andrew McKelvey, the new billionaire funding the anti-gun movement. They believe it's their freedom, and they've hung in there with the NRA.

One of the reasons they continue to support the NRA is they see free people around the world being systematically disarmed. You look at England, you look at Australia. My gosh, the worst public shootings during the last year occurred in nations that have the most restrictive gun laws. If you look at England, crime has skyrocketed. Gun crimes are up 40 percent. In Australia, armed robberies are up 51 percent. Meanwhile, here in the United States, an increasing number of states—we're up to 33 now—have given law-abiding people the right to carry a firearm to protect themselves, and crime has gone down. But at the bottom of that is a very vigilant American public that defends their freedoms to own firearms—and is increasingly taking a stand for the entirety of the Bill of Rights.

That is why I think a lot of politicians are going to see this campaign finance issue backfire this November. Though they think they may have cast a cute little Washington political inside-the-beltway vote, they actually are going to find the American public outraged that they created a privileged, favored class of speech in this country for media conglomerates and politicians above that of the American people as a whole.

RUSH: I'm with you 100 percent on this. And frankly I have been stunned, and I spent hours on my program trying to alert people to what this campaign bill really was, that it was a direct assault from the political class on free speech during elections. This is precisely the kind of speech [America's] founders primarily meant when they wrote the free-speech clause. I was amazed at such apathy. Some people who called me about it had actually fallen for the notion that, well, we've got to do whatever we can, Rush, to get the money out of politics. John McCain had convinced people that money was corrupting Congress, that they were just innocent, God-fearing citizens, representing their elected constituencies, but here comes this money and it corrupts them, so they had to get the money out of the system. But this bill was never going to get money out of the system. Actually it's going to hide where the money is coming from and how much there is. I hope you're right about the public being outraged. On ABC's *This Week* on May 20, you expressed your disappointment with McCain for his assault of the First Amendment. And McCain, in the same program, described the NRA as just "another special interest group." How is campaign finance reform going to affect your group's ability to express itself? And what are the odds that McCain's bill to impose stricter background checks is going to go anywhere? Because that's something he proposed on that show as well.

LAPIERRE: Right after September 11, John McCain and Americans for Gun Safety began to capitalize on the terrorist attacks. This was probably the most crass act of political opportunism I've ever seen. To resuscitate the gun control agenda, they tried to link lawful gun shows to terrorism. They basically make the absurd claim that groups like Hamas and Hezbollah, which are state-sponsored terrorist cabals, are buying one shotgun or pistol at a time from a gun show in, say, Dearborn, Michigan. Under the McCain-Lieberman legislation to fix the so-called gun-show "loophole," background checks will take anywhere from three to seven days, though gun shows only last forty-eight hours. The ultimate goal is to run gun shows out of business. The NRA will aggressively fight this.

As to campaign finance, if you take away the ability of any group to respond to politicians or the media conglomerates with paid media, there's no incentive for the politicians to 'fess up to the truth at all. They'll simply be unchallenged. Not to mention that the whole national dialogue in this country is made possible by the right of groups and American citizens to buy time. The idea of going to a street corner and shouting your point of view is far out of date in America. You take away the right to buy ads and you'll whisper in the wind. That's why I say these politicians want to shut everybody up. And so do the media conglomerates. The question that we're asking—and we were the first, and I'm proud of it, to bring suit against the McCain-Feingold bill—is: Why are the First Amendment rights of media conglomerates any more important than the people's rights?

These big media conglomerates, and I'm talking about Viacom that owns CBS, Paramount, MTV, Showtime, Comedy Central, Paramount Theme Parks, Simon & Schuster, AOL Time Warner owning a whole other chunk, *The Washington Post, The New York Times,* Disney owning another big chunk, and General Electric owning NBC. All those companies spend millions of dollars lobbying Congress every year for what they want. The way the McCain-Feingold bill works is, if you own the network you can say whatever you want. You can spend millions and millions of dollars on programming around your pet cause and your pet politician and it's all allowed. And yet, for the American public as a whole and groups throughout the United States, we are prohibited from running ads criticizing a politician involving a piece of legislation in Congress or talking about a campaign sixty days prior to a general election and thirty days prior to a primary. It stinks. The very fact that Congress has given up on this, and the president has given up on this, and now we're forced to go to the Judiciary to reaffirm our most basic rights as American citizens, is just ridiculous.

RUSH: What are your odds in court?

LAPIERRE: I think they're pretty good. Any way you look at this, if McCain-Feingold is allowed to stand, it guts the First Amendment. Five years from now when kids are taught about the Bill of Rights and free speech in this country, they're going to have to look up McCain-Feingold, not the First Amendment. I'm pretty optimistic, although I don't want to take it for granted. The other thing the bill does is, in effect, give these media conglomerates legislative authority to issue speech licenses around McCain-Feingold. So ABC, NBC, CBS, and CNN can invite anyone on their network for hours of programming—or AOL Time Warner on their website. Rosie O'Donnell, we all know, was all over AOL Time Warner's website in support of Al Gore and bashing George Bush. All of that will still be allowed. In effect, if you own the media, you'll have a speech license to exempt anyone from McCain-Feingold. Maybe I'm naive, but I've got to believe that when the Supreme Court looks at this, maybe there's still a fundamental belief that the Bill of Rights means something. I wish George Bush had said on nationwide American television: "Look, I favor campaign finance reform, but let me tell you this—I favor personal freedom, and if it comes to a choice between campaign finance reform and our Constitutional freedoms, our freedoms come first."

RUSH: Why didn't he do that? I was hoping for the same thing. He's got this unique ability to persuade people because they trust him and believe him. I was longing for that speech. He could have said, "I sent instructions to the Republicans when I was campaigning. I wouldn't sign campaign finance reform if it contained the following. I'm not signing it. I'm going to send it back until they fix it." Why wouldn't he do that, Wayne?

LAPIERRE: I don't know. I think he decided if Congress didn't have the guts to stand up for it, he wasn't going to get in the way of that speeding train and he'd let the [Supreme] Court sort it out.

RUSH: But they were waiting for him.

LAPIERRE: I wish he'd done something different. He did say in his signing announcement that he thought major parts of it were unconstitutional. I wish he had vetoed it, to tell you the truth. And the American public would have been with him.

RUSH: Let me tell you! And that would have helped build his base and his constituency, and it would have led to informing more people about what was at stake. Oh, it was an opportunity.

Let's talk about something I think is good. I want to take you back to the presidential campaign and the debates. I was stunned because I didn't expect it. Al Gore made an entirely un-Democrat-like statement on gun control: he defended hunters, he defended the right of law-abiding people to own guns. Democrats had to have had polling data showing they were on the wrong side of this issue. Then two months ago, *USA Today* ran an article titled "Democrats Divided Over Gun Issue." It reported that Zell Miller addressed an NRA meeting and declared outright that gun owners in states like Arkansas, Tennessee, and West Virginia had cost Gore the election. He said that your 4.2 million members are "the epitome of mainstream America." It seems Democrats know they're losing on this issue. Now I know you don't want to get complacent, but do you see a reason for optimism in all this?

LAPIERRE: In the short term, I see some politicians understanding the politics of the issue and seeing it clearly for the first time in a long time. About four or five months ago I was at, of all places, Harvard, at the Kennedy School of Government. The other speaker was the AFL-CIO head. Polling shows that gun ownership in union households runs from a low of 48 percent in California to a high of 90 percent in states like West Virginia. And in most of your states in the heartland of the country it's somewhere in the 60s, 70s, and 80s. And in the 2000 presidential election, the polling shows, over half of union households that own firearms defected to Bush from Gore based on the gun issue. There's the election right there.

So at Harvard they asked the head of the AFL-CIO, "What's your advice to Democrats on guns?" And he said, "They should just shut the heck up."

I always thought it was crazy, this elite Democratic Party power structure in Washington trying to ban people's guns, make everyone take a federally mandated test before they could own a gun, sue the American gun industry out of business (as President Clinton was trying to do), and to ridicule people who own guns and go hunting. It's just pure elitism, and it cuts to the

heart of the Democratic base in much of the heartland of the country. And Zell Miller told his pollsters, "You are asking your gun questions all wrong." He said, go ask people, "When you hear a politician talk about gun control and he wants to ban your guns, do you think he doesn't understand your values and your way of life?" And 75 percent of the people said yes. And that's the answer.

The American public sees right through the push for gun control as pure elitism on the part of the privileged, because they're always going to have their guns. They're always going to have their bodyguards. They're always going to get their permits. Look at New York City. All the Mayor's buddies and people with wealth have always gotten their permits historically. And yet the Bill of Rights and the Second Amendment was written for the man on the street, the average citizen. Again, that's what I love about the NRA, because that's who we stand up for.

I believe that the Democratic party may have gotten the message that it makes no political sense for them to be trying to pick up that failed Clinton agenda. President Clinton and Al Gore spent eight years trying to center the gun issue. They even said they were going to make the 2000 election a referendum on guns. They did, and it cost them the presidency. I think the much more likely prototype of where we're headed in the future is the Mark Warner gubernatorial campaign in Virginia, where he said he favors the Second Amendment. We'll just have to hold him to it.

RUSH: The Bush Justice Department came out with its "new" interpretation of the Second Amendment, which is a return to the original one. How do you think it's going to affect current legislation and enforcement, and your mission at the NRA? It's got to be helpful.

LAPIERRE: Yes, I think it is. The media has been making a big, big deal about it.

RUSH: Yes, that's been amazing. All Ashcroft does is give a correct reading of the Amendment and they have a cow.

LAPIERRE: Yes, they did. But he put the Administration on the side of 150 years of United States history, understanding that the Second Amendment is clearly an individual right. This idea of redefining the Second Amendment as a government right as opposed to an individual right is not in sync with any honest reading of American history. It was a great moment when he put the government back on the side of the people.

I don't think it's over yet. But constitutional scholars are clearly moving in the direction of, "Let's just be honest, this is an individual right." Seven times in the Bill of Rights "people" or "persons" is mentioned. You can't say six times it refers to individuals but one time it means the government. Congress has taken a look at this issue numerous times in the 1700s and 1800s. Even in 1941 and 1986, Congress clearly took a look at this and said it's an individual right. Through 150 years of U.S. history, whether it's Justice Joseph Story, who was probably the most respected nineteenth-century justice, to all the documents of our Founding Fathers in the framing era, to the fact that forty-four of the fifty states declare right in their state constitution that it's an individual right. I mean, the Second Amendment doesn't start out, "Duck hunting being lots of fun . . ." The Second Amendment is clearly about an individual right to keep and bear arms on the part of the American public.

RUSH: Your opponents say that if the Founding Fathers knew then what we know now, they wouldn't have written it. They're trying to base it on a cultural shift from the founding days to today. They're all wet, but that's the way they're attacking it. In the past they went after the meaning of the Second Amendment, but they've lost on that, and this proves it. So now they're trying to say, Well, the Founders would never have written this if they had know that Uzis and AK-47s were going to be invented. It's a last gasp of a dying movement, but that's what they're trying to say.

LAPIERRE: Yes, and that's about as crazy as saying they never would have written the First Amendment if they had known there was going to be television and radio and the Internet. Even the Kennedy Administration came down on the Second Amendment being an individual right. We just got the documents through a Freedom of Information request. On the other hand, the Second Amendment offers no protection at all to criminals and terrorists. I know the media has been finding a few outrageous cases involving a violent felon as if they're somehow asserting some Second Amendment right.

RUSH: Well, that's a crock. I can find an excess in the First Amendment in Rosie O'Donnell, but I would never say shut down the Amendment because of her.

LAPIERRE: They're going to find, as John Ashcroft correctly asserted in court, the Second Amendment offers no protection to violent felons and terrorists. In fact, if you go back to the documents of our Founding Fathers, they talk about "peaceful citizens" and "law-abiding citizens" and so forth.

RUSH: Yes. You know, before we go here I've got to take you back to one of my favorite appearances of yours. I think it was on ABC's *This Week*. You said to Cokie Roberts, "I've come to believe Clinton needs a certain level of violence in this country. He's willing to accept a certain level of killing to further his political agenda." You caught a lot of heat, because you were right about it. Would you change any of that now?

LAPIERRE: No, I wouldn't change a word of it, Rush. It was true. It needed to be said. The fact is that while the Clinton Administration was doing everything it could to ban firearms owned by citizens, sue the gun industry out of business, make you take federally mandated tests before you could own a gun—my gosh, the so-called Million Mom March was run out of the White House—he even said, which is a completely ridiculous statement, "There's no crime in Europe because there's no NRA in Europe." As I said, crime has skyrocketed in Europe despite all their gun laws. Yet at the same time, his administration was refusing to use the penalty provisions in federal firearms laws on the books against violent felons, violent drug dealers, and violent gangs. They weren't enforcing those provisions.

RUSH: Has that changed since Janet Reno's gone?

LAPIERRE: It is hopefully beginning to change, although I think we have more to do. The events of September 11 diverted a lot of resources. There are many places in this country where we have laws to take violent armed felons with guns off the street, and we need to do more in terms of enforcing those laws against the bad guys. On the other hand, the [Bush] Administration has made a commitment to do that. They have fought for the money in Congress. I believe their hearts are in the right place, and that you will see them carry out that program over the years to come.

RUSH: Wayne, thank you for your time. I appreciate it. And keep it up. Your stand on principle is inspiring.

GUNS FREEDOM ☆☆AND ☆☆ TERRORISM

1

HOMELAND SECURITY: TERRORISM AND TRUTH

To most Americans, the horrific September 11, 2001, terrorist attacks on the World Trade Center and the Pentagon were more than just senseless mass murder. They were also a frontal assault on the very values that made America a target for this kind of madness in the first place: liberty, democracy, justice, and decency.

But to the nation's gun-ban lobby, this catastrophic event was seen as an opportunity: a cynical opportunity to use the genuine shock and revulsion millions of Americans felt in the wake of 9/11 to advance a political agenda.

"Terrorism" has become the new watchword for gun control—and our liberties are at stake as never before.

The gun-ban lobby has seized on terrorism as an excuse to launch a new push for universal gun-owner registration and for laws that criminalize all now-legal sales, trades, and gifts between peaceable persons. If you own a gun, they want your name in a computerized federal database—profiling you on the basis of mere ownership of a firearm.

Ironically, prior to 9/11, the gun-control movement had stalled. That all changed when foreign terrorists—armed with box cutters and a fanatical will to die—committed the worst mass murder in American history. Now, every anti-gun-rights group is reading off the same page—and terrorism has become the vehicle reviving a far-reaching agenda to destroy our Second Amendment freedom.

It started in the press with newspapers running headlines all on the same theme: "Lax Gun Laws Help Terrorists," or "Lax U.S. Gun Control Is Benefit to Terrorists." This is simply a lie.

The laws on the books today firmly deal with any attempts by terrorists or violent criminals to obtain firearms. Period. Under current tough federal laws, firearms commerce anywhere in the nation that involves violent convicted criminals or illegal aliens or terrorists is already illegal. It is a federal crime punishable by tough penalties for those prohibited classes to attempt to acquire any firearm from any source. Possession of any gun by such people is already a crime. Their presence at a gun show or a gun store with the intent to acquire a firearm is in itself a federal crime.

But these indisputable facts have not stopped the anti-gun lobby from camouflaging their firearms-registration agenda in an "anti-terrorism" wrapper. And in no case has this crass opportunism been more evident than with the pronouncements issued by anti-gun zealots.

Even before the flames at Ground Zero could be put out, Sarah Brady sought to exploit this tragedy to further erode the Second Amendment, demonize firearms, and ridicule those who own them.

On September 18, 2001, the Brady Campaign to Prevent Gun Violence issued a statement urging Americans not to respond to 9/11 by buying a firearm. Sarah Brady announced:

> This nation has lost too many lives in the past week. Please don't let someone in your family become yet another casualty of a senseless act of violence.[1]

What gun ownership had to do with the 9/11 attacks must be left to one's own imagination. It is, however, crystal clear that the lack of firearms in the hands of the pilots allowed the hijackers to seize control of those ill-fated planes in the first place. This seemingly obvious truism was lost on Brady, as she urged citizens to forgo self-defense in preference to blindly trusting innocent lives to the government.

Of course, the Brady Campaign was not alone in issuing hysterical anti-gun warnings in regard to terrorist threats in America. On September 21, 2001, the Consumer Federation of America issued a press release entitled "Buying a Firearm Is . . . Harmful . . ." In it, Consumer Federation Firearms Project Director Susan Peschin warned:

> The terrorist attacks naturally made people afraid, but buying a firearm for self-protection gives the consumer nothing more than a false sense of safety.[2]

Peschin went on to assure Americans, "Research that supports the use of firearms for self-defense is flawed."[3] Yet she offered no evidence of the alleged flaws. Instead, people are expected to have full faith in the Consumer Federation, a lobby that believes the federal government should regulate gun designs to ensure "health and safety."

On October 2, 2001, the Coalition to Stop Gun Violence put out its own release bemoaning increased gun sales in the aftermath of 9/11. Coalition President Michael Beard "urged citizens to think twice before bringing guns into their homes, and urged Congress to again take up legislation to prohibit the unregulated sale of guns."[4]

Beard concluded: "In the end, real protection for Americans will mean not arming every family but ensuring that people who should not have guns cannot get them—that means strong gun laws." Beard would have Americans believe thousands died on that horrible September 11 day because of insufficiently strong gun laws—though twenty thousand laws are already on the books, including federal laws that regulate every aspect of firearms commerce in every corner of the nation.

Lost in the hype is the indisputable fact that no system of firearms registration or background checks could have prevented the box-cutter abuse of that day.

On October 1, 2001, the Educational Fund to Stop Gun Violence—a branch of the Coalition to Stop Gun Violence—put out a press release titled "Talking About Gun Control After September 11." The release proclaimed:

> Stronger gun laws must be a part of any plan to reduce the threat of terrorism in our nation. Keeping guns out of the hands of those who wish to harm us at home requires the same policies that can keep guns out of the hands of criminals.[5]

The Education Fund's press release concluded that "people who are looking for protection and solace during this time would be better served to visit a grief counselor, priest, or rabbi, than to buy a gun."

All that was missing from that alert was a twenty-four-hour toll-free phone line for citizens to call for solace and for protection against violent assailants, "terrorist" or otherwise. Even after the worst attack on American territory since Pearl Harbor, the anti-gun forces tried to advance their core message that guns are so dangerous that only government agents could be trusted with them.

Such anti-self-defense dogma fell on deaf ears as Americans, in an emphatic demonstration of self-reliance, flocked in droves to gun stores to purchase handguns for protection. Homeland security meant exercising Second Amendment rights; it meant gun ownership. So much so that instant background checks for firearms purchases were up about 20 percent in the first six weeks after the terrorist attacks in comparison to the same period in 2000.

To the anti-gun lobby, the reality of potential victims actually using a gun to defend themselves against a terrorist or a violent predator, for that matter, is simply not on the radar screen. In fact, many gun banners are convinced just wanting a firearm is evidence of evil intent—or at the very least, a contributing factor in gun violence—and now terrorism.

The Educational Fund to Stop Gun Violence claimed exactly that when it asserted that "as Americans rush to buy weapons for protection, we must remember that others with more sinister motives can just as easily do the same."[6]

The Fund had but one objective—to promote the notion that anyone buying a gun either is a fool or has sinister motives or is helping those with sinister motives. None of these arguments make any sense—but each is designed to advance the core message of the anti-gunners—that guns are both inherently dangerous and easy to obtain.

Hypocrisy was also in ample abundance in the days that followed the 9/11 attacks. *Roll Call,* the semiofficial newspaper of Congress, reported: "Several lawmakers described colleagues—including some advocates of strict controls on handguns—who are now seeking firearms training in hopes of protecting themselves if the need should arise."[7] Since *Roll Call* is deferential in how it reports on members of Congress, no names were used. Nor did any anti-gun members of Congress publicly admit a near-deathbed conversion. But one congressman who whined to *Roll Call* captured the prevailing mood of panic on Capitol Hill:

> I have absolutely no protection in this area. My family is completely unaware of what's going on and completely unprotected.[8]

In truth, members of Congress receive vastly better police protection than most Americans: it is difficult to walk across Capitol Hill without seeing a small army of Capitol police. But despite the size of the army, some members of Congress—like ordinary American citizens—take responsibility for their own protection. A prime example was Warren Rudman, who represented New Hampshire in the Senate from 1980 to 1993 and who, after retiring from politics, wrote a book on his life in Washington, D.C. He had the following to say about the nation's capital and its gun laws:

> Honest people don't have guns and criminals do. I think people have a right to protect themselves. I was outraged to learn that I couldn't have a gun in Washington. Despite the law, I kept one in my office and one in my apartment, because there were plenty of armed criminals roaming the streets of Washington. Until someone figures out a way to disarm criminals, I won't support the disarming of law-abiding citizens.[9]

But the anti-gun lobby will not listen to people like Warren Rudman who speak common sense. They have cynically exploited every failure of the federal government to protect citizens from criminals or terrorists and used them as a pretext to disarm peaceful citizens.

On September 19, 2001, right on the heels of the 9/11 attacks, the Brady Campaign issued a press release announcing that it was joining the National Association of School Psychologists and other organizations in court briefs supporting the Clinton administration's ban on the importation of semiautomatic rifles capable of holding magazines with more than ten rounds.[10]

The ban was imposed by the Clinton administration as part of its campaign to make the 1994 "assault weapons" law far more prohibitive. Once again exploiting the new fear of terrorism in America, the Brady Campaign's Dennis Henigan declared:

> At this time of urgent concern for our national security, it is distressing that a gun company continues to challenge our government's efforts to protect us from military weaponry.[11]

History proves that given the anti-gun crowd's tendency to stretch the definition of "military weaponry," such bans would soon include anything more powerful than a BB gun (which the Consumer Product Safety Commission is working to suppress on other grounds). In short, according to the Brady Campaign, as long as there is concern for "national security," the government is justified in blocking the sale of almost any gun to any person.

None of the gun controllers' hobby horses make any sense. For instance, shortly after 9/11, the Violence Policy Center (VPC) targeted .50-caliber target guns and ammunition. The VPC cited "evidence that Al Qaeda bought twenty-five Barrett .50-caliber sniper rifles" in the 1980s.[12]

The gun-control lobby is desperate if all it can point to is the purchase two decades ago of twenty-five rifles, never used in any known terrorist attack. Moreover, the VPC knowingly distorted the case. As Dave Kopel points out, the guns were actually "paid for and shipped by the U.S. government" since what passed for Al Qaeda then was part of the mujahideen resistance against the Soviet Union, and was supported by the United States.[13]

Is this the best the VPC can do? Apparently so, and, in truth, VPC and its allies desperately applied the terrorism label well before terrorism dramatically entered American life on September 11.

In 1999, Sen. Dianne Feinstein (D-Calif.) denounced those who favored .50-caliber firearms as "terrorists, doomsday cultists, and criminals."[14] No reason to let the facts get in the way, such as the profile of the average .50-caliber-gun owner: a businessman with an above-average income. And this should come as no surprise, as a Barrett rifle sells for more than $7,000. To the VPC, however, such competitive target shooters are really "men in states of arrested adolescence."[15]

Of course, price is no object when the goal is banning all guns—a $70 gun is hated with as much passion as one that costs $7,000. And nothing stirs the passions and seems to stoke the antagonism of anti-gun activists quite so much as gun shows, and the fact that federal rules do not force the occasional purchases from non-dealers to be checked through the National Instant Check System (NICS). Since Congress has said no to shutting down gun shows, these activists looked to September 11 to provide a boost.

"It's actually been documented that terrorists are buying their weapons in this country at gun shows," charged Senator Feinstein.[16] Similarly, John McCain (R-Ariz.) claimed: "Clearly, alleged members of terrorist organizations have been able to secure guns and weapons using the gun show loophole."[17] Senators Kennedy (D-Mass.) and Schumer (D-N.Y.) complained that potential terrorists could walk into gun shows and buy firearms, with no questions asked. Sen. Richard Durbin (D-Ill.) has gone so far as to say that thousands of terrorists are buying weapons in the United States "because we don't check their backgrounds at gun shows."[18]

The terrorist/gun show "loophole" myth has become the cause célèbre of a relatively new gun-control group that calls itself Americans for Gun Safety (AGS). In truth, the group actually has no members, no gun safety programs, and consequently no credibility. It does, however, have the deep-pocket funding of dot-com billionaire Andrew McKelvey.[19]

Staffed by former architects of the anti-gun schemes of Bill Clinton and Senator Charles Schumer,[20] AGS has run an expensive advertising campaign centered around three "terrorists" who purchased firearms at gun shows. AGS leaves one small detail out of its ads—all three men were caught and convicted of committing federal felonies in violation of existing firearms laws. The "loophole" they all fell through landed them in federal prisons. As columnist Sam Francis put it:

> So far from proving there's a "loophole" through which whole armies of terrorists are marching, the examples prove that terrorists who buy weapons at gun shows get caught.[21]

The fact that anti-gunners are attempting to demonize traditional American gun shows in the wake of 9/11 is as nonsensical as it is insulting. Why would terrorist groups such as the Hezbollah that are sponsored or hosted by governments rely on U.S. gun shows?

Commenting on one of AGS's terrorist trio, a man from Michigan, the editor of the *Arab-American News,* pointed out:

> Hezbollah is getting millions of dollars from Iran. They have plenty of weapons. They don't need a few shotguns from Dearborn.[22]

No, they don't need a few shotguns from Dearborn. A January 6, 2002, story in the *Washington Post* reported the Israeli interception of a ship that was part of a smuggling operation coordinated by the Palestinian Authority and Hezbollah. When Israeli commandos seized the *Karine A,* they found her loaded with fifty tons of weapons.[23] According to the Israeli Defense Force chief of staff, the weapons included "long range Katyusha rockets, Sagger and LAW anti-tank missiles, mortars, mines, advanced explosive equipment, weapons and sniper rifles, bullets, and much more."[24] These are hardly items we see while walking the aisles of American gun shows.

The poverty of gun-control arguments and the desperation of the anti-gun movement are evident in their resort to "kitchen sink" attacks. If everything else they try fails, they now demand that the Federal Trade Commission investigate a firearm maker for advertising his product as "homeland security."[25]

Yet while the usual suspects have turned to September 11 as yet another reason to ban guns, the majority of Americans recognize that gun ownership is an important means of combating terrorism. In general, an armed citizenry is better prepared to confront any potential terrorists, whether at a high-rise office building, shopping mall, or school.

Since disarming Americans makes little enough sense given the prevalence of normal street crime, it is far more ludicrous to call for unilateral disarmament when Americans are at war with ruthless killers dedicated to murdering civilians. The very freedom that makes America a powerhouse also leaves it vulnerable to terrorist predators. We have 91,062 schools, 4,000 water treatment plants,

3,329 major malls, 493 skyscrapers, 322 commercial sports stadiums, 103 nuclear reactors, and 190,000 miles of natural gas pipeline. There are more than half a million bridges. The United States will never, and should never, have enough people in uniform to effectively guard them all.[26]

Americans by the tens of thousands—knowing that the future is unpredictable—have become first-time firearms owners since the terror of September 11. They've discovered what the rest of us have known—security means commonsense gun ownership.

With the threat of more terror attacks from Osama Bin Laden and his international terror network, Americans are looking toward the protection of the Second Amendment. The most basic element of that right goes to individual citizens' abilities to protect themselves, their families, their homes, their communities, and, if need be, their nation.

We are at war. Our country has been defiled by terror, our people murdered by terror. This is about evil on a world scale. It is about cosmic hatred by fanatics willing to forfeit their lives on our soil to kill as many innocent Americans as they can. It's about Americans fighting back—from airline pilots to average citizens.

It's about the true meaning of an armed citizenry and our bedrock belief in preserving freedom now and for always.

2

ARMING PILOTS: A MORAL IMPERATIVE

In the world of international terrorism and air piracy, there are three possible definitions for the term "armed pilots."

The first came into being on September 11, 2001, when terrorists armed with box cutters murdered commercial flight crews and seized the controls of four fuel-laden airliners. The fanatics who flew their suicide missions with the intent of killing tens of thousands of Americans were indeed pilots of sorts and they were surely armed—although with edged weapons.

The second definition of "armed pilot" was first reported by the *New York Times* just days after the World Trade Center became a pile of smoking rubble and the nation watched in numbed disbelief as valiant rescuers searched for survivors. "Two mid-level U.S. Air Force generals have been given the power to order the shooting down of civilian airliners that threaten American cities . . ."[1] In this case young American military officers flying fighter aircraft are armed pilots with a mission to kill the hijackers, which also entails killing all of their hostages as well.

The third definition of "armed pilot" covers the 125,000 highly trained men and women we entrust with our lives on any one of the 20,000 domestic airline flights that crisscross America every day.

It means that these good people are prepared—with training and the proper tools—to defend the controls of their airplanes, thus protecting the lives of their passengers and countless innocents on the ground. Unfortunately, that definition did not exist when Osama Bin Laden's terror cadres boarded four commercial flights on September 11, 2001.

Had the pilots and copilots on those ill-fated flights been armed with handguns on that horrific day, the stories that filled the airwaves certainly would have been quite different. Thousands of lives would have been saved. And the news media would have covered a far different story—of terrorist hijackings thwarted by "armed pilots," perhaps of dead terrorists who stormed flight deck doors, stopped cold by "armed pilots."

But this definition of armed pilots, commercial airline captains armed with pistols or revolvers and the training to use them, can only be written with any finality by the Congress of the United States.

It makes no sense that anybody would deny those who continue to meet the needs of America's flying public the right to possess the means to protect their aircraft and their passengers. As the *Washington Times* so aptly put it, "You can't dial 911 at 30,000 feet."[2] Until they touch down, passengers and air crews are on their own. Defense against deadly force is self-contained. There is no help outside that fuselage. The only force that can be applied against armed terrorists must come from within the aircraft.

That certainly was the case with United Flight 93, where brave passengers thwarted the plans of the terrorist hijackers. We will never know Al Qaeda's planned destination, but it was surely to destroy either the White House or the United States Capitol. We all owe those real heroes a huge debt.

Of course pilots should be allowed to carry firearms. Many pilots are former military personnel, and additional training could easily be offered. If you can't trust the pilots, whom can you trust? They already are entrusted with control of airplanes in flight.

Moreover, the pilots, not passengers, are the ultimate targets of any terrorist hijacking. The terrorists' goal is to gain control of the aircraft. Arming pilots is the most obvious way to thwart would-be terrorists from achieving that objective. It is the only way to do so if terrorists breach today's insufficient airport security.

Capt. Stephen Luckey, chairman of the National Flight Security Committee of the Air Line Pilots Association, International, spoke from personal experience when he testified before the U.S. Senate Committee on Commerce, Science and Transportation on July 25, 2002:

> To underscore the risks that we face, I would like to pose three questions and follow them with the answers. First, is there still a risk of terrorists assuming control of an airliner and crashing it into a building? The answer that we are hearing from the Justice Department, the Office of Homeland Defense, the TSA and numerous other sources is an emphatic "yes." Transport aircraft, regardless of whether they carry passengers or cargo, must from now on be viewed as potential human-guided missiles if they fall into the hands of a suicidal terrorist. Osama Bin Laden's henchmen were remarkably patient, thorough, as well trained as any special operations unit in the world, and employed surprise attacks to great advantage using relatively innocuous weapons they knew would go unchallenged through security checkpoints. From their perspective, the operation was a great success, not only in terms of damage, but also with respect to the amount of global media attention their acts garnered. History has shown that terrorists endeavor to repeat successes, so we must prudently assume that our enemies are planning for yet another airliner attack.
>
> Second, if terrorists board an aircraft with the intention of hijacking it, will they be armed only with box cutters as they were before? We think the answer to that is "probably not." The element of surprise from a box cutter–type attack is gone and small knives are now confiscated at security checkpoints, so we must assume that terrorists will be armed with some other weapons,

which could include guns not taken through screening checkpoints and/or undetected explosives.

We have an unfortunate habit in this country of preparing for the type of security breach that most recently occurred—this is the equivalent of locking the barn door after the horse has been stolen. What we must do instead is address, to the best of our knowledge and ability, all of the potential threats that exist, not just those that we have most recently experienced. Many in the airline industry and some in government seem to believe that we should not prepare to counter anything but close-quarters combat by unarmed assailants. Such tunnel vision is foolhardy and leaves us pitifully unprepared for the various types of hijacking attempts that may well lie ahead.

Lastly, do we possess the will to do all that we can to avoid another catastrophe? I can tell you without equivocation that many pilots are willing and prepared to assume the responsibility for training and carrying a weapon. They are willing to do so as both a deterrent against a hijacking attempt and as a means of preventing an attempt from becoming successful. The U.S. House of Representatives has demonstrated with its vote on H.R. 4635 that it is resolved to avoid another catastrophe. We believe that the Senate should also take a stand, which will have a strong deterrent effect against future hijackings and help restore the confidence of the traveling public in aviation.

You may be interested to know that I am one of about a dozen pilots selected in the mid-1970s to be trained by the FBI to carry a firearm while performing my duties as a pilot. My airline's president and the FAA approved that carriage to protect against the hijackings that were prevalent then. From my personal experience, I can tell you that I did not particularly enjoy being armed during the 15 years that I carried a firearm—but it was a duty that I voluntarily undertook. The weapon was worn at all times, which is an inconvenience, and there was definitely an increased

> level of responsibility and restriction of my activity that went with being armed. However, I thought that it was necessary to be armed then, and I believe that it is even more necessary for qualified and properly trained pilots to be armed now. We could wish that our threat situation was such that it would be unnecessary for pilots to be armed, but the events of September 11 and the ongoing threat of further violence against airlines make it a necessity, in our view.

And the widow of one of the pilots killed on 9/11 called for arming pilots as a "last line of defense." Had they possessed guns on 9/11 she said, "it stands to reason that the loss of life and property damage could have been vastly different."[3]

Allowing pilots to carry the tools of self-defense is hardly a radical idea, no matter what some editorial writers might imply. In 1961, the Federal Aviation Administration amended its requirements to allow pilots to be armed (the agency removed that regulatory language in 2001).[4] And for fifty years beginning in 1937, the U.S. Postal Service provided for armed pilots to protect the mail. Columnist Deroy Murdock is not alone in wondering, "Is it asking too much for today's passengers to receive the same protection once afforded their postcards?"[5]

One objection to arming pilots is the claim that federal sky marshals can do the job. The problem here is that there are 20,000 flights per day in the United States compared to only 1,000 sky marshals. To put just one marshal on each flight "would require 20,000 officers—more than twice the number employed by the FBI, Secret Service, and the U.S. Marshals combined," warns the Cato Institute's Robert Levy.[6]

Another contention is that pilots need to concentrate on their jobs. Well, yes, they should fly the plane. But, writes Capt. Tracy Price: "I will not be able to concentrate on flying after terrorists break into my cockpit, kill me, and use my airplane and its passengers as a guided bomb."[7] With a pilot and a copilot, in an emergency one could guard the door while the other landed the plane.

To land a plane even in an emergency takes time—twenty minutes from thirty thousand feet, depending on the proximity to an airport. That is more than enough time to lose control of the aircraft. To have pilots ignore such an imminent threat makes no sense. As Stephen Luckey told Congress:

> Pilots are trained to do numerous tasks simultaneously—individuals who cannot do so are unable to become airline pilots. One of the tasks that they must be prepared to perform is using fire extinguishers if a fire breaks out in the cockpit, regardless of other, pressing duties. A suggestion that pilots should ignore the fire and continue to fly the aircraft would be ludicrous; yet some have suggested that pilots should ignore terrorists breaking into the cockpit and continue to fly the aircraft. This is utter nonsense.

One of the strangest objections to allowing pilots to carry firearms is that liability standards would have to be adjusted, and that doing so would be unfair. Congress would either protect the airlines too much or protect the pilots too little. This is, of course, an objection that could be raised only in a society where liability has run wild, with negligence litigation directed not at making victims whole but at promoting lawyer enrichment.

But as bad as it would be for an airline (and possibly the government) to face cases arising out of an errant shooting where there was no terrorist, imagine the litigation nightmare of another successful terrorist assault. Hundreds of dead passengers, thousands of dead people on the ground, wrecked planes, and buildings reduced to rubble. It shouldn't be hard to choose the lesser evil. Especially if Congress were willing to put the interest of the public ahead of that of the trial bar and to limit potential liability for good-faith defensive efforts.

Don't worries about liability seem almost frivolous compared to the federal government's threat to shoot down a hijacked airplane? Don't forget that in just the first seven months after 9/11 military aircraft responded to 350 "air events," such as when a plane was off course or a potentially troublesome passenger appeared to be on board.

The *Wall Street Journal* captured the arming pilots "debate" in a single sentence—"this isn't really a choice between guns or no guns; it's between giving pilots a last chance to stop a hijacking or having the Air Force shoot down a loaded passenger plane."[8]

So what is the controversy all about? Simple. It's about gun control, about banning guns for self-defense, something that always allows evil to prevail. Where gun-control radicals have tried to disarm ordinary peaceable Americans, they are now trying to make sure that airline pilots are disarmed as well, and in the process they are simply adapting the same arguments that the NRA has been fighting all along. What has never made sense to firearms owners is now beginning to seem absurd—no, just plain crazy—to millions of other Americans as well.

Immediately after 9/11 it would have been hard to imagine any reason to oppose such a straightforward, commonsense measure—armed pilots defending against deadly force with deadly force of their own. Yet arguments were not long in coming from advocacy groups whose sole agenda is to outlaw private ownership of firearms in America.

Leading the charge was the Violence Policy Center (VPC), a tax-exempt firearms prohibitionist lobby on the radical fringe of the issue. To counter the notion of arming pilots, the VPC simply recycled all of its tired and bizarre arguments for making private handgun ownership a crime for ordinary Americans. Those arguments were morphed by major elements of the media into a standardized diatribe against commercial airline pilots bearing arms as a "last-ditch" defense against air piracy and terrorists.

The media's shameless cribbing of VPC talking points has

ironically given Americans of all political hues a crystal-clear look into the political philosophy that drives the anti-gun movement in America today.

What they have seen is a belief system in which evil is painted as essentially unbeatable, and where good is always bumbling, incompetent, and untrustworthy. Aside from this underlying message, the direct pacifist conclusion demanded is simple: when confronted by evil force, you must submit. You can't win. Don't even try.

In *USA Today,* VPC's legislative director, Kristen Rand, lectured America: "A handgun on every plane would mean that the weapon, by definition, would be potentially available to every passenger: from terrorists to unruly or suicidal travelers."[9]

Rand's rant should sound all too familiar. It's merely a "dusted-off" version of the anti-gun lobby's knee-jerk response to Right-to-Carry legislation. To digress, VPC and other gun prohibitionists can't resist creating false images of the American Wild West and then claim the states that pass Right-to-Carry will suffer shootouts as permit holders face off at high noon. So far, thirty-two states have passed "shall-issue" laws (Vermont respects Right-to-Carry without a permit), and the Wild West has yet to reappear. In any event, as historian W. Eugene Hollon has written, "the Western frontier was a far more civilized, more peaceful, and safer place than American society is today."[10] Certainly far safer than the present-day VPC Utopia called Washington, D.C., where honest citizens who have been disarmed suffer a violent crime rate that is more than twice that of the nation.[11]

Rand tells *USA Today* readers: "Experience also teaches that when police fire their weapons, they sometimes make grave mistakes in deciding when deadly force is justified."

Had the pilots of the doomed 9/11 flights been armed with handguns, there would have been no "grave mistakes in deciding when deadly force is justified." That decision was made for them by the terrorists who were slitting the throats of passengers and members of the cabin crews. That decision was made when the terrorists were cutting the throats of the pilots themselves. Self-defense, and defense of the controls of the aircraft, is not a random decision. Self-defense becomes the inevitable and moral response to the actions of attackers. This will never change.

And then Rand wrote:

> Unfortunately, pilots are not infallible. In fact, 84 percent of all fatal commercial air crashes are the result of pilot error. In a nation where states prohibit the use of cell phones while driving, we are relying on pilots of passenger planes, where hundreds of lives are at stake, to be both policeman and pilot.

It may come as news to the VPC, but pilots can talk on the radio and fly at the same time. They don't have to pull over. They are among the most highly skilled, highly trained professionals in the world. These are men and women who countless times a day perform some of the most complex tasks with utter calm and skill.

So there again is the second half of the gun-control belief system—pilots who are able to fly multimillion-dollar wonders of modern digital, hydraulic, and mechanical technology would be transformed into incompetent bumblers when faced with the low-tech mechanics of a handgun. They should not even try.

The positions of the VPC are important only because they are really the sole arguments made against the very concept of armed self-defense of the cockpit by the nation's commercial pilots. They formed the basis for virtually every editorial and news story written opposing arming pilots.

But when polls showed Americans overwhelmingly were rejecting the notion of pacifist pilots, the VPC, and its army of media followers, was forced to try a different tack. In their official comments to the FAA on February 14, 2002, VPC wrote: "Experience teaches that firearms, and particularly handguns, make poor self-defense tools . . ."[12]

But later they argued, "Hijackers will board the aircraft with the knowledge that the pilot is armed, increasing the chance that the hijacker will be determined to smuggle his own firearm on board. Recognizing that he is likely to face an armed pilot will also give hijackers an incentive to do everything possible to take away the pilot's gun."

The VPC's implied message is as simple as it is wholly illogical—"good guys with guns can't win, and bad guys with those same guns can't lose."

The American people were not alone in rejecting such foolishness. On July 10, the House of Representatives passed "The Arming Pilots Against Terrorism Act" on a decisive vote of 310 to 113, making all of the nation's 125,000 commercial pilots immediately eligible for an armed-pilot program. Strongly supported by the NRA, the bill allows, but does not require, qualified and trained pilots to be commissioned as federal law enforcement officers and to carry firearms for cockpit defense.

The day following the House vote, the rabidly anti-gun *New York Times* rushed out a story headlined "Armed Pilots? Many Travelers Are Gun-shy." The *Times* quoted man-on-the-street interviews that unsurprisingly reflected the newspaper's hard-line position on gun control on the flight deck.[13]

The *Times* said one interviewee feared that "a shot fired inside the cockpit might cause unanticipated consequences, from damaging equipment to killing the copilot." And they wrote that another "was reminded of bad guys—the ones who assault police officers and steal their guns. The same, she said, could happen to a pilot."

The *Times* then added that this woman's point "was supported by at least one study, by the Violence Policy Center that found 21 percent of police officers killed with a handgun were shot by their own weapon."

The paper did quote a few people who favored arming pilots, but their views were buried in the story, a story that managed to fail to mention that airline pilots themselves overwhelmingly supported the concept. The AFL-CIO—representing other airline employees—was also for such a simple measure.

When it comes to covering firearms, in any way, shape, or form, the *Times* just doesn't get it. Maybe these words from Al Aitken, a board member of the Allied Pilots Committee for Armed Defense of the Cockpit and an American Airlines pilot, offered after the House vote, will help them:

> Members of Congress now understand what the American people have known for months—only lethal force can stop lethal intent. Tepid measures in response to terrorist attacks and hijackings will not provide the kind of security the American people want and deserve. Americans trust pilots with their lives every day. Arming them with a lethal weapon is simply an extension of that trust.[14]

And Cato's Robert Levy puts it this way: "Imagine that you're a terrorist selecting one of two airlines as your next victim. The first airline boasts in its ads, 'Our Planes Are Gun-Free Zones.' The second says that 'One or More Employees Will Be Armed on Every Flight.' Not much question which one you'd fly. Now picture yourself as a safety-conscious passenger. Still not much question, but the choice won't be the same."[15]

3

TERRORIST BOMB FACTORY IN KABUL? CLOSE THE GUN SHOW IN PEORIA!

Long before 9/11, the so-called "gun-show loophole" was a primary obsession of the anti-gun lobby and its allies at the *New York Times* and the *Washington Post* and in the national TV news media and Congress.

In fact, in the months just before the terrorist attacks, gun shows had been the number one target of the anti-gun forces, who blamed them for just about every crime in the nation except jaywalking. Never mind that a recent Justice Department study—the largest ever conducted—found that less than 1 percent of the guns used in crimes were acquired at gun shows. As usual, facts don't matter to the anti-gun crowd. What did matter to the anti-gun axis was cashing in on "terrorism" as its new excuse for gun control.

The anti-gun lobby seized on the 9/11 tragedies as yet another justification to ban gun shows—and did so with a vengeance. Almost immediately, the cry went from "gun shows = crime" to "gun shows = crime + terrorism."

On October 12, after the House and Senate passed the USA PATRIOT anti-terrorism legislation, Sarah Brady criticized the law, saying, "Nothing in these bills will close the gaps in our federal firearm laws that allow terrorists to amass their deadly arsenals."

Brady shrilly proclaimed: "Incredibly, our soldiers could be gunned down by foreign terrorists armed with firearms purchased at American gun shows." With that said, she inferred that anyone who opposed "closing the gun show loophole" automatically favored the slaughter of U.S. soldiers.[1]

To give the "gun shows = crime + terrorism" theme an even bigger boost, the *Washington Post* obligingly provided space to former Deputy Attorney General Eric Holder, whose past experience in Janet Reno's Department of Justice included countless trips to Capitol Hill to defend the Clinton administration's failure to enforce federal firearms laws. Holder wrote: "Previously convicted felon and terrorist, Ali Boumelhem, went to a Michigan gun show, where he was legally exempt from a background check, and purchased assault weapons, shotguns, ammunition, and flash suppressors that he intended to ship to the terrorist group Hezbollah." A convicted felon "legally exempt"?

Warming to his subject, Holder preposterously claimed that "if Osama Bin Laden, who is under indictment in this country for the bombing of our embassies . . . were to go to a willing or unwary unlicensed gun dealer at a gun show, no mechanism is in place to prevent him from obtaining a weapon of his choice." He went on to contend that "the gaping holes in our current law have likely allowed thousands of undetected firearm purchases by criminals and terrorists."[2]

Holder is flat-out wrong. As a person under indictment, Bin Laden's presence at a gun show would be a felony. Holder ought to know that. Nevertheless, he advocated sweeping new federal controls and a Bureau of Alcohol, Tobacco, and Firearms (BATF) database of every firearm sale, and the anti-gun lobby quickly jumped on his bandwagon.

The Brady Campaign to Prevent Gun Violence (the name Handgun Control, Inc., was discarded when focus groups showed Americans don't like the word "control") issued a press release the same day Holder's article appeared, praising him and telling Americans, "There is one critical need that Congress has failed to address—weak federal firearm laws that terrorists exploit to stockpile deadly weapons."[3]

At the same time, the *Washington Post* editorial page—ever a reliable vehicle for regurgitating anti-gun propaganda—wailed: "A gaping loophole in the laws governing gun sales in this country has been exploited by terrorists in search of quick-and-easy weapons purchases."[4]

These absurd allegations were quickly echoed in the Congress.

In the House, Rep. John Conyers (D-Mich.) bragged that the national reaction to 9/11 would make it a sure thing that Congress would support his attack on gun shows: "We've got the terrorist issue. There are very few in the general population who are going to tolerate a loophole through which these weapons are allowed into the war to support terrorism."[5]

Not missing a beat was the gun-ban cabal in the Senate—led by Senators Charles Schumer, Ted Kennedy, Dianne Feinstein, Hillary Clinton, Joseph Lieberman—and their newest ally, Senator John McCain.

Sen. Dianne Feinstein (D-Calif.) proclaimed: "It's actually been documented that terrorists are buying their weapons in this country at gun shows."[6] Feinstein has since demanded that all now-legal intrastate sales be criminalized—legal commerce between law-abiding citizens would become a crime unless those sales were subject to national registration.

California's senior senator said she "would bring the nation in line with her home state's stringent laws . . ."[7] California now requires background checks, waiting periods, gun-owner competence tests, and confiscatory bans on an utterly confusing list of formerly legal firearms. Strictly private sales are a crime.

In that state, guns have been confiscated from those who tried to register them under the law. Thousands of honest Californians who registered their self-loading rifles—under a deadline amnesty given by the state attorney general—were ultimately told amnesty was not legal. *They were told that their registration was no good.* They were told to give up their property or face prosecution.

Not to be outdone, Senators Kennedy (D-Mass.) and Schumer (D-N.Y.) launched a drive to make the National Instant Check System records on legal sales at federally licensed dealers part of a permanent database—with information on you and me and our families—that would be open to any and all "law enforcement" even for "civil" inquiries. Read: sweetheart deals between big-city mayors and trial lawyers. Read: lawsuits.

But it has been Senator John McCain (R-Ariz.) who has most aggressively led the drive for legislation to close the phony "gun-show loophole."

His absurd efforts to link gun shows to terrorists have been backed by a massive national propaganda campaign paid for by monster.com billionaire Andrew McKelvey through his anti-gun lobbying group, Americans for Gun Safety (AGS). The AGS headlined its big lie: "Terrorist Access Makes Gun Show Background Checks Important to America's Security."[8]

The AGS has spent mega-bucks on TV ads featuring Senators McCain and Joseph Lieberman (D-Conn.) arguing that their anti-gun-show legislation, S.890, would prevent terrorists or criminals from obtaining firearms from private individuals.

When you blow away the fog of disinformation and lies supporting the "gun-show loophole," you clearly see the creation of universal firearms registration—the mechanism for future selective confiscation of private arms from the American people.

How does the gun-ban lobby continue to justify its "gun shows = terrorism" charade? Incredibly, its propaganda is based on a single piece of computer paper with a few paragraphs found in an abandoned house in Kabul, Afghanistan.

With the helpful spin of the media and the gun banners, those few paragraphs have been magically transformed into "pamphlets," then "manuals"—which the spinmeisters cited as "proof" of a terrorist connection to lawful individual gun commerce in America.

Headlines and stories all over America whipped up the same big lies:

U.S. GUN-SHOW LOOPHOLE
CAN BE PUT TO USE BY TERRORISTS[9]

The words on the paper in Kabul said nothing about gun shows. They advised: "In other countries, for example in some states in the USA or South Africa, it is perfectly legal for members of the public to own certain types of firearms . . ." And it said, "In some countries of the world, especially the USA, firearms training is available to the general public."[10]

Gun shows? Nothing. Nothing at all about them. All those words were really saying was that America is a free country and Americans are a free people. It might have said, in America, people are free to travel, free to speak, free to publish or read, free to practice religion, free to own property, and free from racial discrimination.

A few words in the Kabul printout about firearms ownership in America have been turned by the media, anti-firearms-rights groups, and politicians into a whole campaign of blaming innocent Americans for the acts of international terrorists.

Any doubt about the true motives of the gun banners in linking gun shows and gun ownership to terrorism evaporates under close examination.

The fact is, all gun commerce that involves violent felons or illegal aliens or terrorists—anywhere, anytime, under any circumstances—*is already* covered by a host of federal criminal statutes. Simple gun possession by prohibited persons is a federal felony—ten years in a federal prison.

Foreign terrorists? It is a federal felony for an illegal alien to "ship or transport in interstate or foreign commerce, or possess . . . any firearm or ammunition";[11] or to "receive any firearm, or ammunition." That covers everything everywhere.

A prohibited person's mere presence at a gun show could be construed as a federal crime. And if any person acquires a firearm with the intention of violating other laws—anti-terrorism laws, for example, that act is covered by tough federal penalties as well.

Americans for Gun Safety's President Jonathan Cowan has declared: "The only people who should be opposed to the bill by Sens. John McCain and Joseph Lieberman to require background checks at gun shows are criminals, terrorists, and illegal aliens."[12] (It is worth noting that prior to joining AGS, Cowan spent five years with the Clinton administration in the Department of Housing and Urban Development. As a chief of staff to HUD Secretary Andrew Cuomo, Cowan played a key role in HUD's lawsuits against gun manufacturers.)

In reality, however, the McCain-Lieberman legislation does absolutely nothing to cover activities by criminals at gun shows. In fact, the words "felon," "criminal," "terrorist," or "prohibited person" don't even appear in their legislation.[13]

Proponents say their bill is a single-purpose effort to close a so-called "gun-show loophole," but McCain-Lieberman contains numerous complications and loopholes that give a single federal official the ability to register citizens who attend gun shows and impose many other restrictions that have nothing to do with background checks on purchases. Ultimately, the lone federal bureaucrat would have the power to shut down gun shows entirely.

The phrase "in accordance with regulations the Secretary shall prescribe" or similar language occurs repeatedly in the McCain-Lieberman bill. Show operators and vendors would have to supply "any other information" required by BATF regulations. "Any other information" can be as broad as a future BATF administrator desires.

By specifically authorizing extensive regulations for open-ended records-gathering, McCain-Lieberman allows for the collection of far-reaching personal information about people who attend or conduct business at gun shows. The only limit is the curiosity of any administration's Treasury Department.

McCain-Lieberman won't make what criminals or terrorists might do at gun shows any more illegal. *It will make what peaceable citizens do illegal.*

And that is what "closing the gun-show loophole" really is: making innocent people pay the price for criminal violence. McCain-Lieberman is not a "gun-show loophole" bill. It is a gun-owner registration and gun-show prohibition law in the hands of any administration that wants to make it so.

As freedom-loving Americans, we must never be forced to pay the price for foreign terrorists with the loss of our rights.

We must be prepared to fight every single attack on our liberty, no matter how cleverly it is disguised. We must fight political spin with the truth: enforce existing laws against already illegal gun commerce and illegal gun purchases by illegal aliens and criminals.

4

THE SECOND AMENDMENT: PUTTING FREEDOM FIRST

NRA President Charlton Heston said it best when he described the Second Amendment as our "First Freedom." It is also our "best defense."

When the forces of evil launched their attacks on America on September 11, 2001, they had more than murder and mayhem on their minds. They were also waging war on the very "idea" of America. More specifically, they wanted, and still want today, for Americans to question who we are and what we stand for. By doing so, the terrorists reason, they can maximize their attacks from afar by weakening America from within.

Standing in their way are determined leaders, the world's greatest armed forces, and a united people. But, more important, also standing in their way is the overwhelming force of what makes America, America—the U.S. Constitution and its Bill of Rights.

Each amendment in this extraordinary document makes America stronger.

But, as President Heston correctly points out, some rights are more important to the whole than others. And the one right that all the others lean on the most is the right guaranteed in the Second Amendment—the right to Keep and Bear Arms. Why? Because nothing precious can be held for long unless we have the ability to defend against its being taken from us—and the Second Amendment guarantees each one of us that ability.

Since the beginning of our republic, external threats like Al Qaeda have come and gone, and that will still be true long after the current war on terrorism has been won. But the real purpose of the Bill of Rights will remain the same as it has for more than two hundred years now—defending life, liberty, and the pursuit of happiness against all threats.

In the post-9/11 world we now live in, Americans—in order to preserve their liberties—must make a renewed commitment to understanding the historical origins of the Bill of Rights.

Our security, our national defense, and our very survival depend on Americans coming together today behind the same beliefs we have come together on so often in the past—the most central of which is that the government is "We the People."

The brilliant men who crafted our form of government fully understood the importance of the individual rights of their fellow citizens. It is equally fortunate that they drew up the blueprints for a form of government that can maintain its strength through the most trying of times and circumstances. Ours is a nation that endures precisely because of its ability to tolerate and survive through war, assassinations, natural disasters, economic upheavals, and a host of other catastrophes that would crush a lesser form of government.

We have the Founders to thank for that. They were rare men of still rarer vision who understood not only the strengths and weaknesses of themselves and their fellowmen but also the lure and corrupting nature of absolute power.

Above all else, our Founding Fathers sought, fought for, and cherished freedom. Once achieved, they strove to protect and conserve that freedom for generations to come—and this is precisely why they insisted on leaving us freedom's legacy, our Bill of Rights.

While the Founders ranked the Bill of Rights randomly, in order of importance, the Second Amendment is America's first freedom.

The anti-gun lobby vehemently disagrees, but there can be no denying that there is no such thing as a free nation where police and military are allowed the force of arms but individual citizens are not.

The Constitution provides a doorway for freedom of speech and of religion and of assembly. And that doorway to freedom is framed by the muskets that first defended liberty at a place called Concord Bridge. Emerson said it best:

> By the rude bridge that arched the flood, their flag to April's breeze unfurled, here once the embattled farmers stood, and fired the shot heard round the world.

The American Revolution was fueled by British attempts to confiscate arms in Massachusetts and Virginia. As noted constitutional scholar Stephen P. Halbrook has written: "The British resorted to every possible tactic to disarm the Americans—entrapment, false promises of 'safekeeping,' banning imports, direct seizure and finally shooting persons bearing arms."[1]

King George III failed, and in the two centuries that have followed the birth of our nation, there have been many who have challenged us and tried to take away our freedom. We prevailed and survived. And we will prevail and survive again in the war on terror—as long as we don't forget who we are and what makes us strong.

In the wake of 9/11, a fierce struggle is taking place today between those who place their faith in government and those who retain the Founding Fathers' trust in the people. On no single issue is this struggle more apparent than in the debate over the meaning and role of the Second Amendment.

Those in the anti-gun lobby, who attempt to dismiss the Second Amendment as archaic and irrelevant, claim it is a "collective right" granting states the power to raise militias. As always, the anti-gunners are missing the truth—a point that our Founding Fathers understood. In the end, in a truly free society, it is up to the people, and not the government that serves them, to safeguard that freedom.

That was true in the eighteenth century when the threat was the

British army, and it is true today when the threat is international terrorism.

Indeed, the Founders fully expected the people to protect themselves and their liberties from all enemies. Nowhere was this notion more evident than in Patrick Henry's "Give me liberty, or give me death" speech. The context of that oration—the importance of an armed population—has been lost in today's "politically correct" anti-gun climate. Yet, Henry's words are there to defend the embattled Second Amendment. When speaking of the Revolution, Henry proclaimed:

> They tell us . . . that we are weak—unable to cope with so formidable an adversary. But when shall we be stronger? . . . Will it be when we are totally disarmed, and when a British guard shall be stationed in every house? . . . Three million people, armed in the holy cause of liberty . . . are invincible by any force which our enemies can send against us.[2]

Are we now to believe that Al Qaeda is so threatening that these words are no longer true? Are we to verify Osama Bin Laden's conviction that we are "weak"?

Whether it's the World Trade Towers or a sole citizen, terrorists target the unarmed. They particularly target those who live in fear, totally dependent on others for protection. If we abandon the Second Amendment and our right to defend ourselves, terrorists are three-quarters of the way to victory.

In this age of terrorism, too many Americans seem willing to abandon personal freedoms in exchange for government control, for what they naively hope will be a safe, risk-free life.

As Benjamin Franklin warned, the true danger to our freedom and national character comes from those who are willing to yield real freedom for the sake of the illusion of security.

This danger lurks even more ominously today in the post-9/11 world than at any time in America's history. It is this fear that the anti-gunners are now counting on to sway Americans to their side; only the government can be trusted to protect "We the People" from terror.

In this backdrop, the Bush administration recently set the record straight on the "collective" versus "individual" thrust of the Second Amendment.

In a letter to the NRA ILA's executive director dated May 17, 2001, U.S. Attorney General John Ashcroft affirmed that the "plain meaning and original intent" of the Second Amendment is to protect individual rights. This puts Justice Department policy back on its historically correct and original course.

In a matter of months, the Bush administration was joined by a federal court. On October 16, 2001, the Fifth Circuit Court of Appeals' ruling in *U.S. v. Emerson* unequivocally repudiated all versions of the "collective right" theories that have been concocted in recent years by anti-gun lobbies and their ideologues.

"This is the most important and favorable Second Amendment judicial decision in American history," said Nelson Lund, constitutional law professor at George Mason University. "A federal court of appeals has unambiguously held that the right to keep and bear arms belongs to individual citizens and rejected the preposterous but judicially regnant theory that Second Amendment rights belong to governments or can only be exercised in the service of a government."[3]

The *Emerson* opinion—written by Chief Judge William Garwood—noted how the Clinton-Reno Justice Department steadfastly maintained that the Supreme Court's decision in *United States v.* Miller mandated rejection of the individual right interpretation of the Second Amendment.[4]

"We disagree," Judge Garwood wrote, saying the *Miller* decision did not resolve the individual versus collective right issue, but "to the extent that *Miller* sheds light on the matter, it cuts against" the Clinton-Reno position. The court said:

> We turn, therefore, to an analysis of history and wording of the Second Amendment for guidance. In undertaking this analysis, we are mindful that almost all of our sister circuits have rejected any individual rights view of the Second Amendment. However, it respectfully appears to us that all or almost all of these opinions seem to have done so either on the erroneous assumption that Miller resolved that issue or without sufficient articulated examination of the history and text of the Second Amendment.

To correct that deficiency, the court produced its own meticulous eighty-four-page historical examination, concluding:

> We have found no historical evidence that the Second Amendment was intended to convey militia power to the states, limit the federal government's power to maintain a standing army, or applies only to members of a select militia while on active duty. All of the evidence indicates that the Second Amendment, like other parts of the Bill of Rights, applies to and protects individual Americans.
>
> We find that the history of the Second Amendment reinforces the plain meaning of its text, namely that it protects individual Americans in their right to keep and bear arms whether or not they are a member of a select militia or performing active military service or training.
>
> We reject the collective rights and sophisticated collective rights models for interpreting the Second Amendment. We hold, consistent with Miller, that it protects the right of individuals, including those not then actually a member of any militia or engaged in active military service or training, to privately possess and bear their own firearms, such as the pistol involved here, that are suitable as personal, individual weapons and are not of the general kind or type excluded by Miller.

The court's decision in *U.S. v. Emerson* should be read by every American interested in knowing the true meaning of the Second Amendment. It cuts through the distortion and media hype and exposes the real aims of those who press the notion that the right to keep and bear arms applies to only government and not the people.

In its opinion, the court clearly saw the dangers to individual liberty when it defined the Clinton-Reno Justice Department's position as being based on a model where "the Second Amendment poses no obstacle to the wholesale disarmament of the American people." In totally rejecting that position, the court exposed the end game of those who would deny Second Amendment rights to individual Americans.

The ability of the people to bear arms to defend liberty is the immutable right despised by the Osama Bin Ladens of this world and feared by every government that rules through enslavement of its people. It is the "First Freedom"—the right to Keep and Bear Arms—that is taken from the people, followed in rapid succession by the right of a free press, the right to assemble, and the people's right to religious choice and tolerance. There is absolutely no more clear or consistent historical lesson.

A legion of constitutional scholars have described our Second Amendment as the safeguard of all our liberties from examining the words and works of Thomas Jefferson, James Madison, Patrick Henry, Tench Coxe, Richard Henry Lee, Samuel Adams, Noah Webster, Alexander Hamilton, Thomas Paine, Fisher Ames, Elbridge Gerry, and others.

That scholarship did not simply speak to our ability to build, buy, borrow, collect, and inherit firearms, or to—as the anti-gunners like to say in mocking tones—"shoot ducks." The Founders clearly intended the Second Amendment to be a guarantee that Americans will always have the right and means to protect themselves from criminals, despots, and international terrorists.

Thomas Jefferson, who confronted his era's version of terrorism in the Barbary Pirates, studied the works of the great eighteenth-century Italian criminologist Cesare Beccaria. He penned what can be described as an older rendition of today's popular slogan: "When guns are outlawed only outlaws will have guns."

Thomas Jefferson took the time to translate the following from Beccaria's Italian and laboriously copied it in longhand into his own personal file of great quotations:

> False is the idea of utility that sacrifices a thousand real advantages for one imaginary or trifling inconvenience; that would take fire from men because it burns, and water because one may drown in it; that has no remedy for evils, except destruction. The laws that forbid the carrying of arms are laws of such a nature. They disarm those only who are neither inclined nor determined to commit crimes. Can it be supposed that those who have the courage to violate the most sacred laws of humanity, the most important of the code, will respect the less important and arbitrary ones, which can be violated with ease and impunity, and which, if strictly obeyed, would put an end to personal liberty—so dear to men, so dear to the enlightened legislator—and subject innocent persons to all the vexations that the guilty alone ought to suffer? Such laws make things worse for the assaulted and better for the assailants; they serve rather to encourage than to prevent homicides, for an unarmed man may be attacked with greater confidence than an armed man. They ought to be designated as laws not preventive but fearful of crimes, produced by the tumultuous impression of a few isolated facts, and not by thoughtful consideration of the inconveniences and advantages of a universal decree.[5]

The Founders unanimously agreed. "The great object," thundered Patrick Henry, "is that every man be armed."[6]

In short, the Founders and an army of scholars dating from the republics of Plato and Rome to modern-day America agree: self-defense works—criminals fear armed citizens and so do terrorists. And yet, the anti-gunners' argument that we can "all live with a little less freedom, if that's what it takes to live," is a seductive one—even to some who own guns. It's an argument that is not new, as we see in returning to Patrick Henry and the words he spoke at Virginia's state convention on ratification of the Constitution:

> Guard with jealous attention the public liberty. Suspect every one who approaches that jewel. Unfortunately, nothing will preserve it but downright force. Whenever you give up that force, you are ruined.[7]

5

CURRENT FIREARMS LAWS: PROSECUTION IS PREVENTION

It never fails to irritate the nation's firearms owners when statements like the following go unchallenged and uninvestigated by members of the national media:

> I think people around the country are shocked when they realize that we don't have federal laws when it comes to guns.[1]

Sarah Brady routinely makes such outrageous remarks, often to the nodding approval of anti-gun journalists.

So much for the so-called skeptical press, the nation's watchdog, its "Fourth Estate" devoted to digging into the truth.

The fact is, few other consumer products are surrounded by as many federal statutes and regulations as firearms, since federal law covers virtually every aspect of the manufacture, distribution, retail sale, ownership, and use of firearms.

What's more, we in this country have not one *but two* powerful federal agencies whose priorities specifically involve the enforcement of federal firearms regulations.

One is the Bureau of Alcohol, Tobacco and Firearms (BATF). The other is the U.S. Customs Service (USCS). And together with the FBI and other agencies that also enforce a vast array of federal gun laws, restrictions, and regulations, there are plenty of law enforcement agencies to enforce those laws.

The gun-ban lobby only pretends to be so grossly ignorant of just how many federal gun laws there really are. To name just a few:

- The National Firearms Act of 1934
- The Gun Control Act of 1968, amended by the Firearms Owner's Protection Act of 1986
- The Brady Handgun Violence Prevention Act of 1993
- The Youth Handgun Safety Act of 1994
- The Violent Crime Control and Law Enforcement Act of 1994
- The Gun Free School Zones Act of 1996

This expansive federal legal blanket covering firearms and a host of amendments added over the years by Congress have given the federal government the power to:

- Prosecute "prohibited persons." *It is a federal crime for certain classes listed under the law to own a firearm. Prohibited persons include a felon; a fugitive from justice; an unlawful user of, or addicted to, any controlled substance; an illegal alien; anyone discharged from military service under dishonorable conditions; anyone who renounced his or her citizenship; anyone under a restraining order prohibiting harassing, stalking, or threatening an intimate partner or child of an intimate partner; or anyone convicted of a misdemeanor crime of domestic violence.*

- Limit gun possession by age. *No one under twenty-one may legally purchase a handgun or handgun ammunition. Rifle or shotgun (and corresponding ammo) purchases are restricted to those eighteen or older. Except for target shooting, hunting, or other "specifically exempted purposes," no one under eighteen may possess or be given a handgun or handgun ammunition.*

- Impose the requirement of a Federal Firearms License (FFL) for firearms dealers, manufacturers, and importers. *A "dealer" is defined by BATF and federal regulations as anyone "engaged in the business" of selling firearms (wholesale or retail); repairing firearms; making or fitting special barrels, stocks, or triggers on firearms; or who is a pawnbroker. FFL holders have an extensive list of qualifications and regulations (including compliance with all state and local ordinances including zoning) that must be met and a schedule of fees to be paid before a three-year license is issued. BATF also issues a federally approved collector's license. Federal license holders are subject to annual inspections of records and inventory by BATF.*

In addition, federally licensed gun dealers must keep extensive, detailed, and accurate records of inventory and sales. They must make those records available to law enforcement engaged in criminal investigations. Finally, FFL holders must notify BATF of any "multiple" sale, defined as two or more handguns purchased by an individual in a five-day period.

These are just some of the highlights of the mountain of federal laws covering firearms commerce that can be brought to bear against criminal activity.

Of course, with laws come penalties for *breaking* these laws.

And the penalties for breaking America's gun laws are as severe as the list of gun laws is long. To describe just a few:

- Ten years in prison for altering a semiautomatic firearm to full automatic mode
- Five years in prison for possession of an altered semiautomatic firearm
- Five years in prison for trading or selling an altered semiautomatic firearm
- Ten years in prison for a felon to possess any firearm
- Seven-year mandatory minimum prison sentence for brandishing a firearm in a violent or drug-trafficking crime
- Twenty-year mandatory prison sentence for a second conviction for use of a firearm in a violent or drug-trafficking crime
- Life in prison without parole if the firearm used in the second crime is a machine gun or is equipped with a silencer
- Fifteen-year mandatory prison term for firearm possession by a criminal with three prior violent or drug-trafficking felonies
- Ten-year prison term for transferring a firearm knowing it will be used in a violent or drug-trafficking crime
- Ten-year prison term for transporting or receiving a firearm or ammunition in interstate commerce with intent to commit a felony
- Ten-year prison term for shortening a shotgun barrel to less than eighteen inches or a rifle barrel to less than sixteen inches

- Ten-year prison term for traveling from one state to another to acquire or attempt to acquire a firearm with the intent to use it in a violent felony
- Five-year prison sentence for altering the serial number of a firearm
- Five-year prison sentence for possessing a firearm with an altered serial number

Given that litany of laws and punishments, enforcement agencies have all the federal tools needed to scare any would-be armed criminal straight. But that assumption is based on another assumption: federal prosecutors are using these laws to punish criminals. The fact is, all too often they don't.

Under Janet Reno, the U.S. Justice Department rarely enforced the very gun laws the Clinton-Gore administration so revered. In fact, the administration appeared to care much more about scoring political points with the anti-gun media and politicians than ensuring safety for our citizens and our communities.

Case in point: Bill Clinton loved to brag about how the Brady Act "prevented" tens of thousands of felons from purchasing firearms, but a study conducted by the General Accounting Office in 1996 found only seven successful Brady Act prosecutions during the first seventeen months the law was in effect.[2]

How on earth could the administration justify prosecuting *only seven* of these felons? And what about punishments meted out for those who were prosecuted under federal law? Three of the cases involved individuals who lied about drug-related felony convictions and received sentences of one to two years. The other four involved residents of New York who falsified identification cards claiming West Virginia residency. Three of those four received two years' probation. One served six months' home detention and three years' probation.[3]

Bill Clinton and Janet Reno claimed that the Brady Act "prevented" literally hundreds of thousands of, to use their words, "felons, fugitives, and mentally unstable persons" from purchasing handguns. But the federal gun laws are intended to *bring violators to justice*—to arrest, prosecute, and, if convicted, punish criminals. Those tough laws, if enforced, would have removed criminals from our streets and our neighborhoods.

What protection is afforded the public when violent felons who violate federal laws that carry stiff prison sentences are allowed to walk free? How does a government that refuses to punish a violation deter felons from committing violent crimes against you or me?

It doesn't, and therein lies the critical point: we don't have a *gun problem* in America, we have an *enforcement problem.* And when armed criminals go free and violence escalates, the gun-ban lobby uses that malfeasance to push for even more laws restricting lawful firearms ownership.

During the first six years of the Clinton-Gore administration, BATF referrals for prosecution of federal gun laws dropped by 44 percent, from 9,885 to 5,510.[4]

What's more, cases made by ATF and sent to state and federal prosecutors dropped 46.5 percent, from 12,084 to 6,470, during that same period. Sentences under Clinton-Gore-Reno also dropped from a "high" of 57 months in 1996 to 48 months in 1997 to 46 months in 1998.[5]

The National Rifle Association bucked the Clinton administration, the media, and anti-gun extremists in supporting the model of success in using federal gun laws to slash armed violent crime in our communities—Richmond, Virginia's *Project Exile.*

Project Exile is a federal, state, and local effort led by the U.S. Attorney's Office in Richmond that prosecutes violent felons in possession of guns. When law enforcement apprehends a criminal with a gun, he is "exiled" to federal prison for a minimum of five years.

In 1997, Richmond had the second highest per capita homicide rate in the nation.[6] After implementing *Project Exile,* the number of homicides dropped 45 percent.[7] In 2001, Richmond experienced the lowest number of homicides since 1983.[8] So remarkable was *Project Exile's* enormous success that it was quickly expanded to other Virginia cities and ultimately statewide.

Under *Project Exile,* Richmond Police Department officers and Virginia State Troopers carried a laminated card listing the types of criminals targeted for *Project Exile* prosecution under federal law. That list included a person who had a gun and was a "convicted felon (state or federal), drug user or addict, fugitive who had fled another state (or) is under indictment for a felony." When a police officer made an arrest, the officer called the twenty-four-hour pager number listed on the card to determine if federal law had been broken. If it had, *Project Exile* initiated federal prosecution immediately.[9]

The U.S. Attorney for the Eastern District of Virginia, whose office initiated *Project Exile,* told the *Newport News Daily Press* on January 23, 1998, that "officials were shocked . . . at the extent of (*Project Exile*) suspects' criminal records. Several had between four and eight convictions for offenses as serious as robbery, abduction, and murder."

Project Exile officials said the federal system offered the advantages of prompt indictments, less likelihood of bond (therefore no pretrial release), a requirement that 85 percent of sentences be served, and prisons less accessible to family and friends. Press reports showed that a felon-in-possession case in state courts took about a year to prosecute, during which time most defendants were back on the streets, free on bond. The same court case took seventy days and bond was denied in 80 percent of *Project Exile* cases.

The U.S. Attorney reported that publicity was essential to the program's success, and NRA-member dollars helped fund advertising to spread the word about *Project Exile.* Thousands of business cards were printed and distributed with the slogan "An illegal gun gets you 5 years in Federal Prison," and the message was repeated on billboards and in advertising on radio, television, and city buses. In a letter to the U.S. Attorney, one *Project Exile* criminal complained that the sentence of six and a half to eight years recommended for him was unfair because "even the bus and the billboard says [sic] five years."

Federal law requires a mandatory minimum five years in prison for illegally possessing a firearm or ammunition, and under *Project Exile,* prosecutors did not plea-bargain a sentence below the mandatory minimum. *Project Exile* assisted law enforcement in other ways, too. As reported in the *Daily Press* in 1998:

> When *Newport News* (VA) police arrested a convicted felon a few months ago for injuring a person with a gun, witnesses refused to testify . . . The charges against him seemed to be going nowhere. But a program called "Project Exile" breathed new life into the case. Instead of dropping it, officials charged the man with federal offenses (being a felon in possession of a gun). Last month, he was indicted by a federal grand jury and faces up to 10 years in prison . . . "We don't need the witnesses now," said *Newport News* Detective Rick Reid . . . "Without the federal charges, he might have just walked."[10]

In Richmond, career opportunities for armed criminals rapidly diminished. Hundreds of violent felons were put in prison for long mandatory sentences.

Project Exile put into practice what the NRA had been saying all along. Armed criminals were arrested and "exiled" from innocent citizens through absolute and certain federal prosecution and prison under existing laws. Criminals such as drug dealers, felons, and fugitives—all those categories that make revolving-door statistics of the Brady Act so obscene—were in deep trouble in Richmond if they possessed any gun. Punishment was swift with no escape for the guilty. The word spread.

As governor of Texas, George W. Bush took the program

statewide as *Texas Exile*. In his race against Al Gore, Governor Bush promised that the Bush administration would concentrate on enforcing existing firearms laws against violent predators and felons rather than pushing new gun-control laws that infringe on the rights of law-abiding citizens.

President Bush has fulfilled that pledge. The U.S. Department of Justice, under a program called Project Safe Neighborhoods, has committed significant resources to beef up federal, state, and local prosecutions of armed violent criminals. Said U.S. Attorney General John Ashcroft:

> The objective of Project Safe Neighborhoods is to encourage all levels of law enforcement to work together in a strategic and coordinated fashion—so that gun criminals can be tried in either federal or state courts—whichever venue provides the toughest sentences for that particular crime. We want the states to do what the states do best and the feds to do what the feds do best.
>
> Where federal prosecution is involved, I have directed each United States Attorney to prosecute, to the fullest extent possible, the following groups of offenders: violent offenders and organizations who use guns, illegal gun traffickers, and individuals who are prohibited from lawfully possessing a gun—such as felons in possession of a gun and those who attempt to purchase a gun in violation of the Brady Act. Under the nation's tough federal sentencing guidelines, criminals will serve hard federal time if convicted of one of these crimes.[11]

The success of *Project Exile* was based on holding individuals accountable for their actions by using the tough penalty provisions under existing federal laws that cover every corner of America. *Project Exile* was instituted not to look tough in the press but to actually put criminals who terrorize our streets and neighborhoods behind bars and keep them there, where they belong.

6

SELF-PROTECTION: WOMEN AND GUNS

While it is common knowledge that Franklin and Theodore Roosevelt were firearms enthusiasts and hunters, it is less known that Eleanor Roosevelt carried a revolver for personal protection after she moved into the White House in 1933.

"From nearly the first day that Eleanor Roosevelt became First Lady, she refused to be a victim, and she exercised her choice to carry a handgun for protection," according to a recently published, well-documented article penned by scholars at the Independence Institute.[1] A firearm, not a bodyguard or the FBI or the Secret Service, was her constant companion as she recalled in an autobiography:

> Driving my own car was one of the issues the Secret Service people and I had a battle about at the very start. The Secret Service prefers to have an agent go with the President's wife, but I did not want either a chauffeur or a Secret Service agent. After the head of the Secret Service found I was not going to allow an agent to accompany me everywhere, he went one day to Louis Howe [FDR's secretary], plunked a revolver down on the table and said, "Well, all right, if Mrs. Roosevelt is going to drive around the country alone, at least ask her to carry this in the car." I carried it religiously.[2]

Upon leaving the White House, Mrs. Roosevelt moved to New York City where she obtained a permit to carry a concealed handgun in light of numerous death threats she had received. To the anti-gun lobby, she would be excoriated today for taking charge over her life. As the Independence Institute Scholars noted:

> If [Eleanor Roosevelt] were alive . . . Hillary Clinton would lecture the old woman about how people shouldn't own guns for protection. But the old lady probably wouldn't listen to Hillary any more than she listened to all the other people who told her what she wasn't supposed to do . . . What a perfect example of how the Second Amendment is really the cornerstone of our Bill of Rights, the guarantor of all others.[3]

Mrs. Roosevelt's self-reliance sharply contrasts with the gun-ban lobby's credo: No matter what happens—don't resist. Indeed, in 1993 Sarah Brady announced to the *Tampa Tribune*, "To me, the only reason for guns in civilian hands is for sporting purposes." And her husband, Jim Brady, identified the circumstances in which he believes people should be allowed to possess handguns: "For target shooting, that's okay. Get a license and go to the range. For defense of the home, that's why we have police departments."[4]

As Sarah Brady told the *New York Times*, her long-term goal is enacting a "needs-based licensing" system.[5] The local police chief would decide if a person who wanted to buy a gun had a legitimate "need"—as if self-defense were a privilege, not a right.

The fundamental right of self-defense has been affirmed repeatedly by America's greatest legal scholars. Chancellor James Kent's multivolume commentaries, first published in 1826, became the leading American law book. Kent's *Commentaries on American Law* explains that Americans have "the natural right of self-defense, in all those cases in which the law is either too slow or too feeble to stay the hand of violence." Kent explains that homicide in self-defense is justifiable, not merely excusable, and that an individual's right to self-defense "cannot be superseded by the law of the society."[6]

U.S. Supreme Court Chief Justice Joseph Story, the most influential legal mind of the period between the American Revolution and the Civil War, believed in the natural-law right to self-defense since "self-preservation" was one of an individual's natural duties. Thus, "a man has a perfect right to his life, to his personal liberty, and to his property; and he may by force assert and vindicate those rights against every aggressor."[7]

The U.S. Supreme Court's most famous exposition of the right to self-defense is the 1921 decision *Brown v. United States,* written by the great Oliver Wendell Holmes. The case began at a federal naval yard in Texas where a man named Hermis had twice assaulted Brown with a knife, and warned that the next time, one of them "would go off in a black box." One day, Hermis again attacked Brown with a knife whereupon Brown ran to get his coat, which contained a pistol. Hermis pursued, and Brown shot him four times, killing him. At trial, the judge instructed the jury that Brown had a duty to retreat, if he could do so safely.

When the Supreme Court decided the case on appeal, Justice Holmes, a legal historian, traced the duty-to-retreat rule to an earlier period in English history when the law did not even recognize a legal right to self-defense. "The law has grown," Holmes wrote, "in the direction of rules consistent with human nature." Thus, declared Holmes, there is no legal duty to retreat before using deadly force. Nor should a victim's response to a criminal attack be second-guessed at leisure by a judge: "Detached reflection cannot be demanded in the presence of an uplifted knife."

The *Brown* decision was the culmination of numerous cases from the turn of the century in which the Court vigorously protected and expanded the right of self-defense.[8]

Joining Holmes's unanimous opinion for the Supreme Court was Justice Louis Brandeis, who once wrote, "We shall have lost something vital and beyond price on the day when the state denies us the right to resort to force . . ."[9] These justices would be horrified to learn what is going on today, when people who use firearms to defend themselves against violent attacking criminals are criminally prosecuted.

The nineteenth-century French philosopher Frederic Bastiat, in his classic *The Law,* wrote that when "law" is used to protect criminals and to render victims defenseless, true law has been destroyed. He observed that "sometimes the law places the whole apparatus of judges, police, prisons, and gendarmes at the service of plunderers and treats the victim—when he defends himself—as a criminal. In short, there is a legal plunder . . ."[10]

Consider a modern-day situation: a mother in a rough Los Angeles neighborhood moments after an escaped, psychopathic murderer has broken into her house. The woman has a good reason to fear that the intruder is about to slaughter her three children. If she does not shoot him with her revolver, the children will be dead before the police arrive. Is the woman's moral obligation to murmur "violence engenders violence," and keep her handgun in the drawer while her children die? Or is the mother's moral duty to save her children and shoot the intruder?

The gun-prohibition lobbies know that they can't convince the American public that self-defense is immoral, so instead they argue that the average citizen is too incompetent to use a firearm for protection—especially when more and more women choose to own firearms to protect themselves and their families. The great irony is, and always has been, that the only people who benefit from women being disarmed are the very people who wish women harm, particularly rapists.

John Lott, in his book *More Guns, Less Crime,* found that rape declines about 5 percent when states enact laws allowing licensed, trained women to carry handguns for lawful protection.[11] Dramatic proof of how much rapists fear armed victims was provided in the late 1960s, when the Orlando Police Department sponsored firearms safety training for women.[12] The Orlando police instituted this program when it became evident that many women were arming themselves in response to a dramatic increase in sexual assaults in the area. The year following the well-publicized safety-training program witnessed an 88 percent drop in the number of rapes in Orlando. As Gary Kleck and David Bordua note: "It cannot be claimed that this was merely part of a general downward trend in rape, since the national rate was increasing at the time. No other U.S. city with a population over 100,000 experienced so large a percentage decrease in the number of rapes from 1966 to 1967 . . ." Furthermore, that same year, rape increased by 5 percent in the state of Florida and 7 percent on the national level.

In objecting to women arming themselves for protection, gun banners claim that a rapist will seize the gun and use it against his victim; proponents of this argument, however, seem unable to cite real-world examples of this theory. In his book *The Best Defense,* Robert Waters cites countless cases of women, even grandmothers, using firearms to stop rapists and other predators.[13]

Further, as Attorney Jeffrey Snyder elaborates:

> Rape, robbery, and attempted murder are not typically actions rife with ambiguity or subtlety, requiring special powers of observation and great book-learning to discern. When a man pulls a knife on a woman and says, "You're coming with me," her judgment that a crime is being committed is not likely to be in error. There is little chance that she is going to shoot the wrong person. It is the police, because they are rarely at the scene of the crime when it occurs, who are more likely to find themselves in circumstances where guilt and innocence are not so clear-cut, and in which the probability for mistakes is higher.[14]

Another common claim of the gun prohibitionists is that women who are threatened by stalkers, batterers, and their ilk can protect themselves by getting a restraining order. Of course, this is nonsense—

anyone who is prepared to violate the laws against rape and murder isn't going to be stopped by a piece of paper.

As for the notion that citizens can always rely on the government for protection, consider the case of Linda Riss, a young woman who telephoned the police and begged for help because her ex-boyfriend had repeatedly threatened, "If I can't have you no one else will have you, and when I get through with you, no one else will want you."[15]

The day after she pleaded for police protection, the ex-boyfriend threw lye in her face, blinding her in one eye, severely damaging the other, and permanently scarring her features. "What makes the City's position particularly difficult to understand," wrote a dissenting opinion in her tort suit against the City, "is that, in conformity to the dictates of the law, Linda did not carry any weapon for self-defense. Thus, by a rather bitter irony she was required to rely for protection on the City of New York which now denies all responsibility to her."[16]

Other examples abound. Ruth Brunell called the police on twenty different occasions to plead for protection from her husband. He was arrested only one time. One evening Brunell telephoned his wife and told her he was coming over to kill her. When she called the police seeking immediate aid, they told her to call back when he got there. Mrs. Brunell was stabbed to death before she could call the police a second time. The court held that the San Jose police were not liable for ignoring her pleas for help.[17]

In the case of *Warren v. District of Columbia,* two women were upstairs in a home when they heard a roommate being attacked by men who had broken in downstairs. The women immediately telephoned the police for assistance. Half an hour passed and since their roommate's screams ceased, the women assumed the police had arrived and stopped the assault. In reality, their call had somehow been lost in the shuffle, and the roommate was beaten into silence. When the two women went downstairs, as the court's opinion graphically describes: "For the next fourteen hours the women were held captive, raped, robbed, beaten, forced to commit sexual acts upon each other, and made to submit to the sexual demands" of their attackers.

The roommates later sued the District of Columbia for ignoring the call for help. Having set out the facts of the case, the District of Columbia's highest court exonerated the District and its police, saying there is a "fundamental principle of American law that a government and its agents are under no general duty to provide public services, such as police protection, to any individual citizen."[18] The rule that police have no legal duty to protect an individual, only the community at large, is very well established.[19]

It is hypocritical for armed police administrators who work in buildings protected by government-issue guards, and politicians who live in safe neighborhoods and have ready access to government-paid protection, to cite legal immunity in protecting the individual citizen, and then enact harshly restrictive gun laws to prevent people from protecting themselves.

Like Eleanor Roosevelt, many women today have assumed responsibility for protecting themselves. Recently, the Second Amendment Sisters partnered with the Patrick Henry Center for Individual Liberty to provide gun-safety classes for Virginia women to obtain Right-to-Carry permits. Announcing the new program, the "Patriettes" stated: "In response to the endless parade of the raped, the mugged, the stabbed, the murdered . . . the Patriettes refuse to allow women to be an easy target by empowering them to fight back and defend themselves with a firearm!"[20]

All over the country, NRA-certified instructors teach women how to use firearms to deter violent crime. Women from all walks of life are learning that they do not have to live in fear, they don't always need to entrust their lives to others—and that they can protect themselves. As Eleanor Roosevelt would put it, "No one can make me feel inferior without my consent."[21]

7

THE RIGHT TO CARRY: TRUSTING CITIZENS WITH FIREARMS

On December 17, 1991, in Anniston, Alabama, a restaurant patron defended himself and saved the lives of nearly two dozen others held hostage by two armed would-be robbers. The reluctant hero, who was legally carrying his .45-caliber firearm, stopped both assailants before they could complete their crime or injure innocent customers.

On October 16, 1991, in Killeen, Texas, an armed homicidal maniac methodically killed twenty-two people and then himself, facing no resistance from the scores of potential victims, including Suzanna Gratia Hupp. Dr. Gratia Hupp, who lost both her parents in that shooting, went on to become one of the leading advocates for an individual's right to carry a concealed weapon. She has testified numerous times across the country on Right-to-Carry and made a convincing case wherever she spoke:

> That tragedy will be forever etched in my memory. My parents were brutally murdered, and I was helpless to protect them. None of us in that restaurant could control our own destinies, for Texas politicians had seen fit to keep us disarmed.
>
> State law prohibits the concealed carrying of firearms, denying me or someone else the right to have a gun that day to protect ourselves and our loved ones from the rampages of a madman.

> That's flat-out wrong. And I intend to do everything in my power to change that ill-gotten law to avert needless suffering by others.
>
> The violent incidents in Anniston and Killeen ended far differently because of the laws governing the concealed carrying of firearms. Alabama has a fair concealed-carry law, but in Texas the government has said, in effect, that decent citizens can't be trusted to carry firearms for self-protection. The facts simply do not justify that conclusion.
>
> Clearly, concealed-carry laws translate to saving the lives of loved ones in a manner similar to health or life insurance. If ever there arises that time when it is needed, no substitute will do, and I don't intend to be victimized again.
>
> The question of carrying a concealed handgun is one that is highly personal and should be made by the individual. And it is a choice that should not be forbidden to an honest citizen like myself by an overprotective government, particularly one that has no responsibility to provide real protection when my life is threatened.

That testimony was presented before the Virginia Senate Courts of Justice Committee on January 25, 1995, by Dr. Suzanna Gratia Hupp, who for the past decade has urged legislatures all over the United States to adopt Right-to-Carry laws to save innocent lives. To date, thirty-three states including Virginia and Texas respect the rights of honest citizens to carry concealed handguns for self-defense.

As battles over the issue heated up in state after state, many more women would join the ranks of Dr. Gratia Hupp in speaking forcefully to lawmakers in urging passage of such laws.

On February 28, 1995, Dr. Mary L. Cannon gave expert testimony before the Texas Senate Crime and Criminal Justice Committee on pending concealed-carry legislation. As a forensic psychiatrist, Dr. Cannon has served as a consultant to the courts in Dallas and Tarrant Counties, the federal prison at Seagoville, the Dallas County Sheriff's

Department, and the Dallas County Mental Illness Court. With that extensive background, Dr. Cannon told the committee, "I feel I am well-qualified to speak on the issue before us." Her testimony was riveting:

> Briefly, I would like to tell you about a young man that I examined in August of last year. He had turned 18 years old two weeks before I saw him. He had been indicted on three counts of capital murder in a drive-by shooting. He has never married, but he has two daughters, ages 18 months and 6 months. When he was 10 years old, he beat and stabbed a 101-year-old woman nearly to death—she did survive. He spent the next five or so years in various rehabilitative centers . . . I questioned this young man about his feelings regarding the killings. I asked him, "Does it bother you to have killed these people? Do you feel badly about it?" In a flippant, almost sarcastic manner he replied, "No, if you don't have something you want and you see somebody else has it, you take it." I asked what he took at the drive-by shooting. His reply was "Nothing. Those people were—. They didn't deserve to live."
>
> What does this have to do with the concealed-carry weapon bill? A lot! Because we are almost constantly told that weapons cause violence. I am here to tell you that people cause violence . . . We must learn to place responsibility for behavior on the individual rather than a particular instrument or tool.
>
> Until we learn to do this, the law-abiding citizens of this state must have some relief. The predators are out there. They are not going to go away. Until great changes are made, they will continue to see their own value and worth in terms of the amount of destruction and chaos they can create. These young men see their very manhood defined by the killing of others. Obviously, the police cannot be everywhere. The well-trained law-abiding citizen must be given an even chance.

In the mid-1980s, only a half-dozen states routinely issued permits for trained citizens to carry concealed handguns for personal protection—and these permits were rarely given to persons other than retired government employees and other people with political connections.

Today, however, states comprising over half the nation's population grant concealed-carry permits to law-abiding citizens.

In what would become a nationwide campaign, the reform movement began in the early 1980s when gun-rights activists in Florida joined with law-enforcement organizations such as the Florida Chiefs of Police Association to fix the state's law. Under the leadership of Marion P. Hammer of Unified Sportsmen of Florida, legislation was introduced entitling any law-abiding adult citizen who cleared a fingerprint-based background check and passed gun-safety classes to receive a permit to carry a concealed handgun for protection.

Although the legislature passed the Right-to-Carry bill several times, it was vetoed repeatedly by Democratic Governor Bob Graham. His successor, Republican Governor Bob Martinez, signed the bill in 1987, and since then, a steady progression of states have adopted concealed-carry laws modeled on Florida's, and more will follow.

Of course, whenever a state legislature first considered a concealed-carry bill, the anti-gun lobby warned of horrible consequences: permit holders will slaughter each other in traffic disputes, bars will become shooting galleries, and would-be Rambos will shoot bystanders in incompetent attempts to thwart crime—and on and on and on.

But, like clockwork, these apocalyptic warnings soon began to drop off the media's radar screen as none of the anti-gun lobby's dire predictions came true.

In Florida, then Licensing Division Director John Russi noted that there had been "no record of any accidents or incidents from a lack of training . . . and that Florida's concealed weapon law had been very successful. All major law enforcement groups supported the original legislation, and in the eight years the program has been in place, none of these groups has requested any changes . . . [S]ome of the opponents of concealed weapon legislation in 1987 now admit the program has not created the problems many predicted."[1]

In a March 15, 1995, official correspondence to state officials, Department of Law Enforcement Commissioner James T. Moore wrote: "From a law enforcement perspective, the licensing process has not resulted in problems in the community from people arming themselves with concealed weapons. The strict provisions of 790.06, Florida Statutes, preclude the licensing of convicted felons, etc., thus allowing the permitting of law-abiding citizens who do not routinely commit crimes or otherwise violate the law."[2]

Both John B. Holmes, Harris County district attorney, and Glen White, president of the Dallas Police Association, initially opposed concealed carry in Texas but have subsequently embraced it. Holmes said, "I [felt] that such legislation . . . present[ed] a clear and present danger to law-abiding citizens by placing more handguns on our streets. Boy was I wrong. Our experience in Harris County, and indeed statewide, has proven my initial fears absolutely groundless." And White said, "All the horror stories I thought would come to pass didn't happen . . . I think it's worked out well, and that says good things about the citizens who have permits. I'm a convert."[3] Clearly, Right-to-Carry laws are vital tools in the fight against violent crime.

Perhaps most frustrating of all to the anti-gun lobby is the fact that about a quarter of those who apply for and receive carry permits are women. When Alaska Governor Walter Hickel signed concealed-carry legislation in 1993, he explained that the constituents he found most compelling were "the women who called and said they worked late and had to cross dark parking lots, and why couldn't they carry a concealed gun?"

It is no surprise, therefore, that one of the most visible advocates for Right-to-Carry laws is Dr. Suzanna Gratia Hupp, now married, the mother of two boys, a member of the Texas State Legislature, and a strong proponent of Second Amendment rights.

When George Hennard rammed his pickup truck into Luby's Cafeteria in Killeen, Texas, in 1991, many diners were sprayed with glass fragments, and one man was caught underneath the truck. Hennard exited the truck, shouting, "This is for what the women of Bell County did to me!" It was later revealed that Hennard considered his mother a "viper" who had ruined his childhood. Most, but not all, of his victims would be women.

A man pinned under the truck pulled himself out and was immediately shot in the head. Hennard was armed with a pair of handguns. There were 162 people in the restaurant, but—with one important exception—no one offered any resistance.

Over 17 minutes, Hennard killed 22 people and wounded 21.

Along with her parents, Dr. Gratia was in Luby's Cafeteria when Hennard opened fire. Her .38 Special revolver, however, was in her car in the parking lot.

Why?

Because Dr. Gratia Hupp was afraid that if she were caught carrying a gun, she could lose her chiropractor's license.

As she later testified to the Missouri legislature:

> After Hennard drove in and opened fire, well, my father and I immediately put the table up in front of us and we all got down behind it. Your first opinion is, is this guy robbing this place? What's the deal? And then what he's doing is simply shooting people.
>
> As he was working his way toward us, I reached for my purse, thinking, "Hah! I've got this son of a gun." Now, understand, I know what a lot of people think, . . . they think, "Oh, my God, then you would have had a gunfight and then more people would have been killed." No, I was down on the floor; this guy is

> standing up; everybody else is down on the floor. I had a perfect shot at him. It would have been clear. I had a place to prop my hand. The guy was not even aware of what we were doing. I'm not saying that I could have saved anybody in there, but I would have had a chance.
>
> My gun wasn't even in my purse . . . it was a hundred feet away in my car.
>
> My father was saying, "I gotta do something! I gotta do something! This guy's going to kill everyone in here!" So I wasn't able to hold him down and when my father thought he had a chance, he went at the guy! The guy turned, shot him in the chest, and my dad went down.
>
> It made the guy change directions and he went off to my left. Shortly after that somebody broke out a window in back and I saw a chance to get out. I grabbed my mother and tried to get her up, hoped she was following me, and I grew wings on my feet. As it turned out, my mother crawled over to my father and stayed with him; and this—I'm trying to think of a civil word to use—this person eventually came around and shot her also.

Police told Dr. Gratia Hupp that they had seen her mother cradling her father's head in her lap. She looked up at Hennard, and then bowed her head just before he shot her.

A police training class was taking place in a hotel near the cafeteria, and when police arrived on the scene, a marksman wounded Hennard, who retreated and fatally shot himself.

A search of Hennard's home later revealed a videotape in his VCR: a documentary about the 1984 mass murder at a McDonald's in San Ysidro, California. There, James Huberty had walked out of his home and announced that he was going "to hunt humans." He entered the McDonald's and opened fire with three different guns. A police SWAT team sped to the restaurant and swiftly had Huberty in their sights. But the SWAT team did not open fire. Instead, they watched Huberty as he methodically reloaded, strolled over to victims who lay wounded but alive, and shot them in the head. The SWAT team was under strict orders not to fire until their lieutenant arrived on the scene. The lieutenant was stuck in a traffic jam.

Shortly after the Killeen massacre, Killeen's police chief suggested that citizens ought to be able to carry guns for protection. Earlier that year, the Texas State Senate had passed a bill to allow trained, licensed adults to obtain permits to carry concealed handguns for lawful protection. There were enough votes to pass the bill on the floor of the Texas House. The House Rules Committee, acting in secret, killed the bill by keeping it from coming to the House floor for a vote.

Even if the bill had passed the legislature, Governor Ann Richards would have vetoed it, as she did when a handgun-carry bill passed the next legislature. That veto played a major role in Richards's 1994 election defeat by Republican George W. Bush. In 1995, Bush signed a Right-to-Carry bill nearly identical to the one vetoed by Governor Richards.

As Dr. Gratia Hupp testified, if only the laws had been different in Texas in 1991—as they were that year in Alabama, just two states away—her parents might be alive.

Two months after Killeen, a pair of criminals with stolen pistols herded twenty customers and employees into the walk-in refrigerator of a Shoney's restaurant in Anniston, Alabama. Hiding under a table in the restaurant was Thomas Glenn Terry, armed with the .45 pistol he carried legally under Alabama law. One of the robbers discovered Terry, but Terry shot and killed him. The second robber, who had been holding the manager hostage, shot at Terry and grazed him. Terry returned fire and wounded the robber. Twenty-two people died in Killeen, Texas, where carrying a gun for self-defense was illegal. Twenty lives were saved in Anniston, Alabama, where self-defense permits were legal—and remain legal today.

The Shoney's restaurant was hardly the only place in America where a rampaging mass murderer was stopped by an armed citizen. And America is hardly the only country where firearms save lives from rampaging murderers. In Israel, it has become almost commonplace—although it is not something you commonly hear about from the anti-gun media.

The American media, and indeed the world's media, almost always give saturation coverage to *successful* terrorist attacks on innocent Israelis. They give far less coverage, however, to terrorist attacks *that fail*—especially when they fail because of the fast thinking and action of *armed Israeli civilians.*

Here are just a few recent examples, buried deep on the back pages of the media, of how guns in the hands of armed Israeli citizens have prevented murder and tragedy at the hands of armed terrorists:

March 9, 2002—The *Jerusalem Post* reported that a would-be suicide bomber fled the Israeli town of Karkur on Thursday, March 7, after an Israeli citizen carrying a pistol confronted him.[4]

April 6, 2002—The *Boston Globe* reported that gun sales in Israel were skyrocketing, "particularly since an Israeli shoe salesman used his own weapon to fatally shoot a 46-year-old Palestinian who had opened fire in a Tel Aviv restaurant on March 5 and killed three Israelis. The Interior Ministry says applications for licenses have tripled during the past month, overwhelming its staff and forcing it to shift employees from other departments to handle the deluge. The Israeli government, meanwhile, has moved to ease once-tight restrictions on owning a gun . . ."[5]

May 29, 2002—The *Jerusalem Post* reported, "An Israeli teacher and a school security guard teamed up Tuesday night to shoot a pair of Al Aqsa terrorists who were attacking a high school, and who had already killed three students."[6]

May 31, 2002—The *Ha'aretz Daily* reported, "A Palestinian man was killed early Friday morning after he opened fire and threw grenades at a kindergarten and homes in the West Bank settlement of Shavei Shomron . . . David Elbaz, a grocery shop keeper in the settlement, saw the attacker and shot him twice. The Palestinian returned fire at Elbaz, who managed to take cover and avoid being hit. Elbaz then went around the building behind which the infiltrator was hiding, shot the man in the back and killed him."[7]

When it comes to efficacy of citizen self-defense in America, Dr. John Lott's second edition of *More Guns, Less Crime* provides solid statistical evidence. Lott's study, conducted with David Mustard of the University of Chicago, analyzed the FBI crime statistics for all 3,054 American counties from 1979 to 1992. According to Professor Lott:

> Our findings are dramatic. Our most conservative estimates show that by adopting shall-issue laws, states reduced murders by 8.5%, rapes by 5%, aggravated assaults by 7% and robbery by 3%. If those states that did not permit concealed handguns in 1992 had permitted them back then, citizens would have been spared approximately 1,570 murders, 4,177 rapes, 60,000 aggravated assaults and 12,000 robberies. To put it even more simply: Criminals, we found, respond rationally to deterrence threats.
>
> The benefits of concealed handguns are not limited to just those who carry them or use them in self-defense. The very fact that these weapons are concealed keeps criminals uncertain as to whether a potential victim will be able to defend himself with lethal force. The possibility that anyone might be carrying a gun makes attacking everyone less attractive; unarmed citizens in effect "free-ride" on their pistol-packing fellows.[8]

In short, all of us would be safer from criminals and from foreign or domestic terrorists if the seventeen holdout states without a fair, nondiscriminatory, shall-issue law would allow citizens to protect themselves.

Tragically, the anti-gun lobby fights these reasonable laws every step of the way. They say you should remain defenseless against criminals and terrorists. They say you should be terrified at the thought of people like Dr. Suzanna Gratia Hupp carrying a licensed gun. They say you shouldn't own a gun; you should depend on the government to protect *you.*

Lott's data, however, clearly show that preventing citizens from legally carrying handguns makes them more vulnerable to violent criminal attacks. Lott's conclusions are most telling: many criminals concluded that the risks of encountering a victim who could fight back had simply become too high.

While 1 to 4 percent of the adult population exercise the freedom to carry a handgun for protection, a majority of Americans believe they should have such a choice. Polls show that one-half to two-thirds of the population support concealed-carry laws. Even higher rates are reported when respondents are informed about the various restrictions, such as training requirements. That high level of support is based on the principle that responsible citizens should not expect government to provide them with the essentials of life. More specifically, providing for the safety of one's self and one's family is first of all *a personal duty.* It is also an *indisputable right.*

Constitutional law professor Nelson Lund has long argued that the Second Amendment "unambiguously and irrefutably" establishes an individual right to keep and bear arms. He also believes this meaning clearly and logically extends to the right to carry arms. Of its fundamental purpose, Professor Lund has asserted:

> That purpose is to secure the natural right of self-defense, which is no less threatened when government deprives its citizens of the tools for resisting criminal predators than it would be if the government itself turned outlaw.[9]

8

MEDIA MISREPRESENTATION: AND THAT'S THE WAY IT ISN'T

Along with many Americans, gun owners believe that the mass media by and large have a strong bias that slants toward the left end of the political spectrum. The contrast is even more apparent when you compare the political sentiments that dominate the mass media with those expressed on the Internet—a medium with neither censors nor editors.

This perception is not paranoia, and it's not our imagination. It is statistically measurable, making the mass media a powerful weapon for the anti-gun lobby in its war against the Second Amendment.

In 1999, Brian Patrick, a graduate student at the University of Michigan, examined how five nationally prominent newspapers *(New York Times, Washington Post, Wall Street Journal, Los Angeles Times,* and *Christian Science Monitor)* covered the NRA. He then examined how those same newspapers covered other nationally prominent political groups, such as the National Association for the Advancement of Colored People (NAACP), the American Civil Liberties Union (ACLU), the American Association of Retired Persons (AARP), and Handgun Control, Inc. (HCI). And what he found was instructive, but not really very surprising.

After looking at more than fifteen hundred articles, columns, and editorials, Patrick discovered that the NRA is treated vastly different from those other advocacy organizations.

How? For one thing, the NRA was routinely referred to in negative terms such as "radical gun lobby" or "intimidating lobby of weapons peddlers," while the other groups Patrick studied were given either neutral or positive descriptions: "civil liberties group," "senior citizen advocates," "citizens' lobby," "nonprofit organization," "public interest group," "national civil rights group," "venerable civil rights organization," or "the nation's oldest and largest civil rights organization," and on and on and on.

The result was predictable: a large segment of society was programmed to see NRA as a "Darth Vader" image doing the "evil" bidding of the gun manufacturers who allegedly place profit ahead of lives. Never mind that the NRA's strength comes from its four million nationwide members, responsible Americans whose beliefs cross all cultural, demographic, and political lines. As the saying goes, never let the facts get in the way of the story.

Patrick also found that only 6 percent of articles about the NRA included a photograph of an NRA event or official. What about those *other* organizations? In articles about them, 27 percent of the time there was a photograph of one of their events, or of an official. That may not seem like much, but a photograph of an official makes that person real (not a faceless symbol, and therefore not frightening) and a lot less sinister—definitely not Darth Vader.

Patrick further discovered that NRA officials were much less likely to be properly identified with a title. Handgun Control, Inc., and NAACP officials were given their proper titles 64 and 73 percent of the time, respectively. NRA officers were identified by title less than 20 percent of the time. If that doesn't seem like a big deal, compare the openings of two hypothetical sentences: "According to Handgun Control, Inc., Chairman . . ." and "According to an NRA lobbyist . . ." Which person has a more dignified description, the HCI "Chairman" or some NRA lobbyist?[1]

But while Patrick zeroed in on print bias, rest assured it gets worse when you examine television news. The Media Research Center, a highly respected news watchdog group, found that from July 1, 1997, to June 30, 1999, the four big networks ran 653 stories concerning gun control. Of those, 357 advocated more gun control, 260 were neutral, and 36 were in opposition to more gun control. On one morning news interview show, guests were more than twice as likely to be gun-control advocates than opponents of more gun control.[2]

One powerful assumption shared by journalists who live in New York City, Washington, D.C., and, to a lesser extent, other big cities drives that anti-gun bias. To these self-appointed experts, guns are intrinsically *bad*.

The notion that all guns are evil is typically spawned if you live in New York City, Washington, D.C., Los Angeles, or Atlanta, where your chances of being killed by a violent criminal armed with a gun are dramatically higher than if you live in, say, Boise, Idaho, or Flagstaff, Arizona, or Burlington, Vermont. Rather than admit that in urban America the criminal justice system has crashed, it's a lot easier to blame the instrument rather than to demand and impose tough penalties to curb armed violence.

Political spin does not account for all the anti-gun bias you see in the mass media today. Laziness, deadline and ratings pressure, and the extraordinary influence of the *New York Times* and the *Washington Post* define coverage for all manner of issues facing the nation.

For all the supposed intellectual superiority of those in media, from high-priced anchors on down, many allow the *New York Times* and the *Washington Post* to define what is news and how to think. Watch TV news or read daily newspapers carefully in much of America, and you will start to see how reliant the so-called echo chamber has become on those two industry giants.

Newspaper editors are demanding stories now so that they don't have a big hole in the front page. Television journalists are under even more pressure so that they don't have the evening news anchor sitting there speechless for thirty seconds on the air. Desperate to hit deadlines, too many journalists, especially those working for daily newspapers and television, mimic media spin machines from coast to coast.

Most journalists, I would like to believe, try to make an effort to be accurate and fair. But when your boss is demanding a story now, it's all too convenient to take the easy way out. Since you fundamentally agree with Handgun Control, Inc., why bother calling the NRA to get an opposing opinion? Will anyone who reads your paper really care what the highly demonized "radical gun lobby" thinks?

Media fixation on firearms rather than violent criminals masks the root cause behind horrible crimes: America's failed justice system. In many ways the media's obsessive campaign to promote gun control actually *contributes to violent crime.* Yes, you read that correctly. The news media like to pretend they are only the messengers—that they only report on criminal violence, they don't stoke it. As the following two incidents will show, that's not true—and they know it's not true.

Case in point: in 1989, there were several incidents of mass murder involving semiautomatic rifles. The first involved a mentally ill prostitute named Patrick Purdy. On January 17, 1989, Purdy went into an elementary schoolyard in Stockton, California, armed with a rifle and, in a few minutes, murdered five children and then killed himself with a pistol. For two minutes, terror filled the schoolyard. For those children who survived, the trauma continues for a lifetime.

It was a horrifying crime, rendered even more horrifying by the discovery, after the fact, that it could have been prevented but for California's failed criminal justice system.[3] Purdy had been charged with at least seven felonies in the years before committing this monstrous act. Every one of the seven felonies had been plea-bargained down to a misdemeanor. This allowed Purdy to continue passing California's background check for buying handguns and wander the streets as a dangerous psychopath, instead of being locked up in a mental hospital.

One of the sad and bizarre coincidences in this case was that some of those felonies were plea-bargained down by Los Angeles County District Attorney John Van De Kamp. By the time Patrick Purdy had murdered his way into temporary fame, John Van De Kamp had been elected California's attorney general. Unsurprisingly, Van De Kamp then banged the drum for an "assault weapons" ban, rather than confront the failure of his office to do its job with Purdy.

For months, *Time* and *Newsweek* wrote thinly disguised news accounts about the need for a ban on "assault weapons," giving enormous publicity to what Purdy had done. What happens when you turn a small-time loser into a famous homicidal murderer? In Kentucky, a man named Joseph Wesbecher read those news stories, and it changed his life. Wesbecher, like Purdy, had a history of mental problems: he was receiving disability payments because he was unable to return to his job as a printer at Standard Gravure.

Wesbecher had made at least three suicide attempts before he read about Patrick Purdy. Wesbecher apparently didn't own a gun, but after seeing Purdy become famous, he bought one. When Wesbecher found out that his rifle wasn't the exact same model as Purdy's gun, he swapped it for that model. He kept a February 6, 1989, issue of *Time* that mentioned Purdy and mass murderer Robert Sherrill (who had murdered fourteen coworkers at a post office in 1986) and underlined the headline, "Calendar of Senseless Shootings."[4]

On September 14, 1989, Wesbecher went to the Standard Gravure plant, which apparently he blamed for his problems. He murdered eight people, wounded thirteen, and then, like Purdy, killed himself with a handgun. No rational person can look at the intentional parallels—and the sequence of events—and not see that *Time*'s coverage played a part in converting the suicidal Wesbecher into the homicidal Wesbecher.

Journalists knew these horrifying crimes would encourage copycats. *Newsweek,* in its Purdy coverage, even quoted one of the authors of a book on mass murder: "There's a copycat element that cannot be denied." Yet *Newsweek* and *Time* both gave enormous coverage of Purdy's crime in their pursuit of an "assault weapons" ban—and Joseph Wesbecher responded to the publicity.

Of course, you might argue that these horrifying crimes deserved publicity—and you would be right. But did they deserve so much? Freedom of the press is as fundamental as our freedom to keep and bear arms. But when it is reported that the two twisted teenagers who shot up Columbine High School in Colorado in 1999 had fantasized about being on the cover of *Time*—along with which actors would play them in the movie they were sure would be made about their killing spree—it is clear that some measure of media responsibility must temper their overly sensationalized crime coverage.

Media-made myths have been perpetuated for years to serve as stepping-stones to reshape America's policies on firearms ownership.

In 1965, the *Washington Post* ran a series of inflammatory editorials for seventy-seven straight days calling for harsh firearms laws.

In 1975, CBS ran a hysterical prime-time TV segment that portrayed hunters as irresponsible and unsportsmanlike villains.

In 1982, NBC embarked on a crusade against what it deemed "cop-killer" bullets. The ammunition in question was KTW, used only by law enforcement and without incident for years. Its capability of penetrating some of the protective bulletproof vests worn by police officers is what spurred NBC's attention. Ignoring law enforcement's pleas not to expose this "how-to" for criminals, NBC widely publicized its exposé.

In 1990, the CBS newsmagazine *48 Hours* hired a gunsmith to convert a semiautomatic rifle into a firearm capable of fully automatic fire to show how supposedly easy it is for such a gun to be converted.

In doing so, CBS made the words *"assault weapon"* a household name in America—and then called for a ban on the firearm it had just illegally converted. Of course, CBS neglected to tell its viewers that the conversion violated federal law, which strictly prohibits such an unlawful conversion and is punishable by up to ten years in federal prison and a $10,000 fine.

In its campaign to enact massive new gun restrictions, *Time* magazine once laid out a photo spread called "death by gun," showing more than four hundred shooting victims. It failed to mention that at least half were suicides, many others were engaged in criminal activities, and many of the few remaining were legitimate cases of self-defense.

This brings us back to the question: Do the news media, in pursuit of their gun-ban agenda, give disproportionate coverage to gun mass murder relative to other murders?

Time and *Newsweek* covered fifteen mass murderers in the years 1984 to 1991. Mass murders committed with guns received an average of 14.93 square inches of coverage per victim. Mass murders committed with gasoline received 1.70 square inches of coverage per victim. Why did guns get so much more attention? Was it because *Time* and *Newsweek* weren't trying to get gasoline banned?

It is also noteworthy that neither *Time* nor *Newsweek* covered the embarrassing discovery about the "let's make Patrick Purdy famous" issue of *Time* found marked up in Wesbecher's home. It is unlikely that they didn't know about it—both magazines measurably reduced their coverage of gun mass murders after the Wesbecher incident. Clearly, Wesbecher's choice of reading material was important, because a number of newspapers, including the *Los Angeles Times* and the *New York Times,* did make a point of mentioning that Wesbecher read *Soldier of Fortune* magazine, but neglected to mention the prominent role of *Time* in Wesbecher's actions. To their credit, the Associated Press and the *San Francisco Chronicle* did cover this copycat element.[5]

While not as bloody in its results as *Newsweek*'s and *Time*'s relentless gun-control campaigns, coverage of mass murder in other national news media is aimed at gun control rather than promoting public safety.

In April of 2000, the *New York Times* published a series of four articles about what it called "rampage killers," which it defined as "multiple-victim killings that were not primarily domestic or connected to a robbery or gang. Serial killers were not included, nor were those whose primary motives were political."

The author claimed to describe common characteristics of "rampage killers" based on an examination of 100 such incidents between 1949 and 1999,[6] but the sample was heavily biased toward such crimes that took place between 1995 and 1999, with more than half of these incidents taking place in the last 5 of those 50 years. Why? Because these were the easiest incidents to find by doing computer database searches,[7] and the *New York Times* switched back and forth between two different sets of data from which to draw conclusions. One set was 100 incidents of mass murder (involving 102 killers) between 1949 and 1999; the other data set was derived from "nearly 25 years of homicide data from the Federal Bureau of Investigation." According to the *New York Times,* "The incidence of these rampage killings appears to have increased" in the past decade. Yet the same article also claims that "the best scientific thinking, in a field that is admittedly understudied, now holds that multiple, public murder occurs at a fairly constant level across time and cultures."[8]

Dr. John Lott, who has studied mass murders in considerably more detail than the *New York Times* reporter who wrote this story, found that "there is no upward national trend at least since the mid-1970s."[9] Unsurprisingly, the *New York Times* blamed at least some of this increase that it found—but Dr. Lott could not find—on "semiautomatic pistols . . . with their larger ammunition magazines and faster reloading . . ."[10] Yet Dr. Lott reports that exactly the opposite took place, with the rate of such mass murders *falling* from 1985 to 1995.[11] To the *Times'* credit, it did report on the significant role that mental illness played in these "rampage killings," but instead of a call for reform of our nation's mental health system, the articles focused on the need for stricter gun-control laws.[12]

If the *Times'* goal was to make the world a safer place, a study by John Lott and William Landes on what *reduces* mass murder with guns should surely have been considered newsworthy.

Under a very sophisticated statistical study, Lott and Landes found that gun waiting periods, background check requirements, and "one gun a month" restrictions *had no effect* on mass murder rates and *no effect* on ordinary murder rates. The researchers did find that longer prison sentences, higher arrest rates, higher conviction rates, and the death penalty all reduced murder rates. These results are also no surprise: the longer someone is in prison, the less opportunity that person has to commit murder.

While Lott and Landes found that these factors didn't seem to make any difference for *mass* murder rates, *one* and *only one* factor did: passage of Right-to-Carry laws. States issuing carry licenses saw statistically significant reductions in the number of mass murders committed with guns.[13]

Why didn't the *Times* report that fact? The *Times'* reporter who did much of the newspaper's analysis was familiar with Lott's work, yet this well-documented finding—that there was one and only one known method for reducing such mass murders—never made it into the *Times*. Do you suppose that the *Times'* well-known editorial support for harsh gun laws played some part in that news blackout?

Very clearly, if a government or academic report doesn't agree with the gun-control agenda that the national media support, it is deemed not newsworthy.

Back in 1994, when Congress banned certain semiautomatic firearms and ammunition magazines, some clever member of Congress slipped in a provision requiring the Department of Justice to study the effects of the law, to find out if the law did any good. In March of 1999, the National Institute of Justice (the research arm of the Department of Justice) issued a report titled "Impacts of the 1994 Assault Weapons Ban: 1994–96." The authors of the report were Jeffery A. Roth and Christopher S. Koper, two researchers with the Urban Institute, a research think tank in Washington, D.C.

Now remember, the Clinton-Gore administration was responsible for commissioning this study: not the NRA, not the "gun lobby," and not anyone particularly friendly to so-called "assault weapons" or, more accurately, semiautomatic firearms.

The Roth/Koper report said essentially what gun-rights advocates said before the law was passed—that it wasn't going to do any good because "assault weapons" were rarely criminally misused. This is exactly what the report said, time and time again. On the very first page, the authors acknowledged that they had a hard time "discerning the effects of the ban" at least partly because "the banned weapons and magazines were rarely used to commit murders in this country" before the 1994 ban.[14]

What about the effects of "intimidating" rapid fire and large-capacity magazines? "The ban did not produce declines in the average number of victims per incident of gun murder or gun murder victims with multiple wounds." What about "protecting police officers," one excuse repeatedly offered for the ban? There was a decline in "assault weapons" used to murder police officers, but Roth and Koper also admitted that because "such incidents are sufficiently rare" it was impossible to determine whether the law reduced total gun murders of police officers.[15]

This was an eye-opening government-funded study, but it just vanished into the national news media's vacuum. Can you imagine how much publicity it would have received if it had found statistically significant reductions in any category? This should have been news—but the news media ignored it.

One of the worst forms of media misrepresentation isn't only in the stories reported that aren't true, but in the true stories that they don't report. How often do Americans use guns for self-defense?

There have been more than a dozen surveys that measure how often guns are used in self-defense in the United States, ranging from as few as 108,000 per year (the National Crime Victimization

Survey estimate) to as many as 2.45 million uses per year (the Kleck and Gertz study).

So why do you so seldom see news accounts that mention these self-defense incidents? One of the reasons is that most of the time, a defensive use of a gun means that the criminal ran off at the first sight of a gun. The armed victim didn't call the police, or if he or she did, the police merely filed a report.

But there's another reason you seldom read about defensive uses of guns: the news media simply don't cover it. Sometimes they ignore these cases because they aren't deemed particularly important. If you chase a burglar away from your house, while it might be good news to you and bad news to a burglar, it's not news at all to a reporter, unless someone was wounded or killed. The rule of television news—"if it bleeds, it leads"—is true for newspapers as well.

If the problem was just that defensive uses of guns are ignored because they seemingly lack drama, we could accept that, though it does give a false impression of the benefits of firearms in American society. The news media, however, aren't just ignoring defensive uses of guns they see as non-newsworthy—they are removing defensive uses of guns from events that receive national news coverage because it is contrary to the fundamental assumption of many journalists: "Guns are bad!" and "Only bad things happen when people use guns!"

Just recall the murderous rampage at the Appalachian School of Law in western Virginia in January 2002. It was a major news story. A student learned that the law school was about to suspend him because of poor academic performance. He went to the school and killed the law school's dean, a professor, a student, and injured three others.

News accounts described how law students "subdued" the armed student.[16] But here is what really happened:

> Tracy Bridges, a student at the school and a former police officer from North Carolina, heard the shooting while waiting for class to begin. He and another student, Ted Besen, quickly led their classmates down a back staircase.
>
> Once outside, Bridges stopped at his vehicle, retrieved a pistol, and approached the shooter, Peter Odighizuwa. Upon seeing the pistol, Odighizuwa dropped his gun and held up his hands. Bridges, along with several other students, including former officer Mikael Gross, who had also retrieved a handgun, then physically restrained Odighizuwa until the police arrived.

"I feel he dropped his weapon because we were armed," Bridges later told *America's 1st Freedom.*[17]

That's a dramatic story—and yet virtually all news accounts of the events left out the gun used to prevent more killings. A search of the LexisNexis™ database found 280 news stories about the killings—but only 4 mentioned that students used their handguns to stop the killings. A search of the Westlaw database found 112 news stories about the tragedy—and again, only 2 mentioned the students who used a handgun to prevent more killings.[18] Had the brave young men who stopped this killing not been interviewed on *Today,* it is likely that almost no Americans would know that they used firearms to stop this killing spree. But make no mistake, we learned about it on that show only because one of the heroes himself volunteered it.

As reported in *America's 1st Freedom,* the morning following the attack, Bridges appeared on NBC's *Today* to discuss the shooting with Katie Couric. Bridges described his actions in detail, including the fact that he retrieved a firearm from his vehicle, then confronted the shooter with it and ended the attack.

Did Couric somehow miss the gun mention? Did she experience a kind of temporary mental lapse that somehow caused her not to hear the plain truth coming from Bridges' lips? Was she somehow so distracted by other factors that the mention of the gun managed to slip past her?

The answer is no. Couric, known to push her own anti-gun agenda under the guise of "news reporting," simply chose not to ask the obvious follow-up questions concerning the beneficial use of a firearm. Instead, she quickly footnoted Bridges' statement about arming himself with a tidy little report that summed up the anti-gunners' fallacy that only police officers, not average citizens, can successfully protect themselves and others with a firearm.

"I should mention, Tracy, that you are a police officer . . . ," Couric immediately said after Bridges mentioned his gun. "It must have been incredibly fortuitous that you all had police training and a police background and you were able to act in such a quick and appropriate way."

Bridges, on the contrary, is given to a more realistic attitude toward the entire episode. "The only thing police training gave me was the instinct to act, to being sage in what we were doing," Bridges told *America's 1st Freedom.* "Anyone could have done the same thing."

Journalists can't claim that they didn't consider the story important, because almost all newspapers covered it. Journalists can't claim that they didn't consider the bravery of these young men to be important, because what they did was widely covered. Journalists couldn't claim that the presence of the gun wasn't important, because it left a gaping hole in their stories: *How* did they subdue this guy? Did they tackle the killer while he had a gun in his hand? Did they talk him into putting the gun down?

This isn't the only case. A few years back, there was a burst of senseless violence at several schools, including a tragic incident in Pearl, Mississippi, at Pearl High School. The killer had murdered his mother before coming to the school, where he shot nine students, two of whom died. When the violence started, Assistant Principal Joel Myrick retrieved a handgun from his vehicle in the parking lot. With that gun, Myrick persuaded the killer to put his down, doubtless saving many more lives. And while many news organizations carried the story of the killings at Pearl, and even the part the assistant principal played in ending this tragedy, very few mentioned that Joel Myrick had a firearm he used to "persuade" the killer to surrender.

The news and entertainment media talk about their First Amendment guarantee of freedom of the press, a right that we freely acknowledge and endorse. But with freedom comes responsibility.

For too long the media have swallowed manufactured statistics and utter fabrications from anti-gun organizations that wouldn't know a semiautomatic from a sharp stick—and it shows. As a result, the media have very little credibility among seventy million gun owners and twenty million hunters and millions of veterans who learned the hard way which end the bullet comes out.

Contrary to what the mass media would have the public believe, it is not firearms that are responsible for terrorism or for the daily carnage committed by armed violent criminals left to walk the streets.

Those threats are very real. Most threatening of all, however, is how the gun-ban lobby and its media sympathizers aggressively use the First Amendment to erode, and ultimately destroy, America's Second Amendment rights.

9

MICHAEL BELLESILES: HIS OWN WORST NIGHTMARE

Nothing excites the media elite more than the sudden emergence of a new "expert" with new "evidence" that supports the anti-gun agenda.

Perhaps the greatest example of that twisted standard is Emory University history professor Michael Bellesiles. In 2000, to universal media acclaim, Professor Bellesiles and his book, *Arming America: The Origins of a National Gun Culture,* debuted upon the American scene.

Bellesiles and his much-praised book touted the ancestral lineage of American gun culture as a historical myth. A professor of history from a respected university, Bellesiles had all the credentials to attack the Second Amendment that the anti–Second Amendment crowd could hope for.

Specifically, his book made the following astonishing set of claims:

- Guns were rare in America before about 1840;
- colonial governments did not allow most people to own guns;
- few Americans hunted, even on the frontier; and
- most Americans, if they had an opinion about guns at all, disliked them.

If there were any question about the political focus of the book, its cover text was most telling: "Michael Bellesiles is the NRA's worst nightmare."

Bellesiles's research was based on probate records of colonists' estates and the estates of others up to and including the nineteenth century, or so he said. From those records he concluded that few colonials owned firearms. The few firearms that Professor Bellesiles claimed he traced through probate records were mostly antique, rusted, or broken. The portrait painted by the professor was hardly one of an armed citizenry as proffered by Second Amendment proponents.

Bellesiles's assertions contradicted common sense and the evidence put forward by almost all historians—but his book quickly was seen as a gold mine by anti-gunners who have always been frustrated when trying to confront the logical arguments that America was "born out of the barrel of a gun" and that guns have always been a major pillar in the foundation of American freedom.

The media, in particular, loved him. Television and radio talk-show hosts clamored to interview him. Gun-control zealots delighted in quoting his "scholarship." Bellesiles and his book were a heady duo and cause for nonstop celebration among anti-gun advocates. If his conclusions were accurate—that private gun ownership was a rarity in America before the mid-1800s—then the concept of a militia of individual citizens armed with firearms of their own couldn't possibly be historically accurate. Sarah Brady and her friends, now armed with Bellesiles's work, were ready to redouble their resolve to storm the halls of Congress to renew their legislative assault on gun ownership rights.

Never mind that *Arming America* was written in a heavily dogmatic manner. And make no mistake: it was. In fact, it seemed that nearly all the evidence that Professor Bellesiles found supported his case; almost nothing seemed to point in the other direction. Even if you knew nothing about the subject, for the evidence to be so overwhelmingly in one direction should have aroused suspicions, and it caused at least a few reporters to ask serious questions.

The historian Clayton Cramer, who had raised questions early about the accuracy of *Arming America,* described what happened when *New York Times* reporter Anthony Ramirez contacted him for an opposing point of view:

> I pointed out to Ramirez that many of the early Republic travel accounts mentioned guns as being common items, that Alexis de Tocqueville described how every cabin in Tennessee and Kentucky had a gun in it, and Ramirez's question was along the lines of, "How do we know that those guns worked?" When I told him that de Tocqueville reported that an Alabamian told him that almost everyone carried a gun or knife and that bloodshed was common, Ramirez's response was, "So, de Tocqueville didn't actually see any of this?" It was pretty clear that Ramirez didn't want to hear anything that contradicted Bellesiles's claims.[1]

Ramirez was not alone. Of fifty reviews published in newspapers and magazines in the first few months,[2] only one suggested that Bellesiles's claims defied belief.[3] As it turns out, *Arming America*'s problems were much deeper. The book, put politely, was a *fraud.* Bellesiles altered quotes, altered dates, misrepresented sources, and cited documents that he clearly had not read.

Michael Bellesiles, it seems, may well be the archetypal "educator" for today's segment of society that harangues about the evils of guns and of those who dare express opinions or beliefs contrary to the worldview of gun prohibitionists.

In a delicious bit of irony, the very media that lionized Bellesiles and his book were forced, by academics checking into Bellesiles's research, to take a second, more critical look at the work they so readily clutched to their collective bosom and that they hoped to use to thump the NRA and America's gun owners. They quickly found that the good professor cut more than a few corners in cobbling together his book. A great number of irregularities in what he claimed to be historically documented and true began to emerge. One of the most glaring, exposed by Northwestern University law professor James Lindgren, was Bellesiles's claim to have thoroughly scoured mid-nineteenth-century probate records stored at the San Francisco Superior Court. Professor Lindgren discovered that all the probate records Bellesiles said he studied were destroyed in San Francisco's earthquake and fire of 1906.

Comparing source documents that did exist with Bellesiles's account of the same material continued to reveal the extent to which he either erred in transcribing facts or apparently fabricated so-called historical facts.

Examples? There are far too many to list, but here's a sampling.

Bellesiles claimed that guns were in short supply after the American Revolution, and therefore he asserted the Militia Act of 1792 provided that "further, 'every citizen so enrolled, shall . . . be constantly provided with a good musket or firelock, a sufficient bayonet and belt, two spare flints, and other accoutrements. Congress took upon itself the responsibility of providing those guns . . .'"[4]

The problem is that the Militia Act of 1792 doesn't say "shall . . . be constantly provided." It *actually* says, "That every citizen so enrolled and notified, shall within six months thereafter, *provide himself* with a good musket or firelock . . ." [emphasis added]. The citizen was to *provide* himself with a gun. Congress wasn't going to do it.

When confronted with this very dramatic error, Bellesiles first denied there was any error at all, but eventually, as the weight of evidence accumulated, he admitted that the text was incorrect and explained his error as:

> It took me a while to find my original source at a library in South Carolina, but the phrase "shall . . . be constantly provided with" is in the 1792 Militia Act. But you are right that it is not in any

> version I could find from the 1790s. So I then went carefully through the legislative records and found an 1803 Amendment to the 1792 Act ("An Act in addition to an Act entitled 'An Act More effectually to provide for the National Defense'"). Checking further, I found it as U.S. Statutes II: 207, passed March 2, 1803.
>
> So I was at fault in not reconciling the 1815 version I used with the 1792 version I also read (I assumed that they were just different versions of the same act).[5]

But it turned out that the 1803 law to which he refers doesn't use the language he quoted, either. Bellesiles didn't list the 1803 law in his footnote, but he did list two other sources for his "quote": *Statutes at Large* (the official U.S. law books) and *Proceedings and Debates in the Congress* (the official record of what Congress did). Both sources agree on what that law says, which is to say, they both disagree with Bellesiles.

Since then, Bellesiles has returned to denying that there was any error in his quotation and insisting that his list of sources was correct as well.[6] Similar, convenient misquotations and quotations out of context appear throughout *Arming America*.

Incredibly, Bellesiles wasn't content with just altering quotes of well-known federal laws. He also grossly misrepresented historical documents to fit his claims. Concerning the scarcity of guns in Massachusetts Bay Colony, Bellesiles wrote:

> In 1630 the Massachusetts Bay Company reported in their possession: "80 bastard musketts, with snaphances, 4 Foote in the barrill without rests, 6 long Fowlinge peeces . . . 6 foote longe; 4 longe Fowlinge peeces . . . 5-1/2 foote longe; 10 Full musketts, 4 Foote barrill, with matchlocks and rests," one hundred swords, and "5 peeces of ordnance, long sence bowght and payd For." There were thus exactly one hundred firearms for use among seven towns with a population of about one thousand.[7]

But when you look up Bellesiles's source (*Records of Massachusetts Bay* 1:25–26), it says something completely different. It is not a list of all the arms in Massachusetts Bay Colony. It is not even a list of guns owned by the company. It is merely a list of arms to be brought to the colony by the company. It is also *not* a list of *all* the guns in the colony, as Bellesiles implies when he says there were only "one hundred firearms" for a population "of about one thousand."

Finally, even the year Bellesiles gives is wrong—conveniently wrong.

The dates on the document Bellesiles cites are 26 February and 2 March 1628. Of course, if Bellesiles had given the correct year for this "inventory," most historians would have wondered how the Massachusetts Bay Company could have done an inventory of guns in the colony many months before the colony even existed.[8] There are hundreds of such misrepresentations of documents in *Arming America*.[9]

As example after example came to light, colleagues in academia as well as journalists began to ask for a look at the raw data he used in researching the book. Bellesiles claimed his research files and the documents he consulted were destroyed in a mysterious "flash flood."

Academic investigators seeking to apply the traditional standards of peer review of Bellesiles's scholarship attempted to retrace his footsteps by going to primary sources. Scholars and journalists alike discovered that what the professor claimed to be historical facts were neither factually nor historically accurate. Like so much of the antigun pantheon of "facts," the scholarship provided by their would-be professorial champion proved lacking in substance and credibility.

The consequences to Bellesiles, while slow in coming, were significant. The National Endowment for the Humanities (NEH) withdrew its name from a fellowship for Bellesiles. Chicago's Newberry Library "was in error when it awarded an NEH-supported fellowship" to Bellesiles, NEH Deputy Chairman Lynne Monson wrote to Newberry officials.

That signaled the beginning of a huge academic exodus away from Bellesiles—one so overwhelming that the chair of Emory University's History Department and Bellesiles's boss, James Melton, took the extraordinary step of issuing a formal apology.

Yet in spite of the increasing discussion among academics about the very serious problems with *Arming America,* journalists overlooked this major scandal for more than a year.

In the meantime, Bellesiles received Columbia University's Bancroft Prize (in effect the Nobel Prize for American history) for *Arming America.* Worse still, Bellesiles's claim that colonial governments did not allow most people to own guns and that guns were scarce in early America[10] started to be cited in court decisions, significantly in briefs filed by the Clinton administration in *U.S. v. Emerson.*[11]

When Karen Samples, a columnist for the *Cincinnati Enquirer,* wrote a very positive review of *Arming America* shortly after the book appeared,[12] Clayton Cramer informed Samples that Bellesiles had altered quotes to invert their meaning, and gave her instructions on how to read the Militia Act of 1792 on the Library of Congress's Web page. It would have taken Samples about two minutes to see for herself that Bellesiles had altered the quote. Instead, Samples wrote a column that claimed, "I could go on recounting their [Cramer and Bellesiles's] disagreements, but you get the idea. It would take a time traveler to determine who is more correct."[13]

Or, it would have taken a real, objective journalist who cared enough about truth to spend two minutes checking to see if Bellesiles quoted the Militia Act of 1792 accurately or not.

Along with the many journalists who regurgitated what they were told by Bellesiles and his enthusiastic supporters in the anti-gun lobby—without bothering to ask any hard questions—there were a few journalists who took their responsibilities seriously. Sadly, journalists of this caliber seem to be in short supply. Melissa Seckora at the *National Review* did a series of devastating articles about Bellesiles's dishonest use of historical documents, as well as his use of documents that no longer exist.[14] So did David Skinner at *Weekly Standard,*[15] David Mehegan at the *Boston Globe,*[16] and Ron Grossman at the *Chicago Tribune.*[17]

David Mehegan, in particular, deserves mention. Instead of just reporting the dispute between Professors Lindgren and Bellesiles, Mehegan went and checked some of the documents in dispute. As a result, Mehegan was able to tell his readers that in every example he had checked, Professor Lindgren was correct, and Professor Bellesiles's claims were wrong.[18]

With these few exceptions, the media generally ignored what should have been a major story—a much bigger story than the plagiarism scandals that were embarrassing historians Doris Kearns Goodwin and Stephen Ambrose at the same time. Eventually, months after a few courageous newspapers had investigated and published the serious problems with *Arming America,* the *New York Times* finally ran an article admitting there was a controversy[19] and, two months later, carried an Associated Press story about Emory University's investigation into charges of misconduct.[20]

By comparison, the much less serious charges of plagiarism against historians Stephen Ambrose and Doris Kearns Goodwin were mentioned in at least six stories in the *New York Times* during that same period.[21] The *Washington Post* had a similar confusion about which violation of academic integrity is the more serious offense, carrying six stories about charges against Ambrose and Goodwin,[22] but not a single mention of the charges against Bellesiles.

In retrospect, Professor Bellesiles may actually have done his colleagues, the media, and the American people in general a great service by his blatant attempt to rewrite history. "Bellesiles's phony scholarship was as devastating a blow as the anti-gun crowd has sustained in decades of fighting over the Second Amendment,"[23] wrote gadfly journalist Alexander Cockburn.

Bellesiles's arrogant belief that he could break all the rules of academic integrity was fed, no doubt, by a belief that many, particularly members of the firearm-hating national media, would accept his corrupt thesis with noncritical enthusiasm. "It would seem that *Arming America* represented what a lot of book-review editors already believed, or thought other people ought to believe, so instead of sending it out for review to people who might have argued with some of Bellesiles's conclusions—and even more important, his methods of research—they simply sent it out to people who would treat it as gospel,"[24] noted Michael Korda, longtime editor-in-chief for the publishing giant Simon & Schuster.

"Perhaps," Korda suggested, "Professor Bellesiles should have begun his research by reading the fiction of James Fenimore Cooper, in which the ability to shoot accurately is highly admired, and gun ownership on the frontier—then in upstate New York—was a natural thing in view of Indian raids and warfare with the French. But no. What we are seeing with *Arming America* is another familiar example of history being rewritten to make the past conform to the media's prevailing opinion of the present."[25]

On Oct. 25, 2002, Michael Bellesiles resigned from Emory University after a committee of scholars released an overwhelming indictment of his research: "We are seriously troubled by Professor Bellesiles's scholarly conduct . . . the failure to clearly identify his sources does move into the realm of falsification." On Dec. 7, 2002, Columbia University's trustees voted to rescind the prestigious Bancroft Prize awarded for *Arming America*. Finally, on Jan. 7, 2003, publisher Alfred A. Knopf formally announced its decision to cease printing the highly disputed book.

Michael Bellesiles may have wanted to become "the NRA's worst nightmare," but instead, he became his own. He will stand forever branded as the model of the propagandist who masquerades as a historian.

10

THE MEDICAL ANTI-GUN LOBBY: ISSUING JUNK SCIENCE

"Guns are a virus that must be eradicated," declared Dr. Katherine Christoffel, a pediatrician and gun-control activist who issued that warning to gun owners in 1994 in an interview published in the *American Medical News,* a weekly newspaper for American Medical Association (AMA) members.[1]

It sums up the goals of the medical anti-gun-rights movement, and even more, it symbolizes the contemptuous attitude toward scientific ethics that medical gun-control advocates hold today. The rules of science require finding the facts *before* reaching a conclusion, but the arrogant medical gun prohibitionists believe the rules don't apply to them. They start with the conclusion they like—"owning firearms causes deaths"—and then build a case for harsh new gun laws by cranking out one junk science "study" after another.

Medical activists have put out volumes of "advocacy research" against guns since the 1980s. Remember the claim that a gun owner is forty-three times more likely to kill a family member than an intruder? Drs. Arthur Kellermann and Donald Reay published that infamous factoid in the *New England Journal of Medicine* in 1986 and though disproved, the statistic is still routinely trotted out today by gun-ban advocates.[2]

To reach that ratio, self-defense firearms uses were grossly under-counted by counting only cases in which criminals were killed. In most protective firearms uses, criminals are scared off, captured, or wounded. Additionally, suicides were counted as family member killings, increasing the death count by more than 500 percent.

"Guns!! Guns!! Guns!!" ranted Dr. Lester Adelson in the AMA journal *Archives of Surgery* (June 1992). "Guns create feelings of self-esteem, permitting even the least potent to join 'The Superman Club.' As part of its 'magical' power, a firearm is a key which can unlock any door."[3] This incredible passage, published in a medical journal with claims of scientific objectivity, tells far more about the author than it tells about gun owners.

An irrational fear of firearms permeates the public health literature on guns. It gives rise to lurid fantasies like those of Dr. Adelson, who seems to believe a gun is an evil talisman. The attitude of Dr. Adelson and others like him in the medical anti-gun-rights movement shows not only their own fear but also their own astounding level of ignorance about guns and gun owners. In fact, responsible gun owners know a gun is just a tool that can help protect a family or bring home game for dinner. The last thing to enter their minds is a perverse sense of power arising from having a firearm.

Americans know that owning a firearm is serious business. Standard training in concealed carrying of firearms includes the principle that a person legally carrying a self-defense gun is held to a higher standard of conduct than is the average person. Rather than creating "feelings of self-esteem," a self-defense firearm carried by a responsible person fosters an attitude of sober restraint.

Nevertheless, prominent medical authorities make unbelievably prejudiced statements about guns and their owners. Dr. Deborah Prothrow-Stith, dean of Harvard School of Public Health, wrote in her 1991 book *Deadly Consequences,* "My own view on gun control is simple. I hate guns and I cannot imagine why anyone would want to own one. If I had my way, guns for sport would be registered, and all other guns would be banned."[4]

Legitimate scientists are expected to base their conclusions on hard data and sound analysis of the facts. Ethical researchers don't express their political beliefs under the banner of scientific authority—but that's exactly what this Harvard doctor did in making her outrageous recommendation to revoke the Second Amendment rights of all Americans. And the mass media, along with supposedly scientific groups such as the AMA, let her get away with it.

The Centers for Disease Control (CDC) is often referred to as the Centers for Disease *(and Gun)* Control—and for good reason. CDC official Patrick O'Carroll, M.D., couldn't have stated his agency's agenda for gun owners more clearly than when he said, "We're going to systematically build a case that owning firearms causes deaths." Quoted in the *Journal of the American Medical Association,* O'Carroll went on to say, "We're doing the most we can do, given the political realities."[5] Presumably this government official, whose paycheck came from taxpayers, would confiscate all our guns immediately if "political realities" allowed it.

The CDC's push against gun ownership began in earnest in the early 1990s, with the staunch support of the Clinton-Gore administration. Until then, this federal agency had a distinguished history of legitimate public health work such as stopping infectious disease epidemics and making drinking water safe. But under the direction of the new breed of social activists, the CDC began rapidly to expand its definition of "public health problems."

Suddenly, firearms were likened to a dangerous germ that could cause a disease called gun violence. Under that new approach—"reframing the debate," as they called it—CDC officials openly launched a public relations campaign against guns and gun owners.

CDC grants were given to a select group of researchers whose anti-gun politics were well known. Foremost among these was Emory University's Dr. Arthur Kellermann, author of the "forty-three times" factoid, who eventually received more than $1.7 million of taxpayer money. The CDC funded Kellermann and others to produce the anti-gun junk science intended to build its case against gun owners.

In the Winter 1993 edition of a CDC publication called *Health Affairs,* Drs. James Mercy and Mark Rosenberg and their coauthors wrote the article "Public Health Policy for Preventing Violence," which promoted restrictions on gun carrying in public, gun licensing, waiting periods, banning "dangerous ammunition" and gun imports, and even prohibiting gun ownership.[6] These medical doctors and government employees advocated the entire wish list of the gun-ban lobby using the vast resources of the federal government to advocate the dismantling of gun owners' rights, one "sensible" step at a time.

Casting gun injuries and deaths as a public health problem instead of a criminal justice problem allowed the activists to evade two difficulties. First, by concentrating on the gun they could avoid having to explain the vast differences between responsible American gun owners and violent career criminals, whose misuse of guns cause almost all gun deaths except suicides.

Second, the activists could enlist the support of powerful medical organizations that could wage a public relations campaign against "gun violence." That campaign, of course, would turn out to be a shameless cover for just more gun-control activism.

An example of this strategy was seen in the statement of the CDC's Rosenberg and two colleagues in their article "Let's Be Clear—Violence Is a Public Health Problem," published in the *Journal of the American Medical Association* in 1992.[7] The authors assert "violence between family members and acquaintances accounts for more than half of all homicides. Most violent injuries do not stem immediately from criminal activities such as robbery. They occur as the result of violent arguments among people who know each other."

This half-truth assumes that violent criminals don't have acquaintances (like associates in the drug trade, for example) or families. Criminology research has long shown that violent criminals are very different from the average person, showing a lifelong pattern of violence against the people around them, including family members. Indeed, almost all violent crimes are the work of a very small but highly abnormal group of chronically violent individuals. Rosenberg deliberately tried to minimize the crucial differences between violent career criminals and normal people to more easily blame the gun.

By the mid-1990s the CDC anti-gun junk science machine had run into some serious problems. Scientists and gun owners came to realize the enormity of the CDC's misuse of government funds to go after gun owners. The CDC's scandal came to a peak with the revelation in early 1995 that the agency had given a grant to a California gun-control advocacy group called the Trauma Foundation. The group's *Injury Prevention Network Newsletter* (Spring 1995)—in clear violation of federal law governing CDC grants—advised gun-control advocates to "organize a picket at gun manufacturing sites" and to "work for campaign finance reform to weaken the gun lobby's political clout." The editor noted in the page just before this section that "this newsletter was supported in part by Grant #R49/CCR903697-06 from the Centers for Disease Control and Prevention."[8]

Reacting to this clear abuse of taxpayers' money, Congressman Bob Barr (R-Ga.) wrote to CDC Director Dr. David Satcher asking for an inquiry into the improper use of CDC grant money. Satcher admitted that the CDC's funding of the anti-gun newsletter was inappropriate and disallowed the costs charged to the CDC for publication of the newsletter. Other members of Congress pressured Satcher to justify the broader policy of using CDC grant money to essentially operate an anti-gun junk science factory.

To rev up media spin, Satcher himself wrote an opinion article for the *Washington Post,* accusing the National Rifle Association of mounting a "shotgun assault" on the CDC's National Center for Injury Prevention and Control.[9] Sympathetic media outlets piled on with their own editorials, with the *Atlanta Journal-Constitution* complaining that "the NRA has homed in on its intended target like a heat-seeking missile."[10]

But the CDC's actions had been so open, so well documented, and so incriminating that it was unable to escape congressional scrutiny. Representing its four million members, the NRA asked Congress to investigate the CDC's abuses, and in March 1996 a hearing was scheduled before the House Appropriations Committee. When the dust settled, the CDC's anti-gun research was officially shut down. And to make the point clear, the Appropriations Committee's final report warned the CDC that "the Committee does not believe that it is the role of the CDC to advocate or promote policies to advance gun control initiatives, or to discourage responsible private gun ownership."[11]

That battle with the CDC was merely a temporary setback, as funding from private sources such as the Chicago-based Joyce Foundation with assets of just under $800 million now sustains the dishonest medical research operations.

On the heels of the CDC scandal, medical activists were confronted with remarkable findings about firearms used in self-defense. More than a dozen independent surveys by criminologists confirmed that Americans use firearms in self-defense hundreds of thousands of times each year. That led to a new dishonest tactic: the deliberate suppression of the truth.

In 1995, Florida State University criminology professor Gary Kleck and his coworker Marc Gertz published a groundbreaking piece of research, the National Self-Defense Survey. This carefully planned and executed research project found that Americans use firearms between 2.2 and 2.5 million times each year to defend themselves. Between 1.5 and 1.9 million of these defensive gun uses involved handguns.[12]

Of equal importance at this time was the steady expansion of "shall issue" laws in states allowing law-abiding citizens to carry concealed firearms for self-defense. Passage of right-to-carry laws in more than a dozen states during this period turned out to be an undisputed success. Wildly exaggerated predictions of increased gun crime failed to materialize. In fact, violent crimes tended to drop in "shall issue" states.

In 1997, researcher John Lott and his coauthor, David Mustard at the University of Chicago, published a thorough study of crime rates and concealed-carry permit laws in America. As mentioned in chapter 7, they found that when a state "shall issue" law went into effect in a county, murders fell by 8 percent, rapes by 5 percent, and aggravated assaults by 7 percent. This landmark study later was the basis for Lott's book, *More Guns, Less Crime.*[13]

Blindsided by these studies, medical activists worked to suppress the findings. Editors of medical journals, previously so quick to tackle gun violence issues, rarely if ever mentioned Lott's and Kleck's research. Eventually their failure to acknowledge the stellar work of these researchers cost the medical journals a great deal of respect.

Many physicians and scientists, including well-respected researchers, objected when journals such as the *New England Journal of Medicine* and the *Journal of Trauma* refused to publish or even acknowledge this new research. When pressed, the editors of these journals resorted to ridicule or rejection of the research. They echoed Dr. Jerome Kassirer, then editor of the *New England Journal of Medicine,* who wrote, "Data on [assault weapons'] risks are not needed, because they have no redeeming social value."[14]

Saying that data are not needed to prove a scientific theory is like saying a foundation is not needed to build a skyscraper. Data, or facts, are the foundation of science. But when the subject is guns, a surprising number of otherwise respectable scientists lose their moral compass. In this case, the scientific evidence points to the conclusion that guns in responsible hands save lives, prevent injuries, and protect property. But don't expect the medical anti-gun crowd to see that truth for they are blinded by their anti-gun prejudice; the proof can be seen every day as medical organizations launch routine attacks on gun owners.

But are most physicians themselves prejudiced against gun owners? *Medical Economics,* a magazine for doctors, published a survey in 2000 showing that nearly one-third of physicians own guns. Interestingly, 54 percent of female physicians owning guns said they kept them for self-defense.[15]

As a group, doctors reflect the attitudes toward guns and the gun ownership patterns of most Americans. But the professional organizations to which they belong tend to be dominated by social activists—people who want to remake society in their own vision, rather than respect the collective vision of the citizenry. As a result, some national medical organizations call for an outright ban on certain types of guns, with no consideration of the proven social benefits of responsible gun ownership.

The most aggressive gun-rights foe in organized medicine is the American Academy of Pediatrics (AAP), which long ago called for a ban on handguns. The AAP's official policy, as stated in the journal *Pediatrics,* April 2000, Volume 105, Number 4, "affirms that the most effective measure to prevent firearm-related injuries to children and adolescents is the absence of guns from homes and communities."[16]

The American College of Physicians (ACP) in 1998 published its official policy and urged doctors to become politically active in the fight for more gun-control laws. The position paper, published in the *Annals of Internal Medicine,* called for "strong legislation" against "semi-automatic assault weapons," which the ACP broadly defined to include 9-millimeter pistols.[17]

Another medical group, the American College of Surgeons (ACS), traditionally stayed out of gun-control politics, yet the ACS is now becoming more active in gun-control advocacy. Official ACS policy (which the ACS formerly described as its Statement on Gun Control), as explained on its Web site www.facs.org, supports efforts "to restrict civilian access to those [guns] designed primarily for interpersonal violence."[18] Is that pistol owned for home protection "primarily designed for interpersonal violence"? Does that mean a woman should not be allowed to have it for defense of her children and herself? Apparently that's exactly what it means, according to the American College of Surgeons.

The ACS policy of considering a law-abiding gun owner in the same category as a violent criminal is typical of the mind-set of medical gun-control activists. These doctors think that because they are highly trained to treat people with gunshot wounds, they are also experts on criminal justice policy, the mechanics of firearms, and the law of personal defense.

Confronted with mounting scientific evidence favoring gun owners and the marked success of carry laws, many medical gun controllers have changed strategy. The push for gun control has morphed into a push for gun safety. But the change is in name only.

The American Medical Association published its *Physician Firearm Safety Guide* in 1998 "to offer a primer to physicians who want a broad overview of the public health and clinical issues involved in firearm use."[19] But this bland description doesn't begin to describe the anti-gun-rights message that runs through the entire book. For example, the *Guide*'s authors play up unintentional (accidental) firearm deaths. In 1995, the *Guide* tells us, there were 1,225 accidental firearm deaths. Somehow the authors forgot to tell readers that this number was a new low in accidental gun deaths, the latest low number in a seventy-year record of constantly declining numbers.

The AMA also neglected to tell its readers in subsequent pronouncements that the number plummeted to six hundred deaths in the year 2000—an amazing 51 percent drop in five years. If this trend were to continue, fatal gun accidents in America would become a thing of the past by 2005. Any group concerned with firearm injuries and deaths should applaud such a wonderful development; but the AMA and other medical organizations have been silent about this good news. Why? Because good news about guns is not part of their political message. This is not science; it's propaganda.

Another anti-gun-rights group was formed in 2001 by the New York Academy of Medicine under the direction of its president,

Jeremiah Barondess, M.D. Doctors Against Handgun Injury (DAHI) is a coalition of a dozen medical organizations, most of which have their own anti-gun policies. DAHI's Web site insists, "We are not, in short, a 'gun control' organization." But a quick look at their Web site shows links to anti-gun-rights groups such as the Brady Campaign, Join Together, and the Children's Defense Fund.[20]

DAHI's executive director, Robert Seltzer, was quoted in an article in the *New York Observer* as saying, "I'm sure they [the National Rifle Association] will say that we're trying to take away people's guns—which we're not."[21] But DAHI founder Dr. Barondess stated just the opposite in the *Journal of the American Medical Association.* Along with several of his medical colleagues, Barondess proclaimed, "Ideally, handguns, which account for more than half of all homicides in the United States, should be banned completely, *but we recognize that this strategy is not currently politically feasible* [emphasis added]."[22] Barondess and his fellow doctors go on to call for a nationwide licensing system for gun owners that would force gun owners to be fingerprinted and to "rigorously justify a purpose for owning a gun."

The political message is plain: guns are bad, the average citizen is too incompetent or unstable to handle them, and guns should be banned. Most doctors don't buy into the social activist ambitions of the leaders of these medical organizations. Indeed, many have resigned from the AMA and other medical groups because of their war on gun owners. But politicians and the media see these medical organizations as speaking for *all* their members.

As a counterweight, the Association of American Physicians and Surgeons (AAPS) recognizes Americans' constitutional right to keep and bear arms and has exposed many examples of anti-gun junk science produced by the CDC and others. Physicians interested in learning more about the AAPS can go to the association's Web page at www.aapsonline.org.

As with all groups pushing to eliminate gun rights, the anti-gun medical organizations condone violating people's privacy rights—in their case, the privacy rights of patients.

Most of the anti-gun medical organizations have very explicit policies calling for doctors to ask their patients about guns in their homes. These are often very probing questions, including inquiries about how many guns you have, where you store them, and how you secure them.

The point of such questioning is to make the patient feel that his or her gun ownership is a dirty or shameful thing. Firearms scholar Don B. Kates and his coauthors describe this strategy in their landmark exposé "Guns and Public Health: Epidemic of Violence, or Pandemic of Propaganda?" published in the *Tennessee Law Review.*[23] They quote Robert Tanz, M.D., as having a "plan to do to handguns what their profession has done to cigarettes—turn gun ownership from a personal-choice issue to a repulsive, anti-social health hazard."

For a doctor to ask a patient politically based questions about guns in the home is a violation of medical ethics, according to Dr. Timothy W. Wheeler, director of Doctors for Responsible Gun Ownership. Experts in medical ethics describe such politically motivated questioning as an ethical *boundary violation.* "It is unprofessional conduct, and it should result in the offending doctor being disciplined," says Dr. Wheeler.[24]

According to a survey of physicians published in the *Annals of Internal Medicine,* fewer than 5 percent of surveyed doctors said they "frequently talk to patients about having a gun in the house."[25] Clearly, the overwhelming majority understand how strongly their gun-owning patients may feel about their right to keep and bear arms, and challenging that right could jeopardize patients' trust. But the professional medical organizations they belong to continue to carry on against guns—and even the Second Amendment itself.

The immediate past-president of the AMA, Dr. Richard Corlin, said in his June 2001 Inaugural Address that "the gun lobby loves to use the Second Amendment as a smokescreen to hide the reality of the damage that guns do . . ."[26] He made clear his belief that the Second Amendment does not guarantee an individual's right to own firearms, citing the late Supreme Court Chief Justice Warren Burger:

> . . . the Second Amendment has been the subject of one of the greatest pieces of fraud, I repeat the word fraud, on the American people by special interest groups that I have ever seen in my lifetime . . . The very language of the Second Amendment refutes any argument that it was intended to guarantee every citizen an unfettered right to any kind of weapon.

Dr. Corlin's implication that Justice Burger's personal and outdated view—which was announced in *Parade* magazine, never in an opinion from the bench—is the majority opinion among scholars today cannot be attributed to ignorance but to his declaration of war against firearms owners. But as we have seen, concealing or distorting the truth about guns and gun owners is the AMA approach.

The American Academy of Pediatrics dismisses the Second Amendment with this paragraph on its Web site:[27]

> What about the right to bear arms? We hear that phrase so often. But consider this: The Second Amendment reads as follows: "A well-regulated militia being necessary to the security of a free state, the right of the people to keep and bear arms shall not be infringed." This is often cited as a part of the constitution that establishes individuals' rights to keep guns in their homes. However, the Supreme Court has ruled repeatedly that the individual right to bear arms was not protected by the Second Amendment. This amendment protects the state's right to keep well-organized militias.

Over the past twenty years, modern constitutional scholars have rejected that view. It is dishonest at best for the American Academy of Pediatrics not to acknowledge that theirs is a minority view, and that even politically liberal constitutional law professors believe that the Second Amendment affirms an individual's right to own guns and not some states' right.

But Abraham Lincoln's maxim still rings true: you can't fool all the people all the time. Especially since the September 11 terrorist attacks on America, people have become reacquainted with the wisdom of America's Founders. They have come to remember on a very fundamental level how important it is to be able to protect family and home, whether from foreign invaders or from domestic criminals.

The Second Amendment is an expression of the collective American faith that people are endowed with the inalienable right of self-defense. It is this deep belief in our rights, and our insistence that government respect them, that will ultimately allow gun owners to prevail.

11

THE ANTI-HUNTING MOVEMENT: "ANIMAL RIGHTS" AND MORAL WRONGS

September 11, 2001. As our attention as a nation was riveted on New York City, the Pentagon, and the Pennsylvania crash site of United Airlines Flight 93, a much smaller but nonetheless despicable outrage went unnoticed. "Animal rights" extremists pitilessly chose the moment to take credit for firebombing a McDonald's restaurant in Tucson, Arizona. The fire-damaged store walls were spray-painted with "ALF" and "ELF" (initials of the Animal Liberation Front and the Earth Liberation Front), and an ALF spokesman announced that his office had received an unsigned statement from activists claiming credit for the bombing. He termed their crime "nonviolent destruction."[1]

Today, the FBI ranks both ALF and ELF at the top of its list of domestic terrorism threats. The Bureau estimates the groups have committed more than six hundred criminal acts in the United States since 1996, resulting in damages in excess of $43 million.[2] But most Americans have never heard of these groups.

We have all heard of "animal rights." A few years ago, a caller to Rush Limbaugh's radio program asked the following question: "If there were no humans on the planet, would animals have rights?"[3] Rush relished the question because the answer was emphatically:

No! Nature does not and cannot dole out "rights." God gave man inalienable rights, and absent man or human intervention only the law of the jungle would prevail—only the fittest would survive.

Despite this ironclad logic, the "animal rights" movement in this nation and around the world continues to advance the notion that animals are somehow entitled to rights just like human beings, and those in the movement are growing bolder each and every year. They refuse to admit that there is a very real difference between "animal rights" and animal welfare.

Case in point: in May 2002, Germany became the second European country to guarantee "animal rights" in its constitution. By an overwhelming 543 to 19 vote, Germany's lower house of parliament voted to add the phrase "and animals" to a clause obligating the state to respect and protect the dignity of humans. Germany follows Switzerland, which had passed a similar amendment in 1992.[4]

Germany's legislation is more than just "political correctness" run amok. It could also have real, significant, and powerful effects on many critical aspects of German life—from animal experimentation by pharmaceutical industries, to zoos, to traditional farming methods, to how people treat their household pets, and to, of course, hunting.

In an effort to soothe these obvious concerns, Consumer Affairs Minister Renate Kunast (a member of Germany's environmentalist Green Party) assured citizens that the new law would not diminish human rights and that "people remain the most important."[5] Nonetheless, the amendment speaks volumes to the strength of the "animal rights" movement overseas.

If Germany and Switzerland were isolated incidents with regard to "animal rights," one could simply shrug it off, but that is definitely not the case.

In England, one "animal rights" extremist group called the League Against Cruel Sports has set its sights squarely on the nation's long tradition of foxhunting with dogs. The sport, which has been a staple of British culture for centuries, is now in severe jeopardy, in large part because of the efforts of the League and a legion of British and international celebrities who support it. In addition to fox-hunting, the League considers bird, stag, hare, and mink hunting to also be "cruel."[6]

The League admits that its short-term objectives remain, for now, isolated in England. But its long-term goals, like the "animal rights" movement in general, are global in scope. According to its Web site, www.league.uk.com:

> The League focuses its campaigns on protection for wild animals in Britain (rather than abroad), mostly because of limited resources. However, campaigning against cruel sports in other countries will be an option when hunting is banned in England and Wales (fox hunting was banned in Scotland in 2002).[7]

In America, meanwhile, there are literally dozens of groups aggressively and sometimes violently working to place animals on a par with humans.

These groups include People for the Ethical Treatment of Animals (PETA), ALF, ELF, Greenpeace, and the Humane Society of the United States (HSUS), among others.[8] All are skilled media manipulators—operating collectively in a multibillion-dollar industry—who know how to demonize whole classes of people, from farmers to ranchers to fisherman to hunters. Extremists within the movement believe hunting is "murder" and that eating meat is on a par with "cannibalism." They even believe fish feel pain as humans do, and therefore recreational fishing is a cruel act against nature.

These animal saviors don't care that there is absolutely no scientific evidence behind these assertions. What they care about is promoting an agenda that is anti-capitalism, anti-democracy, anti-West, anti-hunting, and, most pointedly, anti-gun. Even more disturbing, some of these "animal rights" groups condone, promote, and engage in violent acts of domestic and international terrorism.[9]

In 2001 alone, the operatives of ALF and ELF staked public claim to 137 separate violent destructive acts estimated to have destroyed $17.3 million worth of other people's property.[10] ALF published a "primer" for terrorists with detailed instructions on burglarizing, vandalizing, and firebombing any enterprise that, in ALF's opinion, exploited animals.[11]

The tentacles of violence and deception that permeate "animal and environmental rights" extremism are worldwide. In California and throughout the Northwest, "tree spiking" is popular with radical environmental groups. It involves driving a large metal spike into a tree marked for harvest by logging companies. Should a logger's chain saw come in contact with one of these spikes, the consequences could be deadly.

Other forms of "environmental terrorism" by "animal rights" and anti-hunting groups are more indirect—but just as dangerous to themselves and to hunters. Anti-hunting activists march through the woods during deer season, making loud noises and creating a general nuisance. By doing so, they do more than just scare away the deer—they also place themselves and others in dire danger of being accidentally shot and/or killed. Such hunt disruptions abound, including the destruction of traps, shooting stands, blinds, and decoys.

Finally, innocent women—from Minneapolis to Bangor to St. Louis—have been assaulted with vile language and dye or paint for "wearing fur," incidents all too common throughout the nation and indeed the world.

The Global Survival Network, now folded into the animal organization WildAid, is staffed by operatives from the "animal rights" group Environmental Investigative Agency (EIA).[12] EIA was founded in 1984 by Alan Thornton, a former Greenpeace director who fancies himself and his organization as sort of a global "CIA" for "animal rights."[13]

Both WildAid and EIA pride themselves on their influence

within the bureaucracy of the United Nations and various federal and state government wildlife agencies and work closely with other organizations such as Greenpeace and the International Fund for Animal Welfare (IFAW).[14]

Each is a very wealthy, very influential organization that maintains a very careful distance between itself and the more violent factions of its movement. While Greenpeace relishes its ability to perform attention-getting stunts such as scaling skyscrapers and bridges to hang banners festooned with animal and environmental slogans, it avoids being associated with the outright violence and property destruction characteristic of ALF and ELF.

To fully understand the increasing threats of these groups, one must again look to Europe for a glimpse of our potential future.

Great Britain has long laid claim to being the home of the most violent and aggressive behavior by "animal rights" extremists. Buildings and lorries (trucks) owned by meat purveyors, farmers, or furriers have been routinely burned; medical research laboratories, retail fur and grocery stores, and farms have been vandalized, sometimes destroyed when explosive devices detonated.

Despite the proven benefits of using animals in medical research—the practice dates back to the third century B.C.[15] —one biomedical research lab, Huntingdon Life Sciences, with facilities in England and the United States, has become the target of a highly coordinated assault to drive it out of business by militant "animal rights" groups, including PETA, ALF-US, and ALF-UK.[16]

Huntingdon's United Kingdom operation has been on the receiving end of such "protest tactics" as eleven separate car bombings, two arson fires at the homes of researchers whose children were asleep at the time, violent home invasions, and the beating of its managing director by three masked thugs swinging baseball bats. One of the assailants, thirty-five-year-old David Blenkinsop, was caught and jailed for his role in the assault. To date, the most serious injury inflicted by Britain's "compassionate" activists was a shrapnel wound from an explosive device suffered by a baby being pushed in a carriage when the explosion occurred.[17]

On May 7, 2002, the mantle of mindless "animal rights" extremist violence passed from Britain to the Netherlands.

At six o'clock that Monday evening, authorities say Volkert Van der Graaf, thirty-two, approached the Netherlands' most controversial candidate for prime minister, Pym Fortuyn, and shot him fatally. Van der Graaf, described by the media as a "militant animal rights crusader," was arrested for the crime shortly thereafter. The deliberate nature of Fortuyn's assassination shocked Europe, but it was not an aberrant event that could not have been predicted.[18]

Incredibly, Europe's "always blame America crowd" tied the Fortuyn murder to America's violent Hollywood films and tolerance of firearms ownership by average citizens.[19] But the fact is, Fortuyn was murdered by a radical "animal rights" fanatic, because Fortuyn was pushing to end a ban on fur farming.

Van der Graaf, described as working for Vereniging Milieu Offensive (Environment Offensive), apparently revved himself into a murderous frenzy over what he considered the cruelty and abuse associated with so-called "industrial" or "factory" farming. In all, Van der Graaf had been involved in more than two thousand lawsuits against European animal and fur farmers.[20] Van der Graaf's activities against farmers mirrored campaigns waged elsewhere around the world by major animal rights groups, including PETA.

PETA has become increasingly successful in thwarting medical research efforts in this country, even when it comes to sabotaging efforts to end the scourge of AIDS. We'll never know how far the search for a cure may have been set back when in July 2002, Dr. Michael Podell was forced to stop his AIDS research studies and resign from Ohio State University. Why was Dr. Podell forced to give up a tenured position and abandon a $1.7 million project funded by the National Institutes of Health?

According to the *New York Times,* it was because he received death threats after PETA listed his experiments on an "action alert" list. Among those threats, Dr. Podell was sent a photograph of a British scientist whose car had been bombed. A terrorist had scrawled "You're next" across the top of the photo.[21]

Equally disturbing, the front-page *Times* report went on to note the distressing lack of support Dr. Podell received from the university:

> At Ohio State there was intense debate over who should defend Dr. Podell, and how. Reluctant to be his own public defender, Dr. Podell, who agreed to an interview but not a photograph, pressed the administration to take a public stand, perhaps with an opinion article in the local newspaper. University officials resisted, a move that Dr. Podell said contributed to his decision to leave.[22]

Dr. Podell, a veterinarian, was the target of "animal rights" terrorists chiefly because his research involved cats rather than rodents bred for research. Studying why drug abusers may succumb to AIDS more quickly than others, Dr. Podell infected the animals with feline immunodeficiency, then injected them with methamphetamine. Dr. Podell the *Times'* reporter that he did not take putting cats to death lightly but made an ethical calculation: "It's a small number of animals to get information to potentially help millions of people."[23]

A research colleague of Dr. Podell's told the *Times,* "If he was by himself, he probably would have stayed and fought the battle. I think one of his biggest fears was that his children would get labeled the children of a cat killer."[24]

PETA, which was founded by Ingrid Newkirk and Alex Pacheco, has tried hard lately to obtain mainstream acceptance. It recently halted its function as press agent for the underground ALF and called its 2001 donation of $1,500 to the terrorist group ELF a mistake.[25] PETA officers and staff now regularly associate with Hollywood and recording industry stars such as Alec Baldwin. The group holds its gala awards banquets at Paramount Studios.[26]

In a made-for-headlines breakup, PETA cofounders Newkirk and Pacheco recently staged an elaborate parting of the ways. Pacheco headed off to California to create the Humane America Animal Foundation and raise some $2 million before relocating to Pompano Beach, Florida.[27] Pacheco's new group was not the first to clone itself from PETA. In Defense of Animals, known as PETA-West, is yet another.[28] But perhaps the most telling PETA-birthed group is the anti-gun Physicians Committee for Responsible Medicine (PCRM) run by a close Newkirk associate, Neal D. Barnard, M.D. PCRM brings the perception of scientific and medical credibility to PETA's radical "animal rights," anti-hunting, and anti-gun-rights ideology.[29] And if you think "radical" is too harsh a description, consider the following from the *New York Post:*

> Despite its mainstream aspirations, PETA still proudly wears its extremist ideology publicly on its sleeve. Sometimes too proudly. After PETA spokesman Bruce Friedrich proclaimed "It would be great if all fast-food outlets, slaughterhouses, these laboratories and the banks who fund them exploded tomorrow," PETA's board was forced to censure him.[30]

PETA's Newkirk has openly condemned humans as a "cancer" on the environment and rejects any and all research using animals to test any medical procedure, evidently claiming the life of a purposefully bred lab rat is more important than possibly saving the life of an ill child.[31] At the height of the outbreak of hoof-and-mouth disease and "mad cow" disease among British beef cattle, Newkirk told the press that she couldn't wait until a similar fate struck North American livestock.[32]

Alarmed that UK animal extremists may have played a significant role in the spread of the infection in England, Scotland, and

Europe, Canadian authorities reportedly went on high alert against the possibility of such an act of deliberate domestic bio-terrorism, a fact they acknowledged publicly and attributed to Newkirk's theoretical musings.[33]

While PETA's rhetoric and street-theater antics seek media and public attention, the Humane Society of the United States (HSUS) operates quietly at the state, federal, and international levels pressing for laws, regulations, and treaties designed to choke off the lifeblood of the activities and organizations it sees as its ideological enemies.

Since its founding, HSUS has postured itself as the voice of reason as its emissaries make their way throughout the halls of Congress, through state legislatures, and among the various Secretariat offices of United Nations' conventions on environmental regulatory issues.

At every venue—state, federal, or international—HSUS conducts its affairs as business-suit-clad professional advocates for animal welfare and foes of "animal cruelty" and "environmental abuse" in any form. Chief among HSUS's emissaries of legislative concern is Wayne Pacelle, former national director of the anti-hunting group Fund for Animals.[34]

At first perception, it appears that HSUS and PETA operate as independent and separate organizations. Legally, they are in fact distinct; however, for nearly a decade, PETA has quietly succeeded in achieving a bloodless internal takeover of HSUS.[35]

Virtually every administrative and operational level within HSUS is run by and/or filled with former PETA employees.[36] The HSUS vice president for investigations is PETA's former CEO, Richard W. Swain Jr., a retired Montgomery County, Maryland, police officer who just happened to be the responding officer to PETA's infamous "raid" in 1980 to free monkeys from the laboratory of stroke researcher Dr. Edward Taub.[37] John Paul "J.P." Goodwin, formerly of the organization CAFT (Coalition to Abolish the Fur Trade), is now a suit-wearing HSUS employee working on fur issues.[38]

Where PETA acts out an extremist "animal rights" and anti-hunting agenda, HSUS is in a position to implement it. The two are the animal/environmental activist version of the classic "good cop/bad cop" team. The same methodology can be seen in the relationship of groups like Greenpeace and the more sedate and acceptable World Wildlife Fund (WWF). Interwoven among the groups—PETA, HSUS, EIA, and WWF—is a cadre of familiar faces extremely well versed in the political and public relations techniques of "reality versus perception."

While some of its leaders may be different, and their primary goals may differ, the anti-hunting, "animal rights," and anti-gun-rights movements are really all one and the same. They use the same tactics. They are manned by many of the same people. They appeal to the same fears and emotions of the voters they target for support. And they are treated, for the most part, with kid gloves by the mass media.[39]

Hunters especially might want to take note of the following from anti-terrorism experts at the Southern Poverty Law Center. In a new exposé they say that American authorities and their Canadian counterparts are worried about yet another British import—the Justice Department:

> Since it sprang up in 1993, the so-called Justice Department has claimed responsibility for hundreds of violent attacks in the U.K. With an underground cell structure similar to those of the ALF and ELF, the Justice Department has made creative use of letter bombs, which have injured several people, and sent out scores of envelopes rigged with poisoned razor blades. The London Independent called the Justice Department's attacks "the most sustained and sophisticated bombing campaign in mainland Britain since the IRA was at its height."
>
> In January 1996, after the group became active in North America, the Justice Department claimed responsibility for sending

envelopes with blades dipped in rat poison to 80 researchers, hunting guides and others in British Columbia, Alberta, and around the United States. The blades were taped inside the opening edge of the envelopes, poised to cut the fingers of anyone opening the letters. "Dear animal killing scum!" read the note inside. "Hope we sliced your finger wide open and that you now die from the rat poison we smeared on the razor blade." The letter signed off, "Justice Department strikes again."

For Americans who love liberty, the groups are virtually one-minded in a most significant aspect: each wants to dictate how we live and what we believe—and each couldn't care less about citizens' rights or the Constitution of the United States.

12

THE COURT OFFENSIVE: DISARMAMENT BY LAWSUIT

On October 30, 1998, New Orleans became the first city in the nation to file a frivolous lawsuit against the firearms industry,[1] followed two weeks later by Chicago.[2] Within a year, twenty-seven additional cities and counties had filed suit against more than forty gun manufacturers, dealers, and trade associations.

Because politicians did not have to pay for the lawsuits out of their own pockets—and because they often got favorable publicity, regardless of the sham nature of their actions—the lawsuits kept coming. Cities found one outrageous reason after another to blame outside corporations for their own failure to maintain peace and order in their streets. Such lawsuits were nothing but old-time scapegoating.

The assault was on. Most of the municipalities suing the gun industry contended that firearms incurred liability for their manufacturers under the traditional rules of American product liability law.

Under product liability law, all manufacturers are legally responsible for compensating people directly injured by their "defective and unreasonably dangerous" products. The defects can exist in the products when they leave the factory—thus, if Coca-Cola were to manufacture a bottle that exploded upon opening, the company would be liable to those injured by the explosion. Products can also be deemed "defective" because of particular marketing techniques. For example, if a product contained a hidden danger if used in a particular way, and the manufacturer not only failed to warn of this danger but actually encouraged it to be used in that way, the product could be considered "defective" as marketed.

Most of the twenty-nine municipalities demanded damages for harms allegedly caused by inherent defects in the manufacturers' guns. In effect, the municipality claimed that the manufacturers' guns were defective, because criminals could use them. And upon closer examination of the firearms suits, the municipalities also sought to recover damages resulting from the suffering by others. Specifically, the suits asked for reimbursement for medical costs the municipalities incurred by treating gunshot victims in city hospitals, by paying for police overtime to investigate shootings, and by missing out on tax revenue when property values dropped because of high crime rates.[3]

But under law, no one but the victim may sue and recover damages, and even then, victims have rights only against the person who wrongfully caused the damage. The direct victim of a drunk driver, for example, has no recourse against the manufacturer of the car. The direct slip-and-fall victim of a negligently thrown banana peel has no suit against the farmer who planted the banana tree.

Another "nontraditional" theory lay behind several of the firearms lawsuits, most notably Chicago's suit, which charged that the firearm industry's marketing tactics had created a "public nuisance" jeopardizing citizens' safety. It was alleged that manufacturers created this nuisance by legally selling "too many" guns in the suburbs of Chicago, and manufacturers "should have known" that some of these firearms would be transported to Chicago for illegal use. In addition to monetary damages, the Chicago suit also sought complex court orders—for example, an injunction prohibiting:

- any sales to people who had purchased guns in the past thirty days;
- any sales "in excess of lawful demand"; and

- any sales of "firearms that by their design are unreasonably attractive to criminals."

Clearly, the "remedies" sought by Chicago amounted to the court enacting a gun-control statute that begged the question: Aren't courts supposed to apply legal principles, not create new policy?

Many of the lawsuits were raw power grabs camouflaged in public interest rhetoric. Florida Judge Amy Dean, commenting on the Miami–Dade County lawsuit against gun makers, said to the government prosecutors: "If you were to get exactly what you wanted, they'd be taken off the market entirely." Judge Dean rejected the lawsuit, saying: "The County explicitly seeks to regulate aspects of the manufacture, sale, and distribution of firearms. Only the Florida legislature has the standing to authorize such a claim."[4]

Chicago's lawsuit against firearms manufacturers anticipated that other cities' claims of "defective design" would not go far. Indeed, American case law has routinely rejected claims that handguns are intrinsically defective. Some prominent examples among many, many others include the following:[5]

- In 1984, the Seventh Circuit Court of Appeals held in *Martin v. Harrington & Richardson* that liability for producing or distributing a defective product simply did not and could not apply to manufacturers of handguns at large.

- In 1995, the Supreme Court of New York reached the same argument in *Forni v. Ferguson* (the famous "Long Island Railroad Shooter" case).[6]

- In 1989, the District of Columbia Circuit Court of Appeals held in *Delahanty v. Hinkley* (the Reagan assassination attempt case), that gun injuries are not the product of defective design or marketing.[7]

- In 1998, a federal court in New York ruled in *Hamilton v. Accu-tek* that "the mere act of manufacturing and selling a handgun does not give rise to liability absent a defect in the manufacture or design of the product itself . . . [Plaintiff] alleges that handguns are unreasonably dangerous because of the lack of an anti-theft or related safety device. There is no valid basis for this claim."[8]

Chicago therefore relied on the innovative claim that the manufacturers' wrongdoing lay in their marketing of guns. Chicago contended that the selling of firearms in America in general, and in Illinois in particular, created a "public nuisance" in two different ways:

- Currently, law-abiding Chicago residents have the right to buy handguns in Illinois, but they can't legally bring those guns into the city.[9] Chicago investigators who conducted undercover "sting" operations at suburban gun dealers alleged that several retailers were aware that Chicago gang members circumvented federal and local laws by paying qualified buyers to make "straw purchases," with the true purchaser bringing the firearm into the Windy City. Chicago alleged that mass manufacture of guns encouraged this complicity in fraud by retailers and was thus a nuisance.

- Chicago's brief also alleged that gun stores "flooded" with guns made sales without obtaining adequate "proof" that Chicago-based buyers would keep their guns outside the city and without notifying city police whenever a Chicago resident bought a firearm. The city's attorneys ignored the fact that no law requires dealers to obtain such proof or to give such notice. At any rate, the core of this claim was that "too many" guns were sold in Chicago's suburbs and that

> retailers and manufacturers must have known that some purchasers were in fact taking their products into the city.

Chicago's claim was at best imaginative and at worst a flagrant attempt to bypass the legislative process and replace it with a judge's notion of what a gun-control statute ought to look like. Indeed, some aspects of Chicago's claim were self-contradictory. For instance, Cook County was co-plaintiff with the City of Chicago. As a "home rule" unit under Illinois law, the county could have enacted more restrictive gun laws. Cook County's complaint to the court, quite literally, was that it has itself failed to pass appropriate legislation. Cook County's "Reward me as a plaintiff in tort because I didn't legislate" plea must be a "first" in American jurisprudence!

The American Law Institute (ALI), in its authoritative *Restatement (2nd) of Torts,* defines a public nuisance as "an unreasonable interference with a right common to the general public." If I block the road, I create a public nuisance. But Professor David Kairys of Temple University Law School, co-counsel for the plaintiffs in the Chicago case, had urged the adoption of the public nuisance doctrine in gun cases.[10] Unfortunately for Kairys, but fortunately for the rule of law, no case can be made that legal firearms sales constitute a public nuisance. Indeed, Kairys had it backward. It is Chicago's lawsuit and Kairys's argument that constituted a public nuisance under the ALI definition. The sale of guns promotes a right common to the general public—for individuals have a right to protect themselves against criminal conduct.

Far from constituting a "public nuisance," firearms marketing generates a public good. Their production and sale to law-abiding citizens is the opposite of a nuisance. The argument that there are "too many guns" is, pardon the pun, shot full of holes. So is the argument that guns are being marketed so casually as to constitute a nuisance; the manufacture, sale, and ownership of firearms are all highly regulated by federal law.

Economic logic ultimately provided one more compelling reason to reject the "public nuisance" claim. If gun makers reduced the supply of firearms sold to suburban dealers as Chicago wished, then the law of supply and demand dictates that the market price of guns will inevitably rise. Consumers with the most "elastic" demand—that is, consumers who are most sensitive to price changes—will be the ones who reduce or eliminate their purchases. The evidence is clear: the most price-sensitive consumers are law-abiding citizens. By contrast, criminal demand for guns is highly "inelastic" since crooks are willing to pay inflated black-market prices for firearms. Perversely, by restricting the legal supply of guns and thereby raising their price, a successful Chicago lawsuit would have put a greater percentage of the nation's firearms in criminals' hands and a smaller percentage in the hands of honest citizens.

Such a consequence would produce exactly the opposite effect from the public good that comes with widespread ownership. In Maryland, for example, where so-called "Saturday night specials" may no longer be legally sold, criminals may have more confidence that potential victims in poor neighborhoods have been priced out of the defensive handgun market. Despite virtually identical climates, demographics, and cultures, Maryland's violent crime rate is three times that of "Right-to-Carry" Virginia next door. A *Washington Post* analysis of FBI violent crime statistics found that in Fairfax County, Virginia, the crime rate had dropped 36 percent from 1977 to 1997, but in adjoining Montgomery County, Maryland, the violent crime rate had risen 43 percent over the same period. The two counties have virtually identical demographics, but since 1998 law-abiding Fairfax County residents have been allowed to carry concealed firearms.[11]

Finally, any coordinated industry response to a "public nuisance" tort claim would run afoul of federal antitrust laws. Because brands are more or less interchangeable, no single gun maker would agree to cut back production for fear that other manufacturers would take up the slack. Manufacturers that "overproduce" would have to collude in order to jointly reduce production.

Many of the cities that sought to plunder gun manufacturers were themselves guilty of aggressive marketing practices. Walter Olson, an author and expert on lawsuit abuse, observed: "Boston attached no strings when it recently got rid of more than 3,000 police .38s, even though it has now endorsed a new legal theory that private vendors should be liable because they displayed 'willful blindness' to what happened after guns left their hands."[12]

New Orleans was even more brazen. As constitutional lawyer Robert Levy noted:

> In 1998 the city's police department traded more than 8,000 confiscated weapons—40 percent of which were semiautomatic—to a commercial dealer in return for Glocks. Nearly half of the traded guns would have been characterized as "unsafe" in the city's lawsuit against gun makers—including TEC9s, AK47s, and Uzis, banned since 1994. Only a quarter of the guns had safety locks. Still, Mayor Marc Morial signed and approved the deal, paving the way for resale of those guns across the nation.[13]

Apparently, as long as politicians profit, gun sales could do no harm.

Chicago's sorry nuisance argument would have had terrible implications if it had been accepted. Is General Motors liable in tort because the market for cars is "saturated" in southern California, resulting in traffic jams and accidents? Of course not. Rather, individual motorists bear the burden of their choices (where to live, what to drive, how to get to work) and are constrained only by their obligation to take due care in using the automobiles they voluntarily acquire. The extent of highway development is a public policy issue, not a tort issue.

When a state judge asks a state jury in a tort case to determine whether its state has too many cars, or too many knives or guns, this judge is asking the jury to engage in public regulation totally outside its constitutional jurisdiction. If that judge allows a claim that neighboring states allow too many gun sales, as the city of San Francisco requested,[14] he or she is contravening principles of federalism. Never before in our country's history have tort tribunals been asked to interfere so extensively in the legislative process, and never before has individual responsibility been so challenged by a tort suit.

The good news is this: as of this writing, many of these lawsuits, including the Chicago case, have been dismissed with prejudice.

More good news—thanks in large measure to NRA efforts: twenty-nine states have enacted bans on frivolous firearm lawsuits. Similar federal legislation is pending.

You might well ask, "If municipal and county lawsuits are being dismissed, how can firearm litigation still be a threat?" The answer is that several factors combine to transform weak legal cases into effective means of accomplishing a shakedown against the firearms industry and, ultimately, the right to keep and bear arms. Those factors include the use of juries in civil cases, the sheer size of potential damage awards, and the perverse incentives that drive lawsuits when public officials hire private attorneys on a contingent fee basis.

Alone among Western democracies, the United States still provides for juries in civil cases. Whatever the merits of civil juries, they are more willing than judges to overlook legal requirements (assuming jurors understand them), especially when a local injured plaintiff seeks damages from an out-of-state corporate defendant. Juries are also much more likely to be swayed by the pain and suffering of the victim or victims, and by their own personal feelings on, in these cases, firearms. These feelings could be the direct result of the massive amount of anti-gun propaganda emanating from the mass media.

In addition, not only are plaintiffs more likely to prevail if a jury hears their case, but they are also more likely to recover a greater sum when juries evaluate their damage—especially when the jury's own government is the plaintiff. This incredible conflict of interest is an inevitable product of the conflation of private and public ordering. Its effect is to make defendants—in this case it happened to be the firearms industry—more amenable to settlement.

Procedural rules also push defendants toward settlement, even when they have a strong case on the merits. In many jurisdictions, judges are reluctant to dismiss a case prior to far-reaching "discovery." Thus, anti-gun plaintiffs can engage in lengthy and costly "fishing expeditions" for documents or other evidence that might support their case or embarrass defendants in other ways. Even after discovery is complete, a case typically will not be dismissed without trial if there is any conceivable factual dispute over a significant issue.

Yet another intimidating factor for defendants is the potentially enormous damage award that could follow an adverse verdict in a compensation suit. While a defendant might risk going to trial against one private claimant making a radical legal claim, the stakes are much higher when a government is the claimant and the litigation is converted effectively into a gigantic class action.

Responsible CEOs may be loath to "bet the company" on one tort case if the government is offering a settlement that will allow the company to survive. Indeed, when the federal government under the Clinton administration announced that it planned to join the lawsuit against firearms manufacturers, it virtually conceded that it had no desire to see the legal merits of its case debated before a court of appeals. Rather, HUD Secretary Andrew Cuomo frankly admitted that he hoped the mere prospect of facing off against unlimited resources of the federal government would lead the defendants to settle.[15]

The point of all this legal action is simply to make firearms harder to manufacture, harder to market, harder to find, and much more expensive. None of that will deter criminals or terrorists who can easily locate and purchase illegal firearms on the black market. But it potentially makes it much more difficult for average, law-abiding Americans to practice their Second Amendment rights—which is the real motive behind all the lawsuits that were filed.

As of this writing, nine government lawsuits against firearms makers are still pending. Let us hope that courageous mayors, governors, and (yes) judges dispose of them quickly, before any lasting damage is done to the rule of law and to our constitutional rights.

13

GOVERNMENT TERRORISM: PUBLIC HOUSING AND RAW POWER

Every American should be frightened by the raw extortion committed by the Clinton administration against federally licensed firearms manufacturers, distributors, and dealers when President Bill Clinton ordered massive litigation against a perfectly lawful industry.

The *Los Angeles Times* summed it up: "Gun makers can agree now to modest, responsible steps that will cut the flow of guns to juveniles and criminals. Or they can write very large checks to their attorneys."[1]

Extortion. The gun industry litigation, with the federal government as a "super plaintiff," came in the form of class-action lawsuits filed on behalf of 3,200 public housing authorities under the U.S. Department of Housing and Urban Development (HUD) demanding recovery of billions of dollars in damages for criminal violence. HUD suits would piggyback on the scores of lawsuits that had been filed by urban mayors at the administration's urging.

Though the municipal lawsuits were failing one by one in the courts, the Clinton administration could not resist seizing a new opportunity to ban guns. On December 7, 1999, the White House announced that HUD would be bankrolling class-action product-liability lawsuits against firearms manufacturers.

The Justice Department reportedly advised the department that there was no legal basis for HUD's involvement in the lawsuits—but to no avail.[2]

The Clinton administration was determined to demonize firearms—and to do whatever it could to financially weaken the firearms industry and use tort law to torpedo the Second Amendment. The Clinton administration sought to blame gun makers for violence in public housing projects—as an antidote to its abject failures in curbing violent crime.

HUD was renowned for doing a poor job of policing its projects.[3] George Sternlieb, director of the Center for Urban Policy Research at Rutgers University, observed that public housing creates "a moral and psychological bankruptcy" in "the people who live in it."[4] According to a HUD report, *Crime in Public Housing,* "Crime rates in public housing complexes are in some cases . . . ten times higher than the national average."[5] The robbery rate at one large Baltimore public housing project was almost twenty times the national average.[6] In Washington, D.C., in the early 1990s, 80 percent of all violent crime occurred at public housing projects.[7] Yet, despite the perennial failure of HUD to protect either its own public housing residents or their luckless private neighbors, HUD Secretary Andrew Cuomo busied himself blaming gun makers for all the ills.

The Clinton administration worked tirelessly to create the political and publicity atmosphere that would allow trial lawyers to bludgeon gun makers. On March 17, 2000, Clinton announced that Smith & Wesson, the nation's largest handgun manufacturer, had agreed to sweeping new controls over its gun designs and marketing and to new restrictions on gun buyers. Smith & Wesson had been in a precarious financial position and the British-owned company decided it could not financially afford to fight multiple court attacks around the nation and from Washington. The company agreed to a settlement. When not a single additional American gun maker followed suit, the Clinton administration and particularly Andrew Cuomo were humiliated but undaunted.

The "concessions" by Smith & Wesson came in return for promises of government procurement contracts that never materialized and were clearly face-saving devices for the administration—which knew the lawsuit had no legal merit.

The company's settlement exemplified how trial lawyers and politicians abused tort law to attempt to seize absolute power over an industry—and all its customers. The Smith & Wesson settlement also illustrated how political operatives used the coercion of bogus litigation to achieve "concessions" from corporate targets that could never have been enacted through the legislative process.

The Clinton administration pressured Smith & Wesson to sign a "code of conduct" that originated from Clinton's anti-gun dogma. Jeff Reh, general counsel for Beretta (which provides the standard sidearm for the U.S. military), noted that "the 'code of conduct' bans almost all semiautomatic pistols . . . and the manufacture of all small handguns."[8] The code also allowed the possibility for sweeping recalls of previously made guns.

Lawrence Summers, Treasury secretary at the time, hailed the settlement: "Because of the agreement reached today, fewer parents will have to bury their children."[9] HUD Secretary Cuomo, the prime architect of the deal, declared of the new specifications for firearms: "This is a product that did not exist last week . . . This will do to the [gun] industry what FedEx did to the [delivery] industry. This is a better mousetrap."[10] But there was no "mousetrap" and no new "product"—only government press releases based on empty political promises.

According to a HUD press release on the Smith & Wesson settlement, "Within 12 months, handguns will be designed so they cannot be readily operated by a child under 6."[11] For the Clinton administration, the more difficult a gun was to fire, the safer it became. This Rosetta stone was necessary to understand Clintonite claims that the "agreement" improved gun safety. The federal government sought to apply the "childproof cap" panacea to guns. However, according to a study by W. Kip Viscusi, an economist at Harvard Law School, the federal mandate for childproof caps on drug prescriptions actually may lull parents into a false sense of security and make them more likely to fail to keep drugs securely stored away from children.[12]

Besides, while people with a headache usually have some margin of time to struggle with the top of an aspirin bottle, people confronting a burglar cannot request a time-out. In short, the federal government has not yet been able to persuade the "National Association of Home Burglars" to sign a side agreement giving an extra five minutes warning to victims—time for residents to remove trigger locks—before they break into people's homes.

The agreement obliged gun stores to see that "guns and bullets must be kept locked and separated." Since there had been no reports of shootings in gun stores from customers combining guns and bullets in recent years, perhaps HUD's negotiators watched *The Terminator* movie one too many times to concoct this rule.

The agreement required "persons under 18 to be accompanied by adults in gun stores or gun sections of stores." That effort attempted to classify guns as pornography—something so obscene that no child could be exposed to it. Moreover, the agreement required Smith & Wesson to "not market guns in any manner designed to appeal to juveniles or criminals." HUD had no evidence that Smith & Wesson had been running advertisements in prison magazines—but the provision aided the Clinton administration's efforts to cast an aura of illegitimacy around all firearms.

Smith & Wesson was required to "refrain from selling any modified/sporterized semi-automatic pistol of a type that cannot be imported into U.S." That was a far more prohibitive standard than what governed products other American manufacturers can produce and sell. The administration used the Smith & Wesson agreement to leapfrog toward broader firearms bans. When Clinton banned imports of certain semiautomatics in 1997, he justified it because the guns violated the "spirit" of the 1994 assault weapons ban (even though such guns could be legally sold under existing federal law).

There was an exemption for the new design specifications for purchases by law enforcement agencies. Thus, Smith & Wesson could continue to manufacture certain types of firearms that would be otherwise banned—but only for government employees.

The settlement created an "Oversight Commission . . . empowered to oversee implementation of the Agreement. The Commission will have five members selected as follows: one by manufacturers; two by city and county parties; one by state parties; one by ATF." Four government officials and one private representative were the Clinton administration's idea of fairness. This commission would have given government officials practically unlimited power in perpetuity over the nation's largest gun manufacturer. As Beretta's Reh noted, "If the Oversight Commission decides that an ad showing a father and son hunting together make the firearm shown 'particularly appealing to juveniles,' it can ban the ad."[13] Reh also noted that the creation of the commission "surrenders firearm design and distribution to antigun politicians."

The Clinton administration abused tort law to seek far more power over gun makers than either the Constitution or the U.S. Congress would allow. But—because few people realized the degree of the extortion—the Clinton administration bragged that the Smith & Wesson settlement was not achieved with an iron fist.

Clinton's former Secretary of Labor, Robert Reich—one of the most liberal members of his administration—denounced the HUD lawsuit: "The biggest problem is that these lawsuits are blatant end-runs around the democratic process. We used to be a nation of laws. This is nothing short of faux legislation, which sacrifices democracy to the discretion of administration officials operating in utter secrecy."[14]

The settlement was almost fatal for Smith & Wesson, which

was widely denounced by other firearms manufacturers for trying to cut a sweetheart deal with the federal government. Consumers boycotted their products, and many gun dealers refused to accept the onerous new restrictions that Smith & Wesson sought to impose on them. Smith & Wesson announced layoffs of its manufacturing employees. And the company nonetheless continued to be sued by city governments who refused to abandon their opportunity to plunder its remaining assets. Of course, gun owners know that Smith & Wesson, thank goodness, is now back in the hands of American owners.

Even after the Clinton administration flattened one of the nation's most prestigious gun manufacturers, the lawsuits kept coming. A few months after the HUD–Smith & Wesson "settlement," New York became the first state to join municipalities around the country in suing firearms manufacturers. The New York State lawsuit sought to compel gun makers to change how they made and sold their goods. The lawsuit charged: "Illegal guns in New York State cause harm above and beyond actual physical wounds. The presence of illegal handguns impairs residents' ability to use public spaces. In locations around the state, parents do not allow their children to use public playgrounds or to walk home from school alone because gunfire may erupt."[15]

In announcing the lawsuit, New York Attorney General Elliot Spitzer portrayed the government of New York as a reluctant victim of the gun industry: "For more than a year, we sought to achieve reasonable reforms through negotiations with the gun industry. It is now clear that most manufacturers and wholesalers are unwilling to give up the profits they reap from selling guns into the criminal market."[16] And since the gun industry refused to surrender, the government was left with no alternative except to seek to destroy it. HUD Secretary Cuomo showed up at the New York City press conference announcing the suit and cheered Spitzer on: "New York's lawsuit is an important step that increases the pressure on irresponsible gun makers and distributors to agree to reforms that will prevent needless deaths and injuries."[17]

The suit also aimed to force companies to cease manufacturing certain "crime-friendly" firearms. That typical scam by anti-gun politicians aimed to shift the blame for misconduct from the perpetrators to innocent bystanders. The same models of firearms that might have a high rate of criminal use in the Bronx had a low or zero rate of criminal use in the many parts of the Adirondack Mountains in upstate New York. But as long as the politicians could blame firearms for the misdeeds of their armed, violent criminals, it provided an election issue.

The New York State lawsuit did not seek monetary damages: instead, it sought "only" power to dictate how guns must be sold and made in America. Spitzer bragged: "We have the capacity to squeeze manufacturers like a pincers and hurt them in the marketplace."[18] This was a grim warning, since anti-gun politicians will not be satisfied until they have destroyed all sources of private gun ownership—all the while creating exemptions (as did the Smith & Wesson agreement) for law enforcement and the military.

Sturm, Ruger & Company issued a press release offering its candid take on the controversy: "The Attorney General of New York has threatened us with punitive litigation if we do not cede ultimate control of design, manufacturing, marketing, and sales decisions to a 'monitor' appointed by his office, reporting directly to him, with absolute powers. Respectfully, this we cannot do . . . We cannot allow such possibly illegal and wholly inappropriate arrogation of decisions affecting our core business away from our Board of Directors to the Attorney General of one of the 50 states, or even a group of states, in which our products are owned and used."[19]

Robert Delfay, then president and CEO of the National Shooting Sports Foundation, commented: "The responsible manufacturers of firearms attempted over the course of the past year to hold meaningful discussions with Mr. Spitzer but with each meeting it became increasingly clear that responsible discussions were not furthering Mr. Spitzer's agenda and he, not the industry, canceled further meetings." Delfay observed: "It is clear the Attorney General has made the political decision that he can gain more by piling on a misrepresented industry than he might lose by wasting taxpayers' dollars on a frivolous lawsuit."[20]

Spitzer's case was dismissed in August 2001 by New York State Supreme Court Judge Louis York, who ruled: "The relief sought here would have the potential effect of preventing defendants from engaging in activities, i.e., the manufacture and sale of guns, that they are permitted to engage in by law in an area which is strongly controlled by various federal and state statutes. The recognition of a cause of action for public nuisance based on the manufacture and sale of a non-defective product threatens to unreasonably expand the scope of nuisance law."[21]

Ironically, many government agencies could be destroyed by the same methods that anti-gun politicians have sanctioned for use against private enterprises and legal products.

Who would want to defend HUD if it could be held liable for all the damage that public housing projects have done to surrounding neighborhoods and to urban life as a whole? Who would want to defend the Food and Drug Administration if the agency could be held responsible for all the people who died while the agency took years before approving new lifesaving drugs and medical devices? Who would want to defend the Internal Revenue Service if the agency could be held liable for the pain and suffering caused by its annual hundreds of thousands of wrongful levies and liens? What if public schools could be held liable for all the false promises they make to children and parents?

Yet, the government has sovereign immunity, and its officials are immune from such charges. Nonetheless, its power is immense to coerce private, lawful corporations to heel to its political demands. The abuses of the legal process combined with the abuses of the political process create a combination deadly to freedom in America.

14

AUSTRALIA: LOSS OF LIBERTY

On a recent Thursday, as gun owners queue up at a collection center—some stifle tears as they embrace their weapons for the last time.

Roy Burton, a 72-year-old retired chimney builder, seems more downcast than most. Burton's gun belonged to his brother, who was killed in World War II. "It was the only thing I had left of his," Burton says.[1]

Welcome to Australia, circa 1997. Tens of thousands of good people across that nation were forfeiting their personal property to the government under threat of imprisonment and heavy fines.

In reaction to a mass murder committed by a lone sociopath, Australian politicians have criminalized possession of all semiautomatic and pump shotguns and all self-loading rifles (including .22s). Although the media worldwide claimed the ban was on "military-style" or "assault weapons" or "automatic weapons," a huge majority of the 640,000 guns ultimately confiscated were sporting arms. Virtually all of those firearms—save a few the government kept for its museum collections—were hammered, shredded, or crushed into tons of scrap.

The list published by the government of outlawed long guns to be forfeited or confiscated covered every sporting arm manufacturer's products from the golden age of firearms to modern times: Savage, Winchester, Remington, Colt, Browning, High Standard, Ithaca, Franchi, Mossberg, SKB, Beretta, Brno, Smith & Wesson, Marlin, H&K, Ruger, Stevens, H&R, BSA, Anschutz, FN, Walther, Weatherby. From the modern Ruger 1022s to the classic Winchester Model 63 .22 to Peerless Grade Remington 1100s to Winchester Model 12 trap guns—all were outlawed, most forfeited and destroyed.[2]

On May 25, 1997, the *Fort Worth Star Telegram* headlined, "Australians Demolish Guns to Prevent Another Massacre" and described the work at one gun confiscation center:

> Swinging a hammer, Al Egan hacks at a semiautomatic rifle. Soon, the gun is dismembered—the barrel, the wooden butt and metal parts are strewn on his workbench. All around him, in an air-conditioned room filled with the clang of bludgeoning hammers, Egan's mates pulverize an endless line of rifles and shotguns disgorged by a conveyor belt. "A lot of engineering has gone into some of these beautiful pieces, but destroying them does good for everyone," Egan says.

Good for everyone? Consider this. A mass murderer uses a watch to be on time for his killing. Does the government take your watch? A crazed murderer uses an automobile to get to his killing ground. Does the government take your car? Those are absurd notions. Yet, that's exactly what happened in Australia with long-gun owners who were in no way connected to crime, violence, or mass murder.

How do the loss of liberty and the loss of cherished personal property equate with doing good for everyone? They don't, but that was the immediate price extracted from peaceable Aussies to pay for the insanely evil acts of one individual, Martin Bryant.

On the morning of April 28, 1996, Bryant, armed with an illegal CAR-15, invaded the home of David and Sally Martin, a middle-aged couple who ran a bed-and-breakfast near historic Port Arthur in Tasmania. Bryant murdered them and then raided their gun cabinet.

From there, he proceeded to a Port Arthur café where he ordered lunch, sharing the pleasant Sunday tourist atmosphere with about sixty other patrons. Witnesses remember that the strange man with stringy blond hair made some odd comments about "WASPs," then about "Japs" while he was eating.

When he finished lunch, Bryant opened a bag he'd carried with him, removed the illegal carbine, and began firing. He murdered 20 people. The toll of innocent lives snuffed out would rise to 35 before Bryant was finally taken into police custody 12 hours later.

Almost immediately after the shootings, some in the Australian media asked questions involving the culpability on the part of government officials. The headline in the May 5, 1996, *Sydney Sun-Herald* blared, "He could have been stopped," and predicted "the mood of grief at the carnage would quickly turn to anger when people realized the massacre could have been prevented."[3]

In an exclusive investigation, the *Sun-Herald* blamed government inattention and said that "Martin Bryant slipped through the net of health authorities and police at least three times before he embarked on his killing orgy at Port Arthur. His parents pleaded with the Community and Health Services Department for help. But apart from counseling and some medication, close family friends maintain Bryant's case was dropped."

Yet, after the initial coverage, the world media replaced the ghastly details of Bryant's crimes with an antiseptic description that became the mantra of the anti-gun-owner movement in Australia and worldwide. Bryant used a "military type rifle" to murder. That was it.

In reducing the story to the gun he used, the emphasis was moved away from the heartless killer and the horror of his crimes and from possible government culpability. Within days, Australian politicians met to draft a new set of national gun laws—at the top of their agenda was a ban on all semiautomatic firearms.

The firearm Bryant used was an *illegal gun in his hands* under existing law. At the time of Bryant's crimes, Tasmanian law required anyone wanting to own any gun, including an air rifle, to pass a firearms knowledge test, purchase a gun-owner license complete with photograph, and be vetted by police.[4] Bryant fulfilled none of these requirements. It was a serious crime for him to possess any gun.

Weeks before the shootings, Bryant was reported to have taken an illegal self-loading rifle to a Hobart gunsmith for repair. When he handed it to the dealer, the firearm was loaded, with a round in the chamber and the safety off. Since Bryant could not produce a firearms license photo-ID in his name, the dealer refused to return the gun and called police and reported this frightening man. The police did nothing.

For the gun-control movement in Australia, the violent rampage presented the opportunity to enact the gun controls they had previously failed to pass.

In just twelve short days after the Port Arthur Massacre, with a media frenzy fueling panic, the Australian federal government, headed by Prime Minister John Howard, forced an agreement with the six states and two territories on what would be the first-ever national gun ban in Australia.

"The basis for these changes," noted the Coalition for Gun Control, "had been laid in 1990 when the National Committee on Violence (NCV) made about 20 recommendations for improved gun control."[5]

Under the Australian Constitution, the national government possesses no real power to regulate or restrict gun ownership—only the states have such authority. But the government of Prime Minister John Howard, with a massive media campaign behind it, forced the states to address the issue the way he and the press demanded.

The national scheme to criminalize possession of whole classes of long guns—rifles and shotguns—was universally adopted by the states and territories as was the compulsory registration of all firearms.

In Victoria's Parliament, the new long-gun prohibition law came in the form of a 147-page bill that virtually no ministers had seen. It was rammed through in a heartbeat.[6]

In a single stroke, all semiautomatic rifles and all pump-action and semiautomatic shotguns were declared contraband. Future possession was a criminal act punishable by a long stay in prison and heavy fines.

What drove all of this was panic politics at its worst.

The government granted an amnesty and instituted what it euphemistically called a "buyback" under which gun owners would be paid for guns from a published list that covered every make and model of firearm declared illegal for private ownership.

The media loved it. It sounded so benign, almost soothing, as if the people who were about to have their prized property forfeited to government and destroyed by government were getting a good deal. How can the government "buy back" something it never owned?

"Buyback?" This was theft with partial compensation.

Yet many in the anti-gun-ownership crowd called this confiscatory "buyback" voluntary. What is voluntary about "give us your property or go to prison"?

For gun owners in Victoria, where universal gun registration had been law since 1983, civil disobedience—conscientious objection, if you will—was virtually impossible. Police data banks contained information about who owned what firearms and where they were located.

What happened in Victoria proved everything opponents of registration had ever predicted—registration is the inevitable prelude to confiscation. Under the original nationwide amnesty, gun owners were given until September 17, 1997, to turn in their property for destruction.

At the time, when hundreds of thousands of honest Australians were standing in line waiting to give up their firearms, the Coalition for Gun Control condescendingly told those gun owners:

> It is part of the responsibility of being a member of a community that people have some liberties curtailed for the sake of the wider community's interests. Fewer guns in the community will deprive many people of guns who would never use them in violent acts. But it will reduce the ease with which the minority who will use them violently can get hold of them . . . Such imputation of potential criminality is a petty inconvenience to pay for the purposes that are served by these measures.[7]

Loss of liberty is no petty inconvenience. And time has shown that no purpose was served by the long-gun ban, save to whet the appetites of those who seek to further criminalize legal gun ownership.

When all was said and done, the taxpayers of Australia, including those who owned the confiscated firearms, paid $500 million for the government gun collection and gun destruction scheme.[8]

The long-gun forfeiture scheme was puffed as the hope and vision of the future by both international gun-control lobbyists and their American counterparts.

Natalie Goldring, deputy director of the British-American Security Information Council (BASIC)—the major organization pushing for breaching national sovereignty to adopt United Nations bans on "light arms"—told the *Los Angeles Times,* "One of NRA's worst fears is that people in the U.S. will listen to what people in Australia and Japan (which bans all gun ownership) say about gun control."[9]

Lost in the international coverage of the forced "buyback" was the monster—Martin Bryant. On November 7, 1996, CNN covered Bryant's guilty plea, in a news segment: "Laughing so hard at one point he could barely say the word 'guilty,' the man charged with killing 35 people at a Port Arthur, Australia, tourist attraction reversed himself and admitted responsibility."[10]

And he laughed again at his sentencing—to life without parole. No remorse. No human feelings. No morality. There was nothing normal, nothing human about his reaction to any of this, just detachment from the horror and pain he'd caused.

Without a trial, Bryant—the man, the monster—was put away for life. And he was put away by the media and by the politicians as well. Bryant was the forgotten element in Port Arthur. Instead, cruel retribution was heaped upon every honest Australian gun owner, not on the actual killer. *Time* described it this way:

> It is clearly only law-abiding shooters who have relinquished their guns; those with devious intent will hardly do so voluntarily. But the gun control lobby says there is a direct correlation: fewer guns in the community mean fewer shooting deaths.[11]

Where *Time* magazine was puffing the ban to its American readers as effective crime control, the actual proponents of the law said quite the opposite.

Australian Prime Minister John Howard said, "I don't pretend for a moment that this decision [the gun ban] can prevent the reoccurrence of tragedies in the future . . ." And try this: "This proposal will never prevent criminals from possessing firearms and we never said it would." That remark by an Attorney General's Department official was quoted in the *Weekend Australian,* just days after the deadline closed on the long-gun forfeiture amnesty.[12]

Yet *Time* quoted Roland Browne, chairman of Australia's National Coalition for Gun Control: "If you take them out of circulation—out of gun stores, out of people's cupboards—you reduce the chance that people like Martin Bryant will get hold [of] them." People like Martin Bryant? Of the millions of people who have lived in the Australian continent, there has been only one Martin

Bryant. Mass murderers are the rarest of human aberrations. There never was anything normal about Martin Bryant, and because he was allowed to roam free, thirty-five innocent people were murdered and millions of good Australians today pay for his crimes with their freedom.

No matter what kind of guns were banned, for the media, this was never about hardware—it was about tarnishing gun ownership.

Time again led the way: "But few sympathize with [sporting] shooters. 'Port Arthur gave shooting a bad name. Gun ownership became something a lot of people were embarrassed by; a lot of people handed in their guns,' says [Roland] Browne. 'We saw a change of culture, a change in consciousness. To say it's done and we can now sigh with relief is the wrong attitude. Unless the pressure is kept on, there is always the tendency to weaken existing laws.'"

On the same subject, the *Washington Post* on November 7, 1997, reported: "In a country with a long tradition of shooting and gun ownership, the new laws were a startling cultural change. A grief-stricken Australia did overnight what gun-control advocates in the United States have been unable to accomplish in decades."[13]

And the *Post* quoted the husband and father of three of Bryant's murder victims, saying there is "real stigma to guns now. Anybody who brings one of those guns out into the fresh air is marked."

From the coverage, one would assume that the relatives and survivors of the Port Arthur Massacre were all of a single mind. But that simply was not the case. In truth, the views of relatives or victims of Martin Bryant's violence who didn't blame innocent gun owners were blacked out by the media.[14]

Les Ingram, the brother of murder victim Gwen Neander, was quoted as saying, "I think everyone should have their guns to protect themselves." And this from Neville Quin, whose wife was murdered: "This business about gun control is a joke really."

You never saw that in the American media, and you won't. It doesn't serve their purpose.

So what's next for Australia? Is the ban on semiautomatics and pump long-guns the end? Not by a long shot. It will never be over until the last gun is taken from the last free citizen.

The *Fort Worth Star Telegram* on May 25, 1997, gave a very clear warning: "The National Coalition for Gun Control, a private lobby group, estimates there are 4 million guns of all types in Australia—one for every 4.5 people . . . But even if only 1 million guns are eliminated in Australia, 'that's a very good start,' said the coalition's Rebecca Peters."[15]

But what she doesn't say, what they never say, is that for every start, there must be a finish. An end game. A final round of confiscations. The ultimate, total "buyback."

In Australia, the final goals of "gun control" have been very clearly stated. Unlike the gun-control movement in the United States, which still uses syrupy promises never to harm the "sportsman or hunter," the Australian crowd doesn't mince words. Gun control means the public cannot own any guns. Period.

Recently, in response to questions about his government's inability to stop lawless violence committed by criminals wielding illegal guns, Prime Minister Howard told his nation of a new initiative to disarm them: "We will find any means we can to further restrict them, because I hate guns," he said.[16]

The lead on the Reuters story covering his radio interview outburst read: "Australian Prime Minister John Howard said on Wednesday he would do everything he could to tighten the nation's already tough gun control laws, saying the scourge of America was not welcome in the land down-under."

Like everything else in the *global* war against private ownership of firearms, words take on whole new meanings. "Tighten" and "restrict," like "control," now describe an extreme. Howard defines his meaning, saying: "I don't think people should have guns unless they're police or in the military or in the security industry. There is no earthly reason for ordinary citizens . . . to have weapons."

Howard made it clear that the "scourge of America" he was talking about is simple firearms ownership by law-abiding Australians: "Ordinary citizens should not have weapons. We do not want the American disease imported into Australia."

Beyond the new effort to criminalize now-lawful handgun ownership, the anti-gun-owner lobby is now after the long guns that are left.

Gun Control Australia (GCA) gives lie to every politician anywhere in the world who promises that sport and hunting will never be selected as a "gun-control" target. On its Web site, GCA says matter-of-factly, "*The most dangerous guns are hunting guns which are stored in the home, but available for domestic impropriety.*"[17]

GCA further stated: "It has been estimated that one in four Australian homes contains at least one gun . . . [In state parliaments the] police ministers balked at the difficulties facing them in regard to the removal of guns from homes. This was and still is a major difficulty for any regime of gun control, because it required new concepts in gun storage, concepts which have not been adequately debated . . . *No matter how good home storage is, however, the guns are still there* where they are easily accessible to the gun owners and where they can cause the most danger."

As to why ordinary people having guns in their homes is a danger to society, GCA explained, "Active shooters have become a different segment of the community to the majority, a segment that has a fatal attraction to guns and to the killing process. Above all, they constitute a segment that is ill-disciplined, poorly read, and above all too often quite call us."

In reality, gun owners are a diverse cross section of society who have one thing in common—they are good people, who have nothing to do with crime or violence or mass murders. Just like in America.

In Australia in 2002, Rebecca Peters's government gun collection—the "very good start"—is moving into the second phase: all of the anti-gun groups, the media, and politicians are reading off the same page and are now demanding a permanent ban on all handguns that have been tightly regulated since the 1920s. A recent headline in the (New South Wales) *Daily Telegraph,* leading a story about a 440 percent increase in handgun crime since Port Arthur, says it all: "Handguns Declared Public Enemy No. 1."

The Australian press is full of coverage of armed criminals and increasingly brutish violence inflicted on ordinary citizens, yet for the politicians and especially for the anti-gun lobby "down-under," those criminals are not the target.

The Associated Press, in a story headlined, "Call to Clamp Down on Handgun Ownership on the Rise," reported, "Firearms registrations in NSW [New South Wales] have soared in the past two years, with new figures revealing the average license holder owns up to four guns."[18]

The story centered on the reaction of the National Coalition for Gun Control (NCGC), which the AP said "is calling on the government to ban semi-automatic guns [handguns] and tighten the state's firearms law to make it tougher for people to acquire multiple firearms." Mind you, this is in addition to waiting periods combined with registration and licensing and gun-owner testing and police clearances.

The head of the coalition told the AP "that while the soaring registrations showed more people were coming forward about owning a gun, the emerging picture of gun ownership was alarming . . . What we are concerned with in Australia is the number of semiautomatics circulating in the legal market."

Why on earth would people who have obeyed the law and registered their guns and obtained gun owner licenses bother the gun-control crowd? Because, they say, "all guns start out legal before they fall into the illegal market."

In an April 30, 2001, *Newcastle Herald* op-ed, Rebecca Peters took the same concept to its final conclusion, calling ownership of all licensed and registered handguns "a loophole."

Peters claimed, "There are more than 300,000 handguns in

Australia, and each year about 1,000 are stolen from homes, gun dealers and Army barracks around the nation. NSW [New South Wales] has more than 70,000 handguns registered . . . This raises alarm bells about the continued availability of handguns, the premium weapon for robbers and assassins . . . It's time to close this loophole and ban handguns."[19]

"Loophole." That's a word Americans are becoming all too familiar with. Whatever the anti-gun crowd wants will be another "loophole" to close.

Peters's definition of the ultimate "loophole"—private, lawful ownership of firearms—could come to the United States, just as she has. No doubt this is indeed her goal, the reason she is among us. Peters has moved to New York City, where she is a senior fellow at the Open Society Institute and heads a "global" gun-control effort bankrolled by international billionaire financier George Soros.

Remember the logic of these people, for it's coming to America: "All guns start out legal before they fall into the illegal market"; therefore, "remove guns from the homes."

In referring to the government's long-gun confiscation scheme, Peters called it "voluntary," saying, "The emphasis was on getting the guns out of circulation, on prevention."[20] But the long guns the government took from innocent Aussies were not "in circulation"; they were in people's homes.

In the state of Victoria, which already had firearms registration in addition to gun-owner licensing, there was nothing voluntary about it. A police official recently described the advantages for government:

"It means we know who's got what guns and where they are so, if police are called to a house, they know this person may have x, y, and z guns."[21]

In fact, in July 2002, the Australian news outlet www.news.com.au reported the beginning of a general sweep: "Police spokesman Senior Constable Rob Pugh today warned gun owners [that] police had begun conducting door knocks searching for unregistered weapons . . . Persons illegally holding firearms can incur fines of up to $24,000 or four years in prison."[22]

The senior constable warned, "Police are conducting door knocks around Victoria so people illegally in possession of a gun better do something about it."

The key to successful forfeiture or confiscation schemes is always *registration.* Never, ever, forget that watchword.

15

BRITONS: DISARMED AND VICTIMIZED

If there is ever a question about where the U.S. domestic anti-gun-rights movement is heading, Americans need only look to the loss of individual liberty that has resulted from "gun-control" experiments carried out in England and Australia.

In those two nations, formerly free people can tell you about the real nature of "gun control"—where all schemes, no matter how benign-sounding, lead to the same ultimate end: *forced disarmament of peaceable individuals by government.* Be it in the form of gun-owner licensing and registration, or safety requirements, or gun storage, or mandatory training, each step in England and Australia was followed by another step, and another, until law-abiding gun owners were forced into a final step—forfeiting their personal property, and with it their liberties.

Whatever the scheme-of-the-moment touted by American politicians, the media, or the anti-gun-rights lobby as "sensible first steps," the ultimate rebuttal is in two words: England and Australia.

During the late 1980s and 1990s, both of those nations outlawed gun ownership for honest citizens by making possession of whole generic designs of firearms a criminal offense.

Mass forfeitures of registered firearms began in England in 1988 following a murderous rampage by a deranged individual in Hungerford. The government banned whole classes of pump and semiautomatic shotguns and rifles. Then following another rampage, in Dunblane, Scotland, by another madman, Britain criminalized possession of large-caliber handguns, then all handguns. In Australia, semiautomatic rifles and semiautomatic and pump shotguns were banned, following the mass murders at Port Arthur.

In both nations, legal private property was declared contraband and then it was confiscated. The rationale used for this theft of freedom was twofold: that disarming all citizens of their firearms would deprive lone sociopathic mass murderers of the tool with which they killed, or the forfeiture of firearms by innocent, law-abiding people would prevent criminal violence by an always-lawless underclass.

Invariably, the media and politicians said that disarming the public was for its own good. Nothing could be farther from the truth. The wholesale loss of liberty in England and Australia will never stop the murderous acts of single sociopaths. How can it? The answer is obvious.

If curbing violence was the promise of "gun control," it has proved to be a cruel lie and a fraud. In both countries, victims of criminal violence are piling up. Ever since gun confiscation orders were instituted, England and Australia have rushed ahead of the rest of the industrialized world in terms of sheer violence by their criminals against the now-disarmed and vulnerable public. In terms of the likelihood of people becoming victims of crime and violence, England and Australia now rank either first or second in the industrialized world, far outstripping the United States in virtually all categories.

According to the International Crime Victims Survey carried out by the Dutch Ministry of Justice, England and Australia and Wales consistently won the dubious honors of having the highest burglary rates and the highest rates for crimes of violence such as robbery, assault, and sexual assault among the seventeen top industrialized nations.[1]

Conducted in the year 2000 with interviews involving thirty-five thousand individuals, the survey was summed up as a shocker in the British press. The *Guardian* reported the study "shows England and Wales at the top of the world league with Australia as the countries where you are most likely to become a victim of crime."[2]

Among the conclusions, people in the United States took a singular honor in one important category: "Feelings of vulnerability were lowest in the USA . . ." They were highest in Australia.

Violence and shootings—all marked by the mindless brutality of utterly lawless criminals—are controlling and crippling every aspect of modern British society. Yet, self-defense with any of the few firearms allowed for private ownership is a serious crime.

As armed violence has increased, the British and Australian politicians and their media elites have promised yet more gun control. In England, it's now BB and pellet guns they are after.

And on what monster does the gun-ban crowd hook its new antigun scheme? In 2002, the political notion of innocent gun owners paying the price for the acts of madmen has been taken to an even more bizarre extreme by Prime Minister Tony Blair. An April 28 headline in the *Sunday Scotsman* announced, "Prompted by shootings in Germany, Tony Blair orders crackdown on convertible air guns."[3]

This call to "control" air guns was keyed to the murderous acts of a deranged, expelled nineteen-year-old student in Erfurt, Germany, who killed seventeen schoolmates on April 16 with a handgun. That mass killing led to Germany tightening already strict gun-control laws. But what on earth does that have to do with British citizens who own air rifles or air pistols?

Citing those murders, the *Sunday Scotsman* said, "The government is now planning further controls on the lethal weapons (air guns), including an across the board ban, or at least a registration scheme designed to stop them from falling into the hands of youngsters and high-risk buyers."

But air guns owned by citizens who would agreeably fall under a "registration scheme" have no connection with guns used by armed, violent criminals. Criminal predators have guns, and they always will. In fact, criminals in Britain now have an estimated two million illegal guns, including machine guns, smuggled from Eastern Europe.

Yet, Tony Blair, under intense political criticism for his utter failure to deal with armed criminals, would once again punish the innocent.

The *Scotsman* warned that "the shootings in Germany have brought fresh urgency to a gun control debate which was stimulated in Britain by the murderous rampage of Thomas Hamilton through a Dunblane primary school six years ago . . ."

After the murders, Parliament moved in 1997 to ban private possession of all handguns except .22s. There was a "buyback" scheme, and licensed gun owners were told to hand over their property. Included in the buyback were all nature of items associated with shooting—everything from holsters to scopes.[4]

As for small-caliber handguns, they were indeed moved out of private homes. The government permitted licensed owners of .22-caliber pistols and revolvers—under strict police supervision—to keep them under government-supervised security at approved gun clubs. Licensed handgun owners were allowed, under very stringent circumstances, to visit their guns.

But when Bill Clinton's good friend Tony Blair became prime minister with his liberal party in control of Parliament, those remaining small-caliber handguns were forfeited up as well. People were paid for their property, but their property had been taken by government edict. In all, the government took 162,000 registered handguns from licensed owners. The government said the new ban—this confiscation from secure government-approved centralized locations—"prevents legally held guns from falling into the wrong hands."[5]

The final day for licensed British handgun owners to turn in their remaining .22s was February 27, 1998. The Home Secretary proudly announced: "The government fulfilled its pledge to remove all handguns from the streets of Britain today . . ."[6]

When the last registered handgun was forfeited by the last

remaining licensed handgun owner, the Blair government said it had "put a firm brake on the development of a dangerous gun culture in the U.K." The "dangerous gun culture" that Tony Blair stamped out was simply law-abiding citizens who had answered to the "harmless" call for licensing, registration, and whatever other restrictions the government demanded. The banned "gun culture" included Britain's Olympic competitors, who were forced to practice their sport on freer soil—in France, Switzerland, or the United States.

Almost immediately, the level of violence and the brutal nature of that violence exploded against the disarmed civil population. Headlines from British papers tell the story: "Handgun Crime Soars Despite Dunblane Ban"; "Police Move to Tackle Huge Rise in Crime"; "London Gun Murders Tripled in 2001"; "Steep Rise in Violent Crime"; "Top Gangs Getting More Guns, Warn Police"; "Handgun Crime Up Despite Ban"; "Gun Crime Rise in London"; "Gun Crime Trebles as Weapons and Drugs Flood British Cities."

The epidemic of crime and mindless violence is increasing at an alarming rate, as indicated by a new assessment of gun violence, which was released during the first days of 2002. Various news outlets covered the story from a different perspective, but their conclusions were the same—very bad news. Terrible news for ordinary and unarmed British subjects.

The *Daily Telegraph* of January 3, 2002, reported, "Police fear a new crime explosion as school-age muggers graduate to guns . . . the number of people robbed of personal property at gunpoint rose by 53 percent . . . Ballistics experts warn that firearms are now cheap and easily available."[7]

The *London Evening Standard* reported on December 19, 2001, "Gun crime in London is rocketing, with increases of almost 90 percent in some firearms offenses, Scotland Yard reported today. New figures show London murders with guns increased by 87 percent in the first eight months of the year compared with the same period last year."[8]

The *Telegraph* reported, "The number of young people committing serious crimes, including murder and grievous bodily harm, has almost doubled in seven years."

All of this was magnified for the world in a stunning report issued by the UN Interregional Crime and Justice Research Institute in July 2002, which found England and Wales to be far ahead of the rest of the Western world in terms of violent crime.[9]

The headline in The *Independent* laid it out in very simple terms: "Britain is now the crime capital of the West." Among the shocking findings reported were that "nearly 55 crimes are committed per 100 people" and that "England and Wales also have the worst record for 'very serious offenses . . .'"

With nearly half the innocent public falling victim to violent crime, the issue of unbridled street thuggery has overwhelmed all else in terms of British domestic issues. All of this in a nation where personal self-defense—armed self-defense—is a crime.

What was the inevitable response of government to its failed gun-control schemes? Call for more gun control, of course. But there's more—and here's where those who don't own guns, even those who hate guns, should take notice. In addition to calling for more gun control, the Blair government has pressed for laws erasing many of the ancient civil liberties protections that were adopted from English Common Law and incorporated into the United States Constitution. Unlike the United States, Britain has no constitution protecting rights reserved to the people.

If the Blair government succeeds in its wish list, citizens will lose the right to choose trial by jury, the right to remain silent, and the right against self-incrimination. Hearsay evidence—gossip—will be admissible in criminal trials. Double jeopardy—the eight-hundred-year-old legal principle that prevents government from taking a second, third, or fourth shot at trying a defendant—will be lost.

Under the Blair proposals, the new law destroying double jeopardy will be retroactive, so that old cases in which defendants were acquitted can be reopened and retried, and perhaps retried again. Among the legislation put forth by the Blair government in its White Paper is the use of previdеotaped testimony, negating the individual's right to be confronted by an accuser and to challenge that testimony in open court.[10]

The Blair government wants sentencing in criminal cases to be based on something other than firm law, in which punishment is tailored to individual defendants at the whim of judges. If Blair succeeds, British courts will fast become inquisitions.

There are some who might believe that such expedience would be good for our own country. But imagine Charles Schumer or Hillary Clinton as U.S. Attorney General zealously prosecuting defendants accused of violating some new gun-control scheme dreamed up by the likes of the Brady Campaign (HCI), the Violence Policy Center, or Americans for Gun Safety.

And imagine all those honest gun owners and dealers who were prosecuted during the BATF abuses of the 1980s being recharged and retried today.

Our unique Bill of Rights—including the Second Amendment—protects us all. Where Americans are "the people," Britons are still mere subjects, with no protections of a Bill of Rights. They have no Second Amendment safeguard, so the assault on firearms ownership will not end until not one private person possesses legal arms of any type.

The Handgun Network—the British equivalent to the Brady Campaign—has said, "Of course illegal guns are a big problem . . . but we mustn't forget that almost all illegal guns start out legal, so it's not so easy to draw a neat line between the two. Creating a safe society has got to be about cutting down on illegal and legal weaponry."[11]

On its Web site, the Handgun Control Network published an extract in which it admitted crime had gone up since the gun forfeitures . . . but said, "Gun control advocates never predicted that the ban would immediately rid the country of all gun crime."

Of course, that is a flat-out lie. They go on: "Now at least, the police and public don't have to worry about rogue gun club members using their handguns to commit crimes."

If anybody ever thinks that outlawing firearms from the hands of good, decent citizens creates "a safe society," he need but look to England, which proves itself a beacon to armed criminals whose level of violence makes their American counterparts meek in comparison.

The real threat of deterrence by an armed citizenry, which certainly exists under American law, is not possible in Great Britain today, not only because of the firearms confiscations but because using any of the legally held firearms left to British householders in defense of self, family, or property is a crime.

Witness the story of Tony Martin, a fifty-four-year-old farmer, whose home on a 350-acre rural tract had been repeatedly burglarized and robbed. In fact, thieves had broken into his home and outbuildings at least two dozen times. On the night of August 21, 1999, Martin heard burglars inside his home and confronted the criminals with a shotgun. He wounded one thief and killed another. A third house-breaker got away.

The dead burglar had a history of crimes of violence and crimes against persons and property. He had been arrested for twenty-nine different crimes, including burglary, theft, and assaulting police. The two other career criminals had been hauled before the court on criminal offenses fifty-two times and thirty-five times, respectively.[12] But it was Tony Martin who was prosecuted with the greatest zeal. Killing in the act of defending himself with deadly force against three intruders in the dead of night was murder in Britain. He was also charged with illegally owning a pump shotgun, and with wounding one of the criminal intruders. The Crown Court found him guilty and sentenced him to life in prison. He was also sentenced to ten years for wounding the second burglar.

In the meantime, the surviving wounded burglar, Brendon Fearon, was consulted by officials of the Home Office—in prison—

as to whether or not Tony Martin could be subject to parole. Although the Court of Appeals (akin to our Supreme Court) ultimately reduced Martin's sentence after changing his conviction to manslaughter, he is still in prison, serving seven years total.

British citizens, already outraged at this injustice, were in for another stunner. On July 2, 2002, the *London Daily Mail* revealed that the government had given £5,000 of taxpayers' money to burglar Fearon (now a free man) to bring suit against Tony Martin—seeking cash damages for his wounds.[13]

Public outrage was reflected in the words of Malcolm Starr, a businessman and staunch supporter of the jailed farmer, who said: "This news must fill Tony with despair—he has already lost faith in the police and the legal system. But I am sure most right-thinking people will consider it is madness that criminals seem to be protected more than the victims."

The newspaper added, "Fearon, who has convictions for theft, drugs and burglary, was shot in the legs by Martin and walks with a limp. He is thought to be hopeful of gaining up to £50,000."

This is the "safe society" created by the work of Britain's gun-control fanatics:

- Good people in jail for defending their homes against violent criminals and drug addicts
- Good people living in fear of the rule of a heavily armed and ruthless thug-underclass
- Good people disarmed and helpless
- Evil people armed to the teeth
- Good people paying the price for criminals and madmen

That's gun control. It will prove out in America, if citizens ever buy into the notion that there is strength in being defenseless.

Some 2.5 million times a year, according to well-founded research,

Americans defend themselves with firearms.[14] It is force against force. It is good against evil. And it is right.

England and Australia are living laboratories proving, in actual practice, the abject failure of every aspect of gun control at work. As a social laboratory, these governments have demonstrated conclusively and irrefutably that gun control in any facet, any permutation, or any combination does great harm to the public and only emboldens violent, armed criminals.

It gives the absolute ring of truth—the practical proof positive—to the old expression: "When they ban firearms, only the criminals will have guns."

16

LICENSING AND REGISTRATION: "IT CAN'T HAPPEN HERE"

The 1984 John Milius film *Red Dawn* was a depiction of what might have happened had the Soviets and Cubans invaded the United States through Mexico. In one scene, after securing control of a small Colorado town, the Cuban commander in charge of the invaders barks out the following order:

> Go to the sporting goods store. From the files, obtain form 4473. These will contain descriptions of weapons . . . and lists of private ownership.

The film and that scene were, of course, works of fiction—and the popular movie was panned by critics as "unrealistic." But there was nothing unrealistic in that dramatization. In fact, that scene has played itself out in dozens of different countries, countless numbers of times throughout history, always with tragic results.

Case in point: at the start of World War II, as nation after nation was conquered, citizens of those occupied lands were promised death for noncompliance with Nazi disarmament edicts. Gun owners were quickly and easily identified by confiscated gun registration lists similar to those depicted in *Red Dawn.* Sadly, to millions of people who actually lived though the Nazi nightmare, it was *all too real* and *all too realistic.*

Scholars such as Dr. Stephen P. Halbrook have meticulously documented dozens of historical precedents of gun licensing and registration that led to the conditions that allowed whole nations—Germany, Poland, Holland, and Belgium, to name a few—to be disarmed and conquered.

The pattern is the same no matter the era. Privately owned arms were ordered by the government to be registered. The excuses varied but usually concentrated on "keeping civil order" or "deterring crime by undesirable elements." Then shortly after those records were compiled, those same registration lists were used by invaders or police or military or killing squads, such as Hitler's *Einsatzgruppen,* to identify potential enemies of the state.[1]

With the most obvious symbols of totalitarianism such as the Berlin Wall and the oppressive Soviet state now vanquished, few are willing to believe such a bloody era will return. Far too many see that history as extreme and refuse to believe such persecution will ever visit a modern society like ours.

But what happened under Hitler's or Stalin's reign of terror is not the only historic precedents that can be cited. Nor is the tandem of registration and confiscation unfamiliar in recent times—or to be found exclusively in tyrannical regimes such as Communist China, North Korea, and Cuba.

Over the past few decades, registration leading to confiscation has taken place in Australia, Canada, Bermuda, Cuba, Germany, Great Britain, Greece, Ireland, and Jamaica—and the list is growing.

A classic example is Great Britain. Today, few in the public, press, or political circles remember that the people of England enjoyed the right to keep and bear arms for eight centuries prior to Parliament's passage of the Pistols Act of 1903.

That turn-of-the-century statute required a license purchased from the post office before a pistol could be legally obtained. For the first time, English felons and minors were forbidden to buy such items. Prior to 1903, any Englishman or -woman, regardless of criminal past or mental condition, could purchase firearms with no questions asked. However, people of nations dominated by British rule—the Irish, Indians, Africans—were forbidden ownership of firearms lest they revolt against British rule. Popular disarmament was part and parcel to British dominance of foreign lands and their people.

What caused the imposition of gun laws on Britain's own? Simply put, the ruling class became alarmed at the movement among England's commoners demanding social equity within the growing industrial society. They feared a revolution would threaten their social primacy. Control of gun license issuance quickly passed from the benign post office to the police. What was a pro forma requirement became a "needs-based" system in which honest citizens had to convince the constabulary they had "good reason" to own a firearm. In 1967, even the venerable British shotgun came under English registration/licensing requirements.

Today, the application prescribed under England's Firearms Act of 1968 (amended in 1997) is one of the most privacy-intrusive questionnaires imaginable. Not only is detailed information about firearms and ammunition sought, but also information about past traffic violations, any history of epilepsy, and treatment for depression or nervous disorders. Applicants are required to grant permission for police to interview their doctors about their medical histories.[2]

The process also demands affidavits from two "referees" who must provide equally detailed observations about the applicant's character and fitness, or knowledge of any physical disabilities, emotional, or mental problems.

The British system seeks to make the applicant's life an open book and entrust to the police the determination of whether or not a citizen is "fit to be entrusted" with a legal firearm. The results? According to the *London Times* (January 16, 2000), Britain's mandatory gun-licensing system has had no restraining effect on Britain's criminals. Fatal shootings in London more than doubled between 1998 and 1999, and armed crime rose 10 percent over that same period of time.

Indeed, Britain is now the "crime capital" of the West.[3] And this inevitable rise in crime has played itself out in other countries that have imposed mandatory gun registration on their citizens.

In 1996, Australia's registration-and-licensing system escalated into a massive government-mandated gun turn-in that saw 640,000 hunting rifles and shotguns destroyed. During the decade and a half prior to the gun confiscation program, Australia's firearms-related death rate dropped by 46 percent and its firearms-related homicides fell by 63 percent. The years immediately following the Aussie gun-ban saw armed violent crime soar.

On February 16, 1995, Canadian gun owners listened to Justice Minister Allan Rock's political siren song that "there is no reason to confiscate legally owned firearms." Less than a year later, Parliament passed the Canadian Firearms Act that resulted in 553,000 legally owned and registered handguns being declared illegal contraband. Gun owners could sell them to gun dealers or the few legally qualified individuals, render them inoperable, or surrender them to the government. A similar promise that confiscation would not result was made to Canadian gun owners in 1934 when the National Handgun Registry legislation became law.[4]

The Canadian Firearms Act also requires a license to purchase or possess a rifle or shotgun and registration of all long guns, effective January 1, 2003. Much to the government's surprise, Canada's gun owners expressed serious reservations about the credibility of government assurances that what happened to their registered handguns wouldn't happen to their registered rifles and shotguns. Imagine that.

When Americans hear these stories, they almost always respond with, "It can't happen here." But it can happen here. *It has* happened here. *And it is* happening here.

Back in 1911, we got our first taste of gun-owner registration with the passage of the Sullivan Law in New York. (Five years earlier, Mississippi enacted a registration law for firearms retailers.)[5] Political boss Timothy D. "Big Tim" Sullivan lent his name to the infamous New York firearms licensing law, heralded as a way to deter crime by such ethnic groups as Italians.[6] Twenty months after the Sullivan Act went into effect, the *New York Times* editorialized on May 24, 1913, that the

> law has not worked as well as was expected by those of us who commended it. This is a fact too obvious for denial. Criminals are as well armed as ever, in spite of the sternness with which the law has been applied to a few of them.[7]

In 1967, Mayor John V. Lindsay signed into law a rifle-shotgun registration ordinance passed by the city council, giving his assurance that the registration system would "protect the Constitutional Rights of owners and buyers."

Interestingly, only six years later, Mayor Lindsay began taking the next steps toward disarming honest citizens, advocating New York City–style gun control for the entire nation. Lindsay's push for federal gun-control legislation included:

- Registration of all firearms,
- Licensing of all gun owners,
- Restricting handgun ownership licenses to "only those demonstrating a specific, over-riding legitimate need,"
- Banning manufacture and sale of any handgun "not suitable for sporting use" and
- A two-year "buy-back" of "all firearms from civilians who want to turn them in . . . the federal government would destroy all such firearms."[8]

The state of Maryland introduced a unique twist on gun registration when, in 2000, its legislature in Annapolis passed the nation's first law requiring new handguns to be "ballistically fingerprinted" before they can be sold in the state. This high-tech version of registration involves the purchase of a $1.1 million computer/software package (IBIS) that stores data regarding the bullet and shell casing fired from a specific handgun.

There are literally dozens of other examples around the United States. And the call for licensing and registration by the gun-ban lobby reached a fevered pitch shortly after the 9/11 attacks.

On December 19, 2001, the Brady Campaign to Prevent Gun Violence issued a report entitled "Guns and Terror: How Terrorists Exploit Our Weak Gun Laws." In introducing the report, Brady Center president and former congressman Michael Barnes announced: "For terrorists around the world, the United States is the Great Gun Bazaar." Barnes further declared:

> This report makes one thing crystal clear: terrorists and guns go together. Firearms are part of the essential tool kit of domestic and foreign terrorists alike. Guns are used to commit terrorist acts, and guns are used by terrorists to resist law enforcement efforts at apprehension and arrest . . . Ensuring true "homeland security" means combating the threat of terrorism in all its possible forms, with all its potential weapons—especially guns.

The Brady Campaign tried to capitalize on a few video clips to create a presumption that all guns are potentially terrorist "weapons"—regardless of the owner. The report did not explain, could not explain, how—even if Congress enacted all the statutes the Brady Campaign demands—Osama Bin Laden would have been stopped or would be prevented from carrying out another horrific terrorist attack.

The Brady report further implied that vast numbers of terrorist "weapons" have been amassed in the United States. "The loopholes and weaknesses in current law, by definition, make it virtually impossible to know how many other terrorists, domestic or foreign, have been able to amass weapons and escape detection." The Brady anti-gun rhetoric found echoes among demagogues on Capitol Hill. Rep. Henry Waxman (D-Calif.), who appeared at the press conference releasing the report, declared: "Our current gun laws are so weak that our country serves as a virtual arsenal for terrorists."

To "solve" this terrorist-with-guns crisis, the Brady Campaign, along with a number of other gun-ban groups, is pushing for the federal government to create a national registration database of all gun purchasers and, eventually, all gun owners.

Specifically, the Brady Campaign called for "requiring background checks on all gun sales to prevent criminals, and would-be terrorists, from obtaining guns, and retaining records of gun purchases, so that weapons can be traced if they are used in a crime or terrorist act."

The Brady Campaign favors the ending of all protections for gun owners' privacy: "Congress should repeal the provisions of the McClure-Volkmer Act and the Brady [Handgun Violence Prevention] Law that prohibit centralized records of gun transactions."

Sen. Charles Schumer (D-N.Y.) and Sen. Ted Kennedy (D-Mass.) introduced a "Use NICS in Terrorist Investigations Act" designed to force the Justice Department to create a national registration list of gun buyers.

Specifically, the bill would make National Instant Check System (NICS) records—gun purchasers not disqualified by the criminal record check—available to "any federal, state, or local law enforcement agency in connection with a civil or criminal law enforcement investigation."

Current law requires that all such records of cleared purchases be destroyed. On the other hand, records of felons, fugitives, illegal aliens, drug users—all persons whose possession or purchase of any firearm is a federal crime and who are blocked by the NICS system if they attempt to buy firearms—are required to be kept indefinitely. Those records are already always available to law enforcement.

The Schumer-Kennedy bill, therefore, is gun-owner registration, plain and simple, and the Brady Campaign and the gun banners know it.

Again, federal law specifically forbids "that any system of registration of firearms, firearms owners, or firearms transactions or dispositions be established." In fact, other than a unique number referencing a lawful firearms transaction, federal law demands that the system (NICS) "destroy all records of the system relating to the person or the (firearm) transfer."

Under the Schumer-Kennedy legislation, this required destruction wouldn't apply to records given to *other* federal, state, or local agencies as part of an ongoing civil or criminal probe. Once the personal information is out of the hands of the feds, it becomes part of a permanent record elsewhere.

Clearly, the Brady Campaign and their gun-ban allies in the Senate are fully aware of these laws and why they were written—to protect gun owners' rights. Their determination to circumvent these laws is just as clear.

What gun registration programs around the world have in common is this: registration has almost always preceded a compulsory roundup of guns. Whenever the creation of a national database of gun owners is proposed, the advocates insist that people have nothing to fear because politicians will not abuse the power inherent in such a database. But as far back as the 1960s and 1970s, people on both sides of the political spectrum were concerned about the consequences of licensing and registering firearms.

In 1975 Senator James A. McClure (R-Idaho) addressed the U.S. Senate with these words:

> Gun registration is the first step toward ultimate and total confiscation, the first step in a complete destruction of a cornerstone of our Bill of Rights.

That same year, anti-gun advocate and head of the Washington, D.C., office of the American Civil Liberties Union, Charles Morgan, told the House Subcommittee on Crime:

> I have not one doubt, even if I am in agreement with the National Rifle Association, that that kind of record-keeping procedure is the first step to eventual confiscation under one administration or another.

There is another reality of registration that hits home regardless of one's overall view on firearm ownership—and that argument is couched in the Fifth Amendment of our Bill of Rights.

In 1968, the Supreme Court reached a landmark decision in *U.S. v. Haynes*. Miles Edward Haynes was a convicted felon who decided to fight his arrest for possession of an unregistered barrel-shortened shotgun. Haynes's argument was short and to the point. Convicted felons were forbidden to purchase, possess, own, or use firearms under federal law. Since registering a firearm would force Haynes, a felon, to admit he was violating the law by claiming ownership of such a gun, Haynes argued that registration laws violated his Fifth Amendment protection against self-incrimination. The Supreme Court agreed: by a count of 8 to 1, the Supreme Court said *felons* were immune from registering their illegal firearms.

Only the law-abiding are subject to these privacy-violating statutes. Only those who commit no crime can be punished under registration and licensing systems, which cannot apply to criminals.

In a later scene in *Red Dawn,* Soviet and Cuban troops are seen tossing hundreds of books into a bonfire. Fiction? Yes. But another all too realistic dramatization of what can happen to *all* of our freedoms once the Second Amendment is lost. And make no mistake: *it can happen here.*

17

GOING BALLISTIC FOR "FINGERPRINTING"

As the frightening drama of the D.C.-area snipers' October 2002 rampage drew to a close—with suspects apprehended, their twisted motives revealed, and the administration of justice underway—gun banners rushed to exploit these serial murders by demanding that a national database of ballistic "fingerprints" for individual firearms be created.

Even a passing glance at ballistic "fingerprinting" proposals introduced in the U.S. Congress revealed that such a system would be flawed and unworkable. Moreover, such a proposition would infringe on the rights of tens of millions of law-abiding citizens, for it would set the foundation for building a national registry of gun owners in violation of federal law.

As always, the antigun political agenda trades on ignorance about how firearms work. But this time, they're also trading on confusion between the legitimate process of ballistic imaging used to compare crime scene evidence and the nonexistent magic of ballistic "fingerprinting." Moreover, the proposals ignore research showing that "probably fewer than 2% of handguns and well under 1% of all guns will ever be involved in even a single violent crime."[1]

Gun owners have long supported H.R. 3491 and S. 2581, the Ballistic Imaging Evaluation and Study Act introduced in the U.S. House by Rep. Melissa Hart (R-Penn.), and in the Senate by Sen. Zell Miller (D-Ga.). It directs the U.S. Justice Department to study ballistic "fingerprinting," evaluate its effectiveness as a law enforcement tool and make recommendations to Congress. But the legislation has been stuck since March 2002 in a House subcommittee.

Senator Miller had this to say about his legislation:

> Four months before the first sniper attack in the Washington area, I introduced a bill in the Senate that calls for a study by the National Academy of Sciences on "ballistic fingerprinting" of firearms. As a lifetime member of the National Rifle Association and a lifetime member of the Georgia Peace Officers Association and Georgia Sheriffs Association, I, like Jack Webb of *Dragnet,* just want the facts.
>
> Not enough is known about this new technology and I think it is worthwhile for an objective and prestigious organization like the Academy to take a good hard look at it before false hopes are raised and millions of dollars spent on something that may not even be feasible.
>
> The first question that jumped to my mind was that there are 200 million guns already out there, and I presume they could not be included in a ballistic database.
>
> And while I'm no expert I do know that it's pretty simple to replace various parts of a firearm to give it a new ballistic identity. I also know that not all guns even generate markings on cartridge casings.
>
> But obviously there is a debate brewing on this subject and it is not going to go away. A lot of misinformation will go back and forth from each side. That's why I wanted this unimpeachable source to conduct such a study. I believe that's the sensible way to deal with this controversy.[2]

Here are the facts, and the fakery, behind the issue.

When a rifle or handgun is fired, the shell casing and bullet are imprinted with marks unique to that firearm at that point in time.

The shell casing is marked by the gun's mechanical system of loading, firing, or ejecting, while the bullet is marked by the rifling in the barrel. These markings are distinctive to that gun as long as nothing significantly changes—for example, extended use or intentional alteration.

Typically, ballistic imaging is used to determine whether a bullet or a shell casing recovered from one crime scene matches those from another crime scene. If the incidents occurred in a short enough time frame, comparing the ballistic imaging can help investigators determine if the same firearm was used in both. An excellent example of this crime-fighting tool was seen in the D.C.-area sniper case.

Ballistic imaging and comparison technology is currently at the disposal of many law enforcement agencies through the National Integrated Ballistic Information Network (NIBIN), which is operated by the Bureau of Alcohol, Tobacco and Firearms (BATF). Proper use of ballistic imaging techniques requires that BATF comply with strict restrictions imposed by Congress. For example, use of NIBIN is expressly restricted to imaging of data associated with guns *known to have been used in crimes.*

Ballistic "fingerprinting," however, is a misleading and dishonest phrase intentionally misused to advance the gun-owner-licensing and gun-registration agenda of America's disarmament movement. Fingerprints, or DNA, or other biometric data do not change over time and can't as yet be altered. But the markings a firearm leaves on cases and bullets can change for a variety of reasons, including normal wear and tear and improper maintenance. Additionally, any criminal amateur, in a matter of minutes, can use a metal file or other simple tools to create entirely new markings—a whole new identity the imaging database can't recognize.

Researchers David Kopel and Paul H. Blackman noted the most significant flaw in ballistic "fingerprinting" in a column in *National Review Online:*

> Supposedly, the government can collect a barrel print from every gun, or at least every new gun, and then a crime bullet can be compared to the sample. Obviously, that also requires knowing who owns each gun associated with a particular bullet, which is one reason why the program requires universal gun registration. If it's okay to require that all rifles and handguns be sampled and clearly associated with the owners who own the barrel that can make such markings, it's hard to see why it would not be okay to require fingerprints and DNA samples from everyone. There are far more crimes that can be solved with fingerprint or DNA analysis than with bullet-striation analysis.[3]

In the wake of the sniper attacks, ballistic "fingerprinting" bills were rushed into both houses of Congress. In the Senate, S. 3096 was pushed by the usual anti-gun zealots, including Charles Schumer (D-N.Y.) and Dianne Feinstein (D-Calif.). In the House, Robert Andrews (D-N.J.) offered H.R. 408, which he claimed would allow "investigators [to] begin to establish leads based on information available to them via the *gun registry database* (emphasis added)."[4] For these bills to work as offered, all of the following assumptions must materialize:

- That all 200-plus million firearms lawfully possessed by Americans are brought into labs and fired to gather individual ballistic "fingerprinting"
- That all violent criminals, and people who might become criminals, also bring in their firearms for "fingerprinting"
- That all ballistic "fingerprinting" files are stored in a national database
- That the firearm barrel and firing pin have not been modified, replaced, deformed from normal use, or intentionally falsified with new ballistic markings

- That an expended bullet or shell casing be recovered from a crime scene
- That the bullet or shell casing conclusively match the ballistic "fingerprinting" of a firearm owned by a person stored in the database
- That the firearm has not been sold, transferred, stolen, or gifted to another person
- That the person, now a criminal suspect, still possesses that firearm at the current address

Besides the impossibility of this sequence of events, there's serious debate within the law enforcement community on whether such ballistic "fingerprinting" would be practical. Police criminalists and forensic scientists have studied such a system and called it "impractical."

So it defies reason why a criminal or terrorist intent on violence would not avail himself of a firearm never subjected to "fingerprinting," one with a new barrel, one altered into anonymity, or one imported from another country.

These reasons are why ballistic "fingerprinting" of handguns in Maryland and New York, the only states that require it, hasn't yet solved a single gun crime.

The costs of ballistic fingerprinting alone are astronomical. In their *National Review* column, Kopel and Blackman detail the high costs associated with the Maryland program:

> Maryland has mandatory sampling of all new handguns, at a cost to handgun buyers of about $20 per gun (the cost to collect the sample). For the state of Maryland, cost of the equipment and manpower to operate the equipment amounts to $5,000 per handgun sold. The system has thus far solved no crimes. Thus, so

> far, every dollar spent by Maryland for the sampling scheme has been wasted money, money that could—in a state currently suffering a budget crisis—have been spent on more detectives or in other ways that really do solve crimes.[5]

Maryland and New York taxpayers might rightfully ask whether the millions of dollars required to create and maintain such a system could be better spent on vital law enforcement needs. Before squandering billions of dollars to deploy such a system nationwide, American taxpayers—despite national alarm in the wake of tragedy—should ask that question, too.

But it's already been answered. Last year, the most comprehensive ballistics study to date was conducted by the Bureau of Forensic Services of the California Department of Justice.

Their experts concluded:

> Automated computer matching systems do not provide conclusive results . . . When applying this technology to the concept of mass sampling of manufactured firearms, a huge inventory of potential candidates will be generated for manual review. This study indicates that this number will be so large as to be impractical and will likely create logistic complications so great that they cannot be effectively addressed.[6]

And after Maryland and New York imposed their ballistic "fingerprinting" laws, a discussion began in Belgium to set up such a database. But first, the issue was studied by Belgium's Department of Justice, which issued a report that concluded:

> While the ballistic fingerprinting database is presented as a *ne plus ultra* solution for solving crimes where firearms have been used, its realization and usefulness become very doubtful for the following reasons:

1. In European countries, less than 5% of the firearms which were used in most crimes are in legal possession. Consequently, most of the searched firearms are not in the ballistic fingerprinting database and searching the database is thus useless.
2. The costs of installing a database in a retroactive way, in order to include all the firearms which are already in legal possession, will be extremely high.
3. The manufacturers of the automated correlation systems do not provide clear information on the discriminative power for the products for this type of huge databases. This does not allow one to make an estimate of the cost of exploiting such a database.[7]

The Fraternal Order of Police (FOP) also has enormous concern and expressed reservations about the concept. In its press release entitled "FOP Viewpoint: Ballistic Imaging and Comparison Technology," the FOP concluded:

> The FOP believes that several questions must be answered. First, since ballistic imprints, unlike fingerprints and DNA, can be altered, either deliberately or simply through normal use, how will we ensure the validity of the findings? Second, how would such a database be compiled and what would be the cost to create and maintain it? The F.O.P. does not support any Federal requirement to register privately-owned firearms with the federal government.[8]

Among its many unanswered questions on system efficacy, the FOP said: "Even if such a database is limited to firearms manufactured in the future, the cost to create and maintain such a system, with such small chances that it would be used to solve a firearm crime, suggests to the FOP that these are law enforcement dollars best spent elsewhere."

Noting that "there are limits to technology, especially in a free society . . . ," the FOP concluded by saying it "supports greater study of this issue . . . ," thus staking out the exact same position as the National Rifle Association on ballistic "fingerprint" technology.

The nation's firearms owners will continue to support objective evaluation of the entire concept of ballistic imaging, or any other technologies, in search of reasonable and genuine contributions to the process of law enforcement. Asking them to support the creation of a federal registry of law-abiding gun owners is another matter entirely.

As John Lott, author of *More Guns, Less Crime* and a resident scholar at the American Enterprise Institute, recently wrote:

> While registering guns by their ballistic fingerprints is a relatively new concept, we have had plenty of experience using gun registration in general, and it has come up woefully short. A couple of years ago, I testified before the Hawaii state legislature on a bill to change registration requirements. Hawaii has had both registration and licensing of guns for several decades.
>
> In theory, if a gun is left at the crime scene, licensing and registration will allow the gun to be traced back to its owner. Police have probably spent hundreds of thousands of man-hours administering these laws in Hawaii. But despite this massive effort, there has not been a single case in which police claimed that licensing and registration have been instrumental in identifying a criminal.
>
> The reason is simple. First, criminals very rarely leave their guns at a crime scene, and when they do, it is because the criminals have been killed or seriously wounded. Second—and more important for ballistic fingerprinting—would-be criminals also virtually never get licenses or register their weapons. The guns that are recovered at the scene are not registered.

> Good intentions don't necessarily make good laws. What counts is whether the laws actually work, and end up saving lives. On that measure, ballistic fingerprinting—a useless diversion of valuable police resources—fails conspicuously, and it should be opposed by anyone who wants to live in a safer society.[9]

Finally, let us remember that gun registration has been an effective tool for gun confiscation—just ask gun owners in New York City, Australia, and England. Logic dictates that law-abiding citizens will register their firearms but criminals won't. Law-abiding citizens will have no choice but to surrender their firearms should the government one day decide to outlaw their possession by ordinary citizens.

18

KIDS AND GUNS: TEACHING AND TOLERANCE

The National Rifle Association works unceasingly to teach firearms safety and responsibility to America's young people. Safety training—whether it consists of teaching kids how to swim, how to ride a bike, how to avoid strangers, or how to be safe around firearms—is about preventing accidents and saving lives. And that's what the NRA's Eddie Eagle GunSafe® Program is all about: preventing accidents and saving young lives.

Offered free of charge, the Eddie Eagle GunSafe® Program helps schools and law enforcement teach gun safety to children in grades K–6. A study in the October 2001 *Journal of Emergency Nursing Online* rated Eddie Eagle the best child gun safety program in America. Author Patricia Kunz Howard, a registered nurse, wrote:

> The Eddie Eagle Program best met the criteria. Strengths of the Eddie Eagle Program include educational material appropriate for intended developmental level and presentation appearance of the printed material. The Eddie Eagle material is colorful, well presented, and available in English and Spanish languages.[1]

Eddie Eagle uses teacher-tested materials, including an animated video, CDs, cartoon workbooks, and fun safety activities. The hero, Eddie Eagle, teaches a simple safety lesson: "If you see a gun: STOP! Don't Touch. Leave the Area. Tell an Adult." It has been endorsed by the National Sheriffs Association, the Police Athletic League, and state legislatures all over the country. And it won the 1993 Outstanding Community Service Award from the National Safety Council.

Since its introduction in 1988, the Eddie Eagle program has reached more than sixteen million children, thanks to more than twenty-thousand instructors, including schoolteachers, police officers, and other community leaders. From its inception to today, the accidental death from firearms rate for children has declined 56 percent, reaching the lowest levels ever recorded in American history, according to the National Center for Health Statistics.

As columnist Paul Craig Roberts chronicled: "Today, water is 19 times more dangerous to a child than a firearm. In 1996, 805 children died from accidental drowning and 42 died from firearm accidents. Bathtubs are twice as dangerous to children as guns. Fire is 18 times more dangerous to children than guns. Cars are 57 times more dangerous. Household cleaners and poisons are twice as dangerous."[2]

Yet the anti-gun Violence Policy Center (VPC) ran a propaganda campaign against the Eddie Eagle program to smear it, claiming it's just a ploy to sell guns.[3] Never mind that Eddie Eagle never encourages anyone to buy or use a gun. Following the logic of the VPC, then the public should also believe that Smokey Bear markets matches to children, McGruff the Crime Dog markets muggings and drug dealing, and traffic safety programs market cars to kids.

To the gun-ban lobby, Eddie Eagle became a major threat in its drive to indoctrinate America's young people into believing guns are "bad" and "evil"—and they determined to shut this program down at all costs. Thankfully, their smear campaign failed miserably.

Firearms accidents for all ages, including children, are now at an all-time low. What's the latest data on the number of fatal firearms accidents involving children ages zero to fourteen? For 1999, the latest year for which complete data is available, there were eighty-eight, the lowest number ever recorded.[4] And while any child's death is unspeakably tragic, the fact is that the number of toddlers who die from gun accidents is far less than the five hundred children who die in swimming pools each year.[5]

Nevertheless, the gun-ban lobby twists statistics to frighten people with false claims about how many "children are killed by guns." An example of this deceit came during the nationally televised Senate confirmation hearings for Attorney General nominee Sen. John Ashcroft. The culprit was Michael Barnes, president of the Brady Campaign, and he was assisted in his deception by a perennial anti-gun lobby water carrier, Sen. Ted Kennedy (D-Mass.). Their exchange went as follows:

> KENNEDY: Mr. Barnes, as I understand, there are 12 children that die from gun accidents every single day. Is that your understanding?
>
> BARNES: Well, Senator, thank goodness it's a little better now. Thank goodness, it's just under 11 children a day in the United States dying from gun violence.[6]

A "little better"? Both Kennedy's and Barnes' numbers are blatant lies—unless you are willing to concede that a nineteen-year-old gangster who's shot by police during a liquor store robbery is a "child."

The latest data available from the Centers for Disease Control show that the real number of "children"—people age fourteen or younger—who die from firearms misuse every day is just one. But "one" is a pretty far distance from the numbers cooked up by the gun-prohibition groups. The figures are inflated by claiming that legal adults—those eighteen and nineteen years old—are children.[7]

When you hear statistics about "X children a day killed by guns," you should know that the overwhelming majority of those "children" are older male teenagers. According to the Centers for Disease Control (CDC), there were 3,385 firearms deaths in 1999 of persons under age twenty—or 9.3 a day. Eighty-nine percent were homicides; most of the rest were suicides. The killings are very heavily concentrated geographically in urban inner cities, almost all of which have very repressive gun laws.[8]

The persons most likely to be killed by a teenager with a gun are gang members, gang hangers-on, and other teenage criminals.[9] In many killings of inner-city high-school-age persons, the victim is a person who engaged in risky behaviors, such as selling drugs.

A study of teenage gunshot victims in New York City found that 40 percent were shot during hours when they legally should have been in school.[10] Of the children and adolescents injured in drive-by shootings in Los Angeles, "seventy-one percent were gang members."[11] An in-depth study of juvenile delinquents in Philadelphia found that juvenile victims of violent crimes were often perpetrators of such crimes as well.[12] Nationally, a gang member's risk of getting killed is sixty times greater than the general population's risk.[13] A St. Louis study found that the city's youth gang homicide rate unbelievably was one thousand times that of the U.S. general population.[14]

A study of Minneapolis youths arrested for homicide found that 75 percent had been arrested at least once in Minneapolis (the mean number of arrests for this group was 7.8); similarly, 77 percent of Boston youthful homicide perpetrators had a prior Massachusetts court appearance (this group had a mean of 9.7 arraignments).[15] Fifty-nine percent of homicides perpetrated by youths are perpetrated by males while committing another crime, such as robbery or rape.[16]

The solution for nineteen-year-olds who commit murder? It is the same as the solution for twenty-five-year-olds who commit violent felonies: stop the criminal justice revolving door. And stop the revolving door that lets violent predators get away with armed robbery and other violent felonies. If gangsters caught robbing liquor stores couldn't plea-bargain their way out of serious prison time, they wouldn't be on the streets where they could commit a murder. As with *Project Exile,* we need to strictly enforce the federal laws against gun possession by prohibited persons.

But rather than talk about the serious problem of crime in the inner cities, the gun-prohibition groups use phony statistics to make the public think that four-year-olds are being killed in gun accidents all the time. Why are the gun-prohibition lobbies working so hard to terrify Americans out of their wits about "children and guns"? Because it's the foundation of their campaign to demonize guns and gun owners.

An article in *Join Together Online* (a Boston University–based E-mail newsletter and Web site that promotes gun control) interviewed Mark Pertschuk—currently a lobbyist with the Coalition to Stop Gun Violence (which wants to ban all handguns and many long guns) and a veteran of the anti-tobacco wars. The article explained that Pertschuk and other anti-gun leaders believe that concerns "about the dangers that a gun in the home poses to family members has the potential to be a powerful tool for activists—in effect a firearms version of second-hand smoke."[17] And that's where the notion of zero tolerance kicks in.

Our nation's Founders—Thomas Jefferson immediately springs to mind—would be appalled at what is taking place today in the nation's schools under zero tolerance's false banner. "Error of opinions may be tolerated," Jefferson wrote, "where reason is left free to combat it."[18] In our schools today, "reason" has been replaced by "restriction."

Today's restrictions go by the name of zero tolerance, and for once, we have a government program aptly named. To have "zero tolerance" is the same as to have "no tolerance," which is the same as being "intolerant" or "bigoted." And just as we might expect from programs that revel in intolerance, zero tolerance is used by an increasing number of so-called "educators" to suppress the behavior of students who do not follow an imposed "politically correct" norm.

Case in point: on May 9, 2001, a fifth grader was handcuffed at Oldsmar Elementary School near Tampa and taken into custody by police. "That's normal procedure in a situation like this," said school district spokesman Ron Stone. His deed, ferreted out by an alert teacher, had been to *draw some pictures of weapons*. Said Principal David Schmitt, "The boy probably won't return for the rest of the year and probably would be moved to another school." Added Schmitt reassuringly, "The children were in no danger at all. It involved no real weapons."[19]

As originally conceived in the 1980s, zero tolerance had nothing to do with expelling children from school for "thought crimes" involving art projects or playground time. Rather, zero tolerance meant setting strict rules against bringing guns, knives, or other potentially dangerous items to school, and imposing automatic and uniform discipline for violators. The inflexible nature of the system was meant to protect schools against discrimination complaints by racial-minority students who violated the rules.

Zero tolerance, however, has insidiously grown into a thought-control program. In an August 2000 report, Professor Russell Skiba, director of Indiana University's Institute for Child Study, noted, "School punishments greatly out of proportion to the offense arouse controversy by violating basic perceptions of fairness inherent in our system of law."[20]

A perfect example was reported by the Associated Press on January 31, 2001, when "an eight-year-old boy was suspended from school for three days after pointing a breaded chicken finger at a teacher and saying, 'Pow, pow, pow.' The incident apparently violated the Jonesboro [Ark.] School District's 'zero tolerance' policy against weapons."[21]

On May 4, 2001, the Associated Press reported that a third-grade honor student at Lenwil Elementary School in West Monroe, Louisiana, was suspended for three days because he drew a picture of a soldier holding a knife and a canteen. The picture also included a fort filled with appropriate gear, including rifles, handguns, knives, and first-aid kits. The school's principal defended the suspension because the school "can't tolerate anything that has to do with guns or knives."[22]

In fact, the school could tolerate drawings of soldiers, Civil War battle scenes, police officers, and lots of other things that involve guns or knives. They're present in our history books and our monuments all across America, which honor those who have sacrificed their lives for the liberty we Americans now enjoy. The school simply chose to be intolerant. Punishing a third grader for drawing a picture of a soldier doesn't make anyone safer.

Willie Isby, director of Child Welfare and Attendance for the Ouachita Parish School System, called the student's picture "a violent arrangement here"—even though the picture simply depicted a standing soldier and contained no violence. "The punishment is not that bad in this case," Isby continued, "in light of the fact that we have been having all these killings in schools."[23]

Isby's quote goes to the heart of modern zero-tolerance policies, under which third graders are turned into scapegoats and punished although they did nothing wrong, because the real culprits—namely a minuscule number of violent school predators—are beyond the power of school officials to identify.

Recently, a third-grade boy in Pontiac, Michigan, was suspended because he brought a one-and-one-half-inch "gun-shaped medallion" to school.[24] It wasn't a real gun, or even a toy gun, only the symbol of a gun. Punishing a child for wearing a medallion is—like punishing a child for artwork—simply a form of thought control.

Most incredibly, on April 29, 2002, a twelve-year-old student attending the Jack Jouette Middle School in Charlottesville, Virginia, was forced to turn his NRA Sports Shooting Camp T-shirt inside out by a vice-principal who considered the NRA shirt illustrations of individuals involved in shooting sports in violation of school policy. Although the youngster was ordered to forfeit his right to free speech and association under threat of school suspension, at the time of the demand there was no rule that prohibited clothing depicting shooting sports.

The student's parents contacted the NRA when they reached a stalemate in discussing the incident with school authorities. When the NRA's Civil Rights Defense Fund formally notified school authorities that the action violated the student's civil rights, the school reacted by adding a provision for the 2002–2003 school year barring any clothing associated with "weapons" and "violence." Subsequently, the NRA filed a First Amendment lawsuit against the Albemarle County school system on behalf of the young man. Among the twelve counts included in the suit were free speech and due process violations under federal and state constitutions.

The NRA made clear that while it wholeheartedly supported the reasonable prohibition of images on clothing depicting violence in a school setting, to preclude a student from wearing an article of clothing because it ran counter to the viewpoints or political beliefs of some school officials was deplorable. The lawsuit specifically cited *Tinker v. Des Moines School District* in which the U.S. Supreme Court held, "In order for the State in the person of the school officials to justify prohibition of a particular expressed opinion, it must be able to show that its actions were caused by something more than a mere desire to avoid the discomfort and unpleasantness that always accompany an unpopular viewpoint."[25]

The lawsuit also challenged the ambiguity of the new school rule, which would affect not only all NRA logos, but also the Great Seal of the United States, the United States Army logo, and the state seal of the Commonwealth of Virginia—all with images of "weapons" that would fall within the prohibitions of the school's new policy.

It was a clear case of political correctness running unchecked. The student had no disciplinary problems in school, had developed an affinity for the shooting sports, and aspired to represent America in the Olympics. School authorities harassed and breached the youngster's First Amendment rights merely because of his interest in the NRA and the shooting sports.

In a *Richmond Times-Dispatch* interview, the student's father said, "I was kind of dumbfounded we were having this problem. Alan came home that day and he was mad. One day he'd like to shoot competitively. They made him feel like he was doing something wrong."

The lawsuit noted that, ironically, Jack Jouette Middle School is named for an American Revolutionary War hero who is known for his famous ride on the night of June 3, 1781, across forty miles of meadows, thickets, and woods to warn Thomas Jefferson, Patrick Henry, Richard Henry Lee, Benjamin Harrison, Thomas Nelson Jr., and Edmund Randolph that British troops were on their way to arrest them. With the exception of Henry and Randolph, all the others were signers of the Declaration of Independence. Jouette reached the men at Jefferson's home, Monticello, two hours before British cavalry entered Charlottesville. In appreciation for his act of bravery, the Virginia legislature awarded Captain Jack Jouette a sword and a pair of pistols.

Does the process of denying basic civil rights to children succeed in creating a safer learning environment? Does promoting administrative "bullying" really reduce aggression? Not according to Professor Skiba. From a comprehensive review of the literature he concluded that there is

> an almost complete lack of documentation linking zero tolerance with improved school safety . . . Zero Tolerance is a political response, not an educationally sound solution . . . The most extensive studies suggest a negative relationship between school security measures and school safety.[26]

Rand Institute behavioral scientist Jaana Juvonen concluded in the March 9 issue of *Salon* that solutions to combat juvenile violence "may not only be ineffective but may actually backfire." Juvonen singled out zero tolerance policies as being the worst example.[27]

And what of the original core of zero tolerance? Even here, the enforcement has gone way over the edge. Brooklyn high school student Reginald McDonald was suspended for carrying a twelve-inch metal ruler, which the school labeled a "weapon"—even though his shop class required him to have the ruler.[28] In Pennsylvania, a six-year-old was expelled because he carried a nail clipper in his backpack—at least nail-clipper-wielding adults aren't yet expelled from airports.[29]

Under zero tolerance, youngsters can be punished for anything. Random punishment for innocent acts serves to create utter confusion for the victim as well as for those students who witness the punishment. Zero tolerance, therefore, isn't a program to make our children safer. Instead, it's a program to enable the bullying of children by intolerant adults.

Things have gotten so out of hand that children at a New Zealand school must now have a "license" to play with toy guns. That policy was adopted after the school found that a ban on toy guns resulted in the children inventing guns from sticks. So, the Tahunanui Kindergarten in Nelson now requires children playing with imitation guns to carry permission cards fashioned after real-life weapon permits. The children have to handle the guns safely (not point them at other people) and appropriately (no imaginary hunting of endangered species).[30]

Should American children attempt to substitute finger-guns for toy guns, the consequences can be severe. In April 2001, four kindergartners in Sayreville, New Jersey, were suspended for playing cops and robbers on the school playground. Their classmates had overheard the dangerous game and turned them in.[31]

Explained District Superintendent William Bauer, "This is a no tolerance policy. We're very firm on weapons and threats . . . Given the climate of our society, we cannot take any of these [children's] statements in a light manner."[32] In other words, playing cops and robbers with one's finger involves an implicit threat to perpetrate an actual gunpoint robbery. The problem is that many "educators" no longer can tell the difference between fantasy and reality.

A few years back, a friend spoke about the silliness of a ban the city of Boston had just imposed on "Super Soakers"—very large water pistols. The conversation was overheard by a woman who broke in to declare she approved of the Boston ban because "if it can save just one life, it's worth it."

Fortunately, in many parts of the country, parents and students are rebelling against the politically correct absurdities of "zero tolerance" and rallying for firearms education programs, such as the Eddie Eagle GunSafe® Program, to help keep American children safe and free.

19

PARENTS AND RESPONSIBILITIES: SOWING SEEDS OF VIOLENCE OR GREATNESS

One of the unfortunate effects of twenty-four-hour news channels is that it is becoming more and more difficult for Americans to retain a proper perspective on high-profile and highly charged events.

For example, when violence erupts at one of our nation's schools, and we are bombarded with emotional coverage, important facts get blurred. In the drama of the moment, it is all too easy to forget that the overwhelming majority of American kids—twenty-five million of them—are good kids, that the overwhelming majority of our schools are safe, and that the overwhelming majority of American parents are good parents who sacrifice for and worry about their children every minute of every day.

But this is not a perfect world, so we also have to face the harsh reality that a tiny percentage of kids are, for whatever reason, violent kids from whom the rest must be protected. When we fail to recognize clear warning signs for potential violent offenders, when those signs are recognized but not reported to authorities, the results can be horrific.

On April 19, 1999, two deeply disturbed teenagers, Eric Harris and Dylan Klebold, went on a diabolical, murderous rampage at Columbine High School in Littleton, Colorado, that left thirteen innocent victims dead and others wounded. That mindless tragedy shocked the entire nation and spawned a national debate on societal ills.

To the gun banners, however, Columbine was seen as an opportunity to advance their argument against gun ownership, and leading the way was then President Bill Clinton. The White House quickly deployed pollsters, assembled focus groups, and then put forth a series of proposals to further restrict firearms owners' rights.[1]

While the new Clinton anti-gun proposals were field-tested among key demographic groups as part of its national political strategy, they were totally off mark for what should be the objective of any firearms policy: *saving innocent lives.* Nothing in Clinton's agenda would have prevented the terror inflicted by Harris and Klebold in their killing spree against their classmates.

Harris and Klebold spent one year planning the mass murders and broke at least twenty federal and state gun laws, even before they set foot in Columbine High School. It is ludicrous to believe that they would have been deterred if they had to break twenty-one laws instead of twenty.

And Harris and Klebold, of course, did far more than just break gun laws. Almost lost in the anti-gunners' rush to blame the guns used is the chilling fact that Harris and Klebold made and deployed more than ninety bombs. After disarming their explosive devices, Littleton Deputy Fire Marshal Rick Young stated that had it not been for defective fusing, "the death toll at Columbine High School would have exceeded a thousand."[2]

Later on, in a presidential debate, Vice President Al Gore weighed in, claiming that more gun control may have prevented the Columbine murders. That statement was palpably false. What Gore said was this:

> Look, this is the year—this is in the aftermath of Columbine and Paducah and all of the places around our country where the

> nation has been shocked by these weapons in the hands of the wrong people.
>
> The woman who bought the guns for the two boys who did that killing at Columbine said that if she had to give her name and fill out a form there, she would not have bought those guns. That conceivably could have prevented that tragedy.

The truth is this: several months before the Columbine massacre, the killers obtained firearms from two suppliers. The first was a twenty-two-year-old Columbine graduate named Mark Manes, ironically the son of a longtime Handgun Control, Inc., activist.

Manes bought a pistol at a gun show and illegally gave it to the two killers who were under age eighteen at the time. Colorado law prohibits giving handguns to juveniles, with certain exceptions, and Manes has been serving time for this crime in a Colorado prison. The second supplier was an eighteen-year-old fellow student at Columbine, Robyn Anderson, who bought three long guns for the killers at a Denver-area gun show in December 1998. Hers was a "strawman" purchase already prohibited under federal law and punishable by a five-year jail term—a penalty the Clinton administration never pressed. She walked free.

On June 4, 1999, *Good Morning America* presented a "kids and guns" program and flew Robyn Anderson to Washington for the segment.

Diane Sawyer introduced Robyn Anderson and asked: "Anything you hear this morning [that would] have stopped you from accompanying them and help[ing] them buy the guns?" Anderson replied: "I guess if it had been illegal, if I had known that it was illegal, I wouldn't have gone." Yet, on January 26, 2000, testifying before the Colorado House of Representatives Judiciary Committee, Anderson claimed that even if the purchase were legal, had there been a background check of her entirely clean record, she would not have purchased the guns.

Whichever version is true, the facts show that Anderson was not afraid to divulge her identity when showing her driver's license to illegally buy guns for her deranged teenage friends. When *Good Morning America* asked, "And they actually paid for the guns, or did you?" Anderson replied: "It was their money, yes. All I did was show a driver's license." (The exhibitors asked to see a driver's license to verify that she was over eighteen, even though there was no legal requirement that they do so.)

Even if one accepted a version of Robyn Anderson's story that is most supportive of gun control, no gun-show crackdown favored by the Clinton administration would have prevented Columbine. The older of the two killers could have purchased guns in a store legally, since he turned eighteen before the Columbine attack. Indeed, in a videotape made before the tragedy, the murderers said that if they had not obtained their guns the way they did, they would have found other ways. In short, no law can read evil in minds or souls or hearts.

Darrell Scott, whose son Craig watched two of his friends murdered at Columbine and whose daughter Rachel Joy was killed, explained that Columbine showed the need for changing the human heart, not for blaming law-abiding gun owners. Testifying before Congress on May 27, 1999, only a few weeks after the murders, Scott said:

> Since the dawn of creation there has been both good and evil in the heart of men and of women. We all contain the seeds of kindness or the seeds of violence. The death of my wonderful daughter Rachel Joy Scott and the deaths of that heroic teacher and the other children who died must not be in vain. Their blood cries out for answers.
>
> The first recorded act of violence was when Cain slew his brother Abel out in the field. The villain was not the club he used. Neither was it the NCA, the National Club Association. The true

killer was Cain and the reason for the murder could only be found in Cain's heart.

In the days that followed the Columbine tragedy, I was amazed at how quickly fingers began to be pointed at groups such as the NRA. I am not a member of the NRA. I am not a hunter. I do not even own a gun. I am not here to represent or defend the NRA—because I don't believe that they are responsible for my daughter's death. Therefore I do not believe that they need to be defended. If I believed they had anything to do with Rachel's murder I would be their strongest opponent.

I am here today to declare that Columbine was not just a tragedy—it was a spiritual event that should be forcing us to look at where the real blame lies! Much of that blame lies here in this room. Much of that blame lies behind the pointing fingers of the accusers themselves . . .

And when something as terrible as Columbine's tragedy occurs—politicians immediately look for a scapegoat such as the NRA. They immediately seek to pass more restrictive laws that continue to erode away our personal and private liberties.

We do not need more restrictive laws. Eric and Dylan would not have been stopped by metal detectors. No amount of gun laws can stop someone who spends months planning this type of massacre.

The real villain lies within our OWN hearts. Political posturing and restrictive legislation are not the answers.

To those of you who would point your finger at the NRA—I give to you sincere challenge. Dare to examine your own heart before you cast the first stone!

My daughter's death will not be in vain. The young people of this country will not allow that to happen.[3]

Darrell Scott has become a spokesman on violence and teens. He said his congressional testimony "became one of the most publicized articles on the Internet. It opened doors in political, educational, religious, and civic arenas that continue to astound me. It also led to opportunities to share Rachel's story on numerous TV programs, in books, and with thousands of high school and college students."[4]

Rachel's dad has developed a program he hopes will be adopted by schools across America. It includes a one-hour assembly program with six hours of training—two hours focused on peer training, two hours on the culture of the school for youth leaders, and two hours of parent training.

We need more people like Darrell Scott, people who lead by example.

In the spring of 2001, another school shooting that left two dead and thirteen injured took place in Santee, California. Charles Andrew Williams lived with his father; his mother lived on the other side of the continent. Williams's former girlfriend said that the killer craved his mother's attention, but never got it. Williams's father meanwhile was apparently oblivious to his son's severe social and emotional problems, so much so that Charles was allowed access to the keys to the gun safe.[5] No one else seemed concerned, either—despite the fact that the killer told an adult and several students he was going to shoot up the school. They did nothing.

In response to that tragedy in California, more gun laws were passed, proving once again that it's easier to blame the gun than to tackle tough issues like parental responsibility, moral decay, and a well-known host of related issues.

If no one takes action when a youngster is making death threats to everyone who will listen, why then would added gun laws such as California enacted stir them into action? And what about the culpability of the media? Do you think that *Time* regrets putting the two Columbine killers on its cover? Do you think the national media consider for a second how many lives might be saved by simply refusing to continuously broadcast the atrocities of publicity-seeking mass murderers? Do you think the media have the slightest regret for the saturation coverage given the Santee murder and the three copycat crimes that followed within forty-eight hours? For the media, apparently, it's easier to blame the gun and demonize the Second Amendment.

Stunningly, upon hearing the shots at Santee High School, one student grabbed a still camera and another grabbed a video camera to record the carnage. No one tried to tackle the killer during his three reloading breaks.

In the same time frame, the national media virtually ignored the story of the heroic high school students who tackled a deranged teenage killer in Springfield, Oregon.

The killer, Kipland P. Kinkel, added one more tragedy to high school shootings that took place in the months just before and after Columbine. He took innocent lives—and became nationally famous in the process. The heroes who stopped him at great personal risk, Jake and Josh Ryker, didn't. Though Jake lay injured in the hospital, his parents went before the news crews and said the tragedy was not about guns. The media lost interest when they learned that the heroes' father belonged to the National Rifle Association and the entire family opposed gun control.

At Columbine, teacher Dave Sanders was justifiably lionized for losing his life while trying to help students flee. But most people have never heard about the adults and students, like Jake and Josh Ryker, who saved lives in other high school murder sprees in Pearl, Mississippi, or Edinboro, Pennsylvania, by confronting and subduing the rampaging killers.

The anti-gun media conspiracy of silence continued in 2002, when most of the national media refused to tell the public about the heroic law students who used their handguns to stop a mass killer at the Appalachian Law School in Grundy, Virginia.[6]

To the gun-ban lobby and the mass media, civilians who take defensive action—wrestling a shooter to the ground or using a firearm in self-protection—apparently teach the wrong lesson: that we're not all helpless and that brave people can stop violent criminals. That's a lesson that conflicts with its anti-gun-rights message that child safety depends on a government crackdown on the constitutional rights of law-abiding American gun owners.

On April 17, 1999, in a speech at the White House, Hillary Rodham Clinton summed up the true objectives of the gun-ban lobby when she insisted, "Guns and children are two words that should never be spoken in the same sentence." Yet, empirically, youths who are taught about firearms responsibility are the ones who will be most responsible around firearms.

On this point, history is revealing. Thomas Jefferson, writing a letter in 1785 to his fifteen-year-old nephew and ward Peter Carr, advised the teenager about building character through the shooting sports:

> A strong body makes the mind strong. As to the species exercise, I advise the gun. While this gives a moderate exercise to the body, it gives boldness, enterprise, and independence to the mind. Games played with the ball and others of that nature are too violent for the body and stamp no character on the mind. Let your gun therefore be the constant companion of your walks.[7]

Jefferson's views on the importance of arms for youth remained strong two decades later, as expressed in his 1818 *Report of the Commissioners for the University of Virginia:* "the manual exercise, military maneuvers, and tactics, generally, should be the frequent exercise of the students, in their hours of recreation."

President Theodore Roosevelt concluded his Sixth Annual Message to Congress, on December 6, 1906, with this call for the government to help schoolchildren and other citizens develop firearms proficiency:

> We should establish shooting galleries in all the large public and military schools, should maintain national target ranges in

> different parts of the country, and should in every way encourage the formation of rifle clubs throughout all parts of the land. The little Republic of Switzerland offers us an excellent example in all matters connected with building up an efficient citizen soldiery.

Roosevelt would repeat this call with greater urgency in his Seventh Annual Message, on December 3, 1907, demanding that the government do its utmost to encourage youngsters to use guns:

> We should encourage rifle practice among schoolboys, and indeed among all classes, as well as in the military services, by every means in our power. Thus, and not otherwise, may we be able to assist in preserving the peace of the world. Fit to hold our own against the strong nations of the earth, our voice for peace will carry to the ends of the earth. Unprepared, and therefore unfit, we must sit dumb and helpless to defend ourselves, protect others, or preserve peace. The first step—in the direction of preparation to avert war if possible, and to be fit for war if it should come—is to teach our men to shoot.

Of course, President Roosevelt's observations about the role of well-trained citizens in preserving the peace overseas is equally applicable to their role in preserving the peace here at home.

The gun-ban lobby would like to dismiss both Roosevelt's and Jefferson's views as outdated and irrelevant to today's society. Yet the centuries-old tradition of gun ownership passed on from parent to child continues to this day to produce highly responsible children.

A Rochester, New York, Youth Development Study tracked 675 seventh and eighth graders until they reached adulthood. That study, conducted for the Office of Juvenile Justice and Delinquency Prevention, which is part of the federal Department of Justice, concluded that the most important factor affecting how children deal with guns was how they were taught about firearms.

Not surprisingly, it found the most responsible, law-abiding, and nonviolent of all juvenile groups studied turned out to be young gun owners. Not one of the study's adolescents who obtained a firearm from a parent ever committed a crime. Young people who learned about guns from their parents were highly law-abiding, compared with their peers who learned about guns on the street, or who did not own guns at all.[8]

Specifically, the report found:

- Children who received guns from their parents never committed firearm crimes (0 percent). Children who obtained guns illegally often did so (24 percent)
- Children who were given guns by a parent were less likely to commit any kind of street crime (14 percent) than children who lived with no guns (24 percent), or children who acquired a gun illegally (74 percent).
- Children who got guns from a parent were less likely to use drugs (13 percent) than children who acquired a gun illegally (41 percent), or who came from a home without guns (15 percent).

Within these numbers is this simple truth: raising youngsters who are productive and respectful members of society takes time, requires good parenting, and demands educators who are willing to teach children how to make the best real-life decisions based on fact not on wishful thinking. The fact that the sport-shooting Rochester youths grew up so well was grounded in their parents, who were involved in their lives in many ways; sharing participation in the shooting sports was just one way in which the parents chose to make a constructive difference.

The Rochester results were similar to those from the 1996 Tulane University National Youth Study of male tenth and eleventh graders that found that a teenager's involvement in recreational firearms use made it more likely that he or she would own a gun—but had no relationship to the teenager's engaging in illegal activity or carrying a gun for "status."

The same cannot be said of youths who receive their firearms instruction from the street or the mass media. For too many today, that is often the only way youngsters in America's cities can learn about firearms.

To fail to teach America's young people safe gun use, under the supervision of responsible adults, is to sow the seeds of disaster. To refuse to acknowledge the values of firearms training for young people is a disgrace.

Case in point: no one better exemplifies the character-building qualities of the shooting sports than our American Olympic athletes. In the Olympic tradition, the first medal is always awarded in a shooting sport.

In the 2000 Sydney Olympics, the first gold medalist was Nancy Johnson, of Downers Grove, Illinois, in the 10-meter air rifle event. As a seventeen-year-old, Johnson had been told that she might have to spend the rest of her life in a wheelchair, when her legs and arms mysteriously began to atrophy. But she fought back and won her medal at age twenty-six.

At the 1996 Atlanta games, the first gold medal was also awarded to an American. Just a week after her seventeenth birthday, Kim Rhode of California won the gold in double trap.

In an interview in *Women & Guns* magazine, Kim explained how her father taught her to focus, while she was practicing her trap shooting:

> When I'd call for a bird, he'd tickle my neck or the back of my leg with a blade of grass, or he'd toss a chunk of broken claybird

> onto the field in front of me, just as the target was thrown. He intentionally put distractions in my path so I'd learn to ignore everything else, and FOCUS on the target.

When not studying or shooting, Kim Rhode spends much of her time giving motivational speeches to groups of young people. Her message is this: "Dreams really do come true, they do—so set your goal high, and stay *focused!*"

Imagine what a better world we might have if American television worked half as hard at showing America's young people models of sportsmanship like Nancy Johnson and Kim Rhode as it does at publicizing and glamorizing criminals who misuse guns. Imagine further what a better world we might have if the gun-ban lobby were to focus its energy on something more constructive than a war on those who participate in the shooting sports.

Anti-gun advocates claim that they don't have anything against the use of sporting firearms, yet the Brady Center to Prevent Handgun Violence and the American Academy of Pediatrics distribute a brochure that warns parents of preteens and teenagers: "Be extremely cautious about allowing children to participate in shooting activities." The brochure offers no evidence that the shooting sports are dangerous and, of course, does not disclose that school shooting programs are safer than all other school sports.

Contrary to what the gun-ban lobby would have American parents believe, target shooting has a lower injury rate than any other sport, and fights between competitors are nonexistent. What's more, unlike other sports, there has never been an incident of one competitor deliberately harming another in a sanctioned match. In baseball, intentional violence, such as spiking and throwing beanballs, is a traditional part of the game. Hockey, boxing, and football all involve the intentional infliction of physical suffering on the opponent. The shooting sports are nonviolent, accessible to everyone, and wholesome. So that's why Thomas Jefferson recommended against those "ball" games as "too violent for the body."

American culture has changed greatly since Jefferson's day, and the real question we face today is whether or not we still possess the national character to do what it will take to change a culture that produces alienation and violence in some of our young.

Colorado Governor Bill Owens recalls touring Columbine High School and walking through the drama classroom:

> As with many high school drama departments, there were movie posters hanging on the walls. What stuck out in my mind, however, was which movies these posters advertised. Not posters like *Gone With the Wind,* but more like *Natural Born Killers.* Not *Casablanca,* but *The Terminator,* not *The Sound of Music,* but *Die Hard.*

Governor Owens reminded us that "almost 20 years ago, in defining the battle against communism, Ronald Reagan said: 'The real crisis we face today is a spiritual one; at root, it is a test of moral will and faith.'"[9]

America defeated Communism. America will defeat international terrorism. But will we demonstrate the will to halt the national decline of our moral standards? Three decades ago Senator Daniel Patrick Moynihan (D-N.Y.) gave a name to the spiraling decline. He called it "defining deviancy down." We've had fair warning. It is time we act.

20

THE "GUN CULTURE": AMERICA'S CULTURAL WAR

What is the "gun culture"? The answer depends on your point of view.

To millions of Americans, especially those who own firearms, the term refers to America's traditional bedrock values of self-reliance, self-defense, and self-determination. To others, most of whom dislike firearms and do not own them, the term is pejorative, even derisive: it was coined to distinguish the culturally elite who rule the national media as morally superior to the nation's gun owners.

Former President Bill Clinton embraced the term in his all-out war against the nation's firearms owners. Case in point: after two deranged high school students went on a murderous rampage in Littleton, Colorado, Clinton charged that the murders stemmed from "the culture of hunting and sport shooting in America."

In a ghoulish press conference held shortly after the Littleton tragedy, Clinton declared, "When there are no constituents for this movement, the movement will evaporate."[1]

The "movement" to which Mr. Clinton referred consists of honest, hardworking, law-abiding gun owners from every walk of life and counts at least 40 percent of all Americans as its members. His was the opening salvo of a cultural war directed at gun owners and those who espouse freedom, as if we are supposed to pay the price for violent criminals with the loss of our rights.

The "gun culture" includes college professors who target shoot for fun. It includes those who understand the importance of an armed populace for personal and national defense. It includes gun collectors who may never fire their century-old antiques, but feel a sense of connection to the past from holding a gun that may have been carried at Valley Forge or Shiloh or Omaha Beach. It includes combat veterans who still own guns they carried island-hopping across the Pacific, landing at Inchon, or defending the besieged marine base camp at Khe Sanh. It includes moms and dads who worry about their safety and their children's safety. It includes your next-door neighbor who likes to hunt geese every October. It includes highly paid urban professionals who own a gun for self-defense. It includes your coworker down the hall who shoots sporting clays every Friday afternoon. And it includes millions upon millions of voters who add up to an unbeatable political movement willing to "Vote Freedom First" when liberty is on the line.

In short, the "gun culture" consists of astronauts and bus drivers, physicians and farmers, computer engineers and law officers, lawyers and laborers—not at all the stereotype conjured up by the mass media and the anti-gun lobby.

To the gun-ban lobby, the "gun culture" is something that must be suppressed at all cost. Not for safety reasons but because of what gun ownership symbolizes to millions of Americans: freedom, independence, self-reliance, and individuality as opposed to submission, conformity, reliance on government, and the overriding needs of the state.

A classic example of this is the gun banners' obsession with shutting down gun shows, because they know gun shows are major centers of political activity by firearms owners.

They reason that if they can shut down gun shows, or reduce the shows to a shadow of what they used to be, it will seriously hamper voter registration, petition signature-gathering, and political education of many members of the "gun culture." At a minimum, it will make it much more expensive to inform our side about the threats to our Second Amendment freedom.

The real purpose of banning gun shows is therefore very simple: to discourage people who like guns, who enjoy looking at guns, who enjoy collecting guns, who use guns for sporting purposes or hunting from meeting and exercising their First and Second Amendment rights simultaneously. *It's about suppressing our culture, our heritage, and our freedom.*

That is why Michael A. Bellesiles and his book *Arming America: The Origins of a National Gun Culture* were such a hit with the anti-gun lobby and its allies in the media. The notion of academic proof that America's traditional connection with firearms was somehow all wrong was intoxicating. In their minds, if this were true, they would no longer have to deal with the "guns are the American way" argument. Fortunately, the truth won out and Bellesiles and his book were both proved to be fraudulent. Ironically, Bellesiles's scam ended up proving just how determined, and just how far, the anti-gun lobby would go to eliminate firearms from America's culture.

I remember a breakfast a few years back in Leesburg, Virginia, that featured commentator Oliver North as the guest speaker. The restaurant was decorated with hundreds of antique guns and Ollie opened his speech by saying, "I'll need to make this speech fast before the federal government comes to confiscate all these *assault weapons.*"

Oliver North was joking, but he was all too close to the truth. Take the case of Patrick Washburn, a professor of journalism at Ohio University specializing in the history of the wartime press. Befitting his specialization, on the wall of Professor Washburn's office he kept an 1878 Springfield rifle that was passed down from his great-grandfather. Washburn believed the gun to be inoperable, had never fired it, and had touched it only once in fifteen years—when he moved from one office to another. Yet the university police showed up and told him to remove it from campus. Why? Was this just overzealous application of a university's weapons policy?

Unfortunately, no. "OU officials told Mr. Washburn they had

received several complaints from members of the OU community who felt 'threatened' by the antique. Removing it, they reasoned, was the only way to end 'all the distress it is causing.'"[2] This is an antique rifle, purely a wallhanger. Why would anyone feel threatened? Because that gun is a symbol, a reminder that we live in a violent world, and a symbol of how individual Americans are empowered to protect themselves.

Another expression of the cultural war appears through the propaganda campaign against guns from the entertainment industry. The movie and television industry is awash in fierce anti-gun sentiment, including the sneaking of hostility into films in subtle ways.

How many hunters do you see on TV these days? Or nonpolice, nonmilitary, nongovernment characters who own guns? Or average citizens who use firearms to stop a violent crime? Few to none. The overwhelming majority of people depicted on TV who use guns are murderers, rapists, drug dealers, and terrorists.

The entertainment industry insists that its products don't influence people, that violent shows don't encourage violent behavior. But if its productions do not affect public behavior, why do companies pay the movie industry enormous sums for "product placement," the prominent use of particular brand-name products in movies? Corporations believe that seeing their brand of soft drinks or cell phones or automobiles portrayed positively in a movie will help market their products. More directly, television exists on advertising directly influencing viewers to buy particular products. Yet the industry insists that television programs don't influence people to do bad things, as if televisions turn on the "influence viewers" rays only when the commercials start!

When Hollywood isn't directly trying to denigrate legitimate gun ownership, its violent depictions have consequences. Why, for example, did the movie version of *The Basketball Diaries* include a sequence in which the lead character walked through the halls of his high school wearing a black trench coat and armed with a shotgun used to kill his classmates? It wasn't in the book. Without that sequence, would the killers at Columbine High School have expressed their angry alienation in quite that way? They saw the movie and considered it noteworthy,[3] so much so that they decided to act out that scene in real life with deadly and tragic results.

Remember the movie *Jurassic Park*? As it happened, the movie didn't exactly follow the book. Significantly, the book's neutral or even slightly pro-gun message morphed into the movie's anti-gun message. If the movie *Jurassic Park* had appeared out of the blue or if subtle anti-gun messages had appeared in the book, one could chalk this up to an author's anti-gun bias. What's instructive, however, is that the climax of the book was altered to promote a perception of guns as futile forms of self-defense.

Coincidence? Steven Spielberg produced *Jurassic Park*. He also made the critically acclaimed *Schindler's List*. As Dr. John Lott pointed out, "With all the well-deserved publicity for the movie 'Schindler's List,' the movie left out how Schindler, an avid gun collector, stockpiled guns and hand grenades in case the Jews he was protecting needed to defend themselves."[4] Hollywood insiders tell us that the writers who produced the screenplay consciously chose to leave this out for political reasons.

More recently, Spielberg spent $100,000 "revising" his film *E.T.* so that FBI agents did not have guns as they surrounded the extraterrestrial's spaceship. Spielberg apparently made this decision because "Drew Barrymore, who co-starred in the movie, is 'now fanatically opposed to all forms of weapons.'"[5] Ironically, Mr. Spielberg has one of the most extensive collections of firearms in Hollywood.[6]

Then there is Sylvester Stallone, who *Saturday Night Live* once suggested should win an award for "longest machine-gun solo" in *Rambo II*. Stallone has made most of his money producing violent movies in which guns are arguably the most important actors. Yet Stallone supports a ban on handguns. After the murder of actor

Phil Hartman, Stallone told reporters in London that "until America, door to door, takes every handgun, this is what you're gonna have . . . It really is pathetic . . . We're livin' in the Dark Ages over there."[7] Oh yes—Stallone's 24,000-square-foot Miami mansion had an indoor shooting range.[8]

The common denominator in all these cases is the clear hypocrisy of the anti-gun elite in Hollywood and the entertainment world. Firearms are bad for the average person, but perfectly acceptable for the enlightened, the elite, and the wealthy—*people like them.*

John Grisham writes novels, lots of them, and Hollywood gets around to making movies of most of them. As I write these words, Grisham's *The Runaway Jury* is beginning production, but where Grisham's novel is about a lawsuit against tobacco companies, the movie version will be about a lawsuit against firearms makers. Why the change from tobacco companies to gun makers? Hollywood apparently now hates guns more than tobacco.

But, without question, the most crucial battleground in this "cultural war" is the one to win over the hearts and minds of our children. From the schools to the movie and television screens and the daily press, they're telling youngsters the same thing: when it comes to guns, limits, restrictions, compromises, and curtailment are perfectly normal and definitely desirable. It's all they hear.

Ask about the Second Amendment and chances are you'll get a blank stare and a mumbled "whatever." Educators who don't have the faintest idea what the Second Amendment means and don't care pass on that ignorance or indifference to another generation.

Look at your children's textbooks that claim the Second Amendment guarantees government's right to assemble a National Guard—or that it's a "collective right" of society or the states or an obsolete relic of our colonial past. The right to bear arms is misinterpreted or it doesn't exist at all. Whatever the case, the bottom line is that youngsters literally don't get the truth.

Listen to the media's anti-gun messages. For many adults, the background buzz of that bias is so common and so constant that they no longer hear it. *But your kids hear it.* Like infants learning language, they suck it up like a sponge. From Dan Rather to Oprah Winfrey to "Doonesbury" and more, kids are told that guns are dangerous, that gun owners are suspect, and that the right to keep and bear arms doesn't mean what it says.

Every day, slick magazines and national newspapers wage a war of words on the Second Amendment, selling "sensible limits," "modest gun-control efforts," and "reasonable restrictions." Every night, everywhere you look, kids are being indoctrinated into believing guns symbolize evil. Guns and crime. Guns and drugs. And now *guns and terrorism.*

Kids and adults alike are hearing a very similar message about hunting. As a result, many Americans who don't hunt receive a very negative view of hunting in large part because of what they see, read, and hear from the mass media. Consider this gem from Allan Saxe, political analyst for WBAP, a Fort Worth, Texas, radio station:

> Why not mount grandma's head on the dining room wall or in a restaurant? That may sound ridiculous, cruel and outlandish. However, we do affix the severed heads of deer, moose, elk and a variety of other creatures to some of our homes and commercial enterprises. We even stuff many four-legged creatures and place them in prominent living areas. It is done as a matter of pride and attraction. To me, it is as outlandish as if a human head were affixed.
>
> All living creatures are sacred. Humans have attempted to portray themselves as somehow higher, more moral, more valuable than other living creatures. Some may ask, "How can you compare grandmother to a deer?" But to have respect for human life means to have respect for all life. It is too dangerous, too easy, to make distinctions about which lives can be taken and which spared.

Yet, after telling us that all life is sacred and how it is dangerous to make distinctions as to which lives can be spared, Saxe then says:

> Hunting is so basic and common in our lives that even those vehemently opposed to guns often say they would exempt the hunter's weapons. I would reverse the proposition. As a semi-libertarian I hold strongly in the Second Amendment right to bear arms, but only in defense against our fellow humans.[9]

If his argument were simply that hunting wasn't necessary, we could have an interesting debate about how to deal with the problem of overpopulation of wildlife. But asserting that "all living creatures are sacred" except when it comes to self-defense goes against the very distinctions he drew in calling hunting "savage."

I suppose we should be glad that Mr. Saxe is willing to support our right to self-defense; there are plenty of gun-control advocates, as Mr. Saxe observes, who are only willing to "exempt the hunter's weapons" from their schemes for gun confiscation. We should remember the parable from the Talmud about a man with two wives, one young and one mature. The young one wanted her husband to look young, and so she would pull out his gray hairs in his sleep. The more mature wife did not want to look old compared to her husband, and so she would pull the black hairs. Eventually he became quite bald. Between those who consider hunting to be savagery and those who oppose guns for self-defense, we are in danger of finding ourselves with no guns at all.

21

FREEDOM

When the ragtag band of Massachusetts farmers stopped General Gage's Redcoats at the foot of Concord Bridge, they weren't fighting for an obscure idea in some philosopher's dusty textbook. They were fighting for the only right that guarantees the others . . . the only freedom that could allow them to fight for freedom at all. The right to keep and bear arms is our first freedom—the one right that allows all "rights" to exist, because there is no such thing as a free nation where police and the military are allowed the force of arms but individual citizens are not.

Some might rank the First Amendment as the most important of our rights because it provides a doorway for news and commentary to pass through free and unfettered. But that doorway of freedom is framed by muskets, muskets that—in the hands of the farmers and shopkeepers, and the blacksmiths and lawyers who owned them—would sentinel the birth of a new nation. Our revolution began when the British sent Redcoats door-to-door to confiscate the people's guns. They didn't succeed: the muskets went out the back door with their owners.

More than 225 years after our forefathers defended their right to keep and bear arms, America's Second Amendment freedoms are again under attack—this time from an internal foe that seeks to win a war of slow attrition on the Second Amendment that will ultimately result in total gun confiscation.

The next time you hear Sarah Brady or Senators Chuck Schumer or Dianne Feinstein propose some form of "reasonable" gun control, think about England and the tragic loss of freedom there. What happened to good Britons in the name of "gun safety" defines the aims of those in America who use those words as camouflage to hide their true goals.

The war against firearms ownership in Britain was lost one step at a time—with each step being called "common sense" or "reasonable"—first with licensing and registration of firearms owners, then with a series of "safety" measures that included "home storage" rules, complete with local police approval and home inspections. Then came changes in the law that made licensees' continued possession of whole classes of registered long guns—including all semiautomatic and pump rifles, and certain classes of semiautomatic and pump shotguns—a dire criminal offense.

When those long guns were removed from the homes of good, honest Britons, the government turned on licensed handgun owners—who were forced to undergo even more strict police supervision. Licensed owners of handguns larger than .22 caliber were ordered to forfeit their registered pistols and revolvers under what was called a "buyback scheme." The government produced lists of guns it was going to remove and set the price. It did the same for accoutrements like scopes, holsters, sights, and shooting rests.

Licensed handgun owners were allowed to keep their registered .22-caliber handguns—but not in their homes. Those firearms had to be removed to government-inspected gun clubs and kept under government-controlled lock and key, that is until a second handgun "buyback" scheme was dictated, and those remaining guns were taken.

This was gun control—total control, where the private property of ordinary, law-abiding Britons became government property and this theft of liberty was touted worldwide as the very model of "gun control."

When the last legal handgun was taken by the government, armed crime by the violent criminal underclass exploded. According to historian Joyce Lee Malcolm, author of *Guns and Violence: The English Experience:*

> In the two years following the 1997 handgun ban, the use of handguns in crime rose by 40%, and the upward trend has continued. From April to November 2001, the number of people robbed at gunpoint in London rose 53% . . . And in the four years from 1997 to 2001, the rate of violent crime more than doubled. Your chances of being mugged in London are now six times greater than in New York. England's rates of assault, robbery, and burglary are far higher than America's and 53% of English burglaries occur while occupants are at home, compared with 13% in the U.S., where burglars admit to fearing armed homeowners more than the police. In a United Nations study of crime in 18 developed nations published in July, England and Wales led the Western world's crime league, with nearly 55 crimes per 100 people.

England—always touted by America's gun-control crowd as their vision for our future—is the ultimate proving ground. And it is the very model for what America's gun-ban axis have in store for the nation's law-abiding owners of firearms.

The anti-gunner's formula for surrendering our Second Amendment freedoms is clear: first, enact a nationwide firearms waiting period; second, after the waiting period fails to reduce crime, enact a nationwide licensing and registration law; and the final step, confiscate all registered firearms.

The Second Amendment, first among equals in the Bill of Rights, remains a target for such restrictions and ultimate repeal. From schools to the media, the refrain is the same; when it comes to guns, limits, restrictions, compromises, and curtailments are perfectly acceptable. It's all we hear. Every day, slick magazines and national newspapers wage a war of words on the Second Amendment, selling "sensible limits" and "reasonable restrictions." Every night the talking heads on the network news use guns to symbolize all that's "evil." Guns and crime. Guns and drugs. Guns and terrorists. Guns and tragedy. This was the same strategy anti-gun groups in England employed to disarm its citizens.

Wherever you look, an anti-gun fever has emerged. Many well-meaning clergy have fallen for the notion that we can protect our lives by sacrificing our liberties. Voices from the American Medical Association, American Bar Association, and the Centers for Disease Control and Prevention either classify firearms as harmful agents like viruses or germs or prescribe gun bans as some miracle vaccine against terrorism.

While the national media is quick to trumpet the anti-gun agenda, these noble guardians of free speech invade our living rooms with made-for-TV massacres, video games that teach our children to kill, and movies that promote violence and tear down our values—all in the name of entertainment.

The efforts of the anti-gun groups and the media to undermine the Second Amendment, to deride it and degrade it, threaten not only the physical well-being of millions of Americans but also the core concept of individual liberty our Founding Fathers struggled to perfect and protect.

In doing so, these groups play right into the hands of terrorists whose primary goal is to deprive us of our freedoms.

Anti-gunners have shamelessly exploited the tragic events of September 11 and, more recently, the D.C.-area snipers, to promote their anti-gun agenda. To anti-gunners, September 11 became a vehicle to further their campaign against gun shows by shrilly proclaiming that U.S. soldiers could be gunned down by foreign terrorists armed with firearms purchased at American gun shows. Of course, the Brady Campaign neglected to mention that gun commerce involving violent felons, illegal aliens, or terrorists is already a federal felony.

The recent tragedies involving the D.C.-area snipers were seized as an opportunity by the Brady Campaign and others to call for ballistic "fingerprinting" and the national gun-owner database it would require in yet another excuse to gut the Second Amendment.

Anti-gunners and others might point out that our country has a history of temporarily suspending liberties. Similar restrictions, they claim, are needed to fight the war on terror and Second Amendment freedoms aren't the only liberties we're being asked to surrender. In an effort to gain the upper hand on terrorists, the federal government has conjured up a variety of programs to monitor law-abiding Americans, including national ID cards, expanded wiretaps, a database of biometric data (hair, eye color, height, etc.), and thorough and personal searches of property at security checkpoints. Further, the wide variety of electronic data available on most Americans, such as personal finances, employment, medical history and our educational history, not to mention the ability to monitor all manner of electronic transmissions, from telephones to E-mail, already allows the government to prepare highly detailed profiles of virtually all Americans.

The worst mistake we can make is to assume that surrendering our privacy and liberties will somehow make America and the world safer. As long as we have relatively wide-open borders, haphazard immigration enforcement, and no decent system in place to track illegal immigrants and those on expired visas who move about our country freely—all the technological tools available to us will not catch the individual terrorists who invade our borders. Second Amendment liberties surrendered in the name of combating terrorism are unlikely to stop a terrorist who seeks illegal and undetected entry into the United States.

As we face our future, the battle between freedom and terrorism has no end in sight. But that's how it's always been. When the Nazis and the Japanese warlords sought to enslave the world, the forces of freedom fought them. And when the Soviets and Stalin attempted world domination, the forces of freedom fought them. And so it is today.

Terrorists seek nothing less than a massive change in the way we lead our lives. They hate Americans and everything for which we stand. Their hatred is fueled by our freedoms and values. The manner in which the Taliban and Al Qaeda ruled Afghanistan stands in stark contrast to America. Afghans lived in a highly restrictive and monotheistic environment. Freedoms were severely restricted and many activities were forbidden. Icons of other religions were even destroyed. This is the life of a people when their liberties are willingly surrendered!

Terrorists hate us for our values and freedom. The freedoms promised in our Declaration of Independence and fulfilled by our Constitution and Bill of Rights are a threat to terrorists who realize that their repressive regimes could not thrive or survive in an open society.

Our individual freedom ensures that media outlets are free to report the news in an uncensored fashion and not shut down if they are critical of the government. Our schools and universities are open to citizens and immigrants alike, terrifying those who seek a government based upon an ignorant and uneducated population. Our right to vote is afforded to citizens over the age of eighteen regardless of their race, religion, or ethnicity. It is yet another tool that could topple other nations and destroy dictatorships.

When the terrorists selected the World Trade Center, the Pentagon, and the White House as their targets on September 11, they erroneously assumed our strength and power are based on money, and military and political power. They never understood what America is about. But imagine their delight to see America's anti-gunners and some members of the media using their First Amendment freedoms to assail the liberties of the Second Amendment.

There is perhaps no better visual image of what America is about than the sight of the rescuers at the World Trade Center on September

11 who were indistinguishable in the gray dust that covered them head-to-toe. When the dust washed away days later, the world discovered these rescuers were of all faiths: Muslim, Jewish, Hindu, Catholic, and Protestant; all colors: white, brown, black, and yellow, and of many ethnic backgrounds. In no other country in the world would such diversity be found among its rescuers. This, too, inspires hatred in religious extremists and madmen who seek power because our values and freedoms in a global scale would mean an end to their dream of domination and subjugation.

As terrorism continues to spread its evil wings in America, we need only decide whether, as citizens, we'll allow opportunistic assaults on the Second Amendment to succeed and open the door for other freedoms in the Bill of Rights to fall or whether we'll choose vigilance over indifference and reject these assaults on our liberties.

I've come to believe that much of this struggle boils down to freedom-loving Americans versus freedom-fearing politicians who believe society is best served by a diminished access to freedom. They believe we can't be tested. They believe they are more capable of managing our lives than we are. They offer the illusion of security if citizens will just agree to be a little less free, as if we can purchase a safer society with the currency of American freedom. Yet we cannot make ourselves safer by making ourselves less free.

We know from history what can be lost, but so far no one has figured out how to get it back. The more we tolerate forfeiture of our freedom, we become a nation in which privacy is a luxury and freedom is suspect. The more we distrust each other and this government distrusts us, the more our liberties will be frisked, x-rayed, strip-searched, and finally lost. When we consign our firearms, our privacy, our free speech to our government in the name of security, what then?

Only we the people can stop the erosion of our liberties. We must declare that there are no shades of gray in American freedom. It's black and white, all or nothing. There are not flavors of freedom. You can't like yours but not mine. There are not classes of freedom. You can't have more, or less, than me. Freedom is not negotiable or malleable. And there is no temporary suspension of freedom. Once on loan, you never get it back.

American freedom is the most precious way of life the world has ever known. The quality of freedom our ancestors bought with their blood is not ours to squander. Individual freedom is the essence of what America is all about, and it must remain intact. The true patriot is the American who supports the sanctity of American freedom as defined by the Bill of Rights.

In the months and years ahead, every American must stand unflinchingly for the individual personal freedoms guaranteed in the Bill of Rights that make our nation, the United States of America, the finest nation in all mankind. Only then can we pass the torch of freedom to the next generation, unequivocally endorsed well into this millennium and beyond.

E-mail Wayne LaPierre with your suggestions, comments,
or updates to the text at:
updates@gunsfreedomterrorism.com

NOTES

CHAPTER 1

1. Brady Center to Prevent Handgun Violence, "In the Wake of Terrorist Attacks, Sarah Brady Warns About Risks of Guns in the Home," press release, 18 September 2001.
2. Consumer Federation of America, "Buying a Firearm in the Wake of Terrorist Attacks Is More Harmful than Helpful for Consumers," press release, 21 September 2001.
3. Ibid.
4. Coalition to Stop Gun Violence, "Desire for Protection Is Understandable, But Buying More Guns Won't Make Us Safer," press release, 2 October 2001.
5. Educational Fund to Stop Gun Violence, "Talking About Gun Control After September 11," 1 October 2001.
6. Educational Fund to Stop Gun Violence, "Talking Points on Terrorism," Stop Gun Violence Newsletter, 28 (October 2001).
7. "Members Fret About Safety of Families," *Roll Call,* 27 September 2001.
8. Ibid.
9. W. Rudman, *Combat: Twelve Years in the U.S. Senate* (New York: Random House, May 1996).
10. Brady Center to Prevent Gun Violence, "Brady Center and Police, Public Health Coalition Seek to Block Military Weapon Imports," 19 September 2001.
11. Ibid.
12. D. Kopel, "Guns and (Character) Assassination," National Review Online, 21 December 2001, available at www.nationalreview.com.
13. Ibid.
14. Ibid.
15. Ibid.
16. Quoted in T. Eckert, "Advocates Push Gun Control as Anti-Terrorism Measure," Copley News Service, 18 January 2002.
17. Quoted in S. Page, "McCain: Terrorists Bypass Laws by Using Gun

Shows," *USA Today,* 27 November 2001, available at www.usatoday.com.

18. Quoted in J. Johnson, "Senators Use Fear of Terrorism to Push Gun Control," CNSNews.com, 10 December 2001, available at www.cnsnews.com.
19. Background on McKelvey from Americans for Gun Safety Web site at www.americansforgunsafety.com/overview.html.
20. N. Confessore, "Control Freaks; Americans for Gun Safety Set Out to Give Gun Control a Shot in the Arm. Instead They May Give It a Shot in the Head," *American Prospect,* 8 April 2002.
21. S. Francis, "The Gun Control Gestapo Gets 9/11 Wrong," 7 January 2002, available at www.vdare.com.
22. Quoted in J.B. Baker, "Anti-Gun Lobby Misfires; Targeting Gun Shows Won't Stop Terrorism," *Washington Times,* 20 December 2001, A21.
23. H. Rosin, "Israel Says Ship with Weapons Was Loaded in Iran," *Washington Post,* 6 January 2002.
24. A. O'Sullivan, L. Lahoud, H. Keinon, and J. Zacharia, "No Doubt Arms Ship Is PA's. Seized Katyashas Would Have Put Cities at Risk," *Jerusalem Post,* 6 January 2002.
25. R. MacMillan, "'Homeland Security' Gun Not Misnamed—Firearms Dealer," Post-Newsweek Business Information, Inc., Newsbytes, 14 January 2002, available at www.newsbytes.com.
26. D. Bandow, "Fighting the War Against Terrorism: Elite Forces, Yes; Conscripts, No," CATO Institute Policy Analysis No. 430, 10 April 2002.

CHAPTER 2

1. E. Schmitt, "A Nation Challenged: The Military; Generals Given the Power to Order the Downing of Jets," *New York Times,* 27 September 2001.
2. Editorial, "Arm the Pilots," *Washington Times,* 12 July 2002.
3. J. Johnson, "Sept. 11 Pilot's Widow Supports Arming Pilots With Guns," CNSNews.com, 19 July 2002, available at www.cnsnews.com.
4. 14 C.F.R. §108.
5. D. Murdock, "Arming Pilots," National Review Online, 15 July 2002, available at www.nationalreview.com.
6. R.A. Levy, "Invitation to Terror," National Review Online, 12 October 2001, available at www.nationalreview.com.
7. T. Price, "Fear of Flying," *Washington Times,* 4 June 2002, p. A19.
8. Editorial, "Congress Gets It: Pilots Need Guns," *Wall Street Journal,* 11 July 2002.

9. K. Rand, "Armed Pilots Pose Risks," *USA Today,* 27 September 2001.
10. W.E. Hollon, *Frontier Violence: Another Look* (London: University of Oxford Press, 1974), p. x.
11. FBI, *Crime in the United States,* 2000 (Washington, DC: Government Printing Office, 2001), p. 5, 77.
12. Violence Policy Center, "Comments of the Violence Policy Center to the Federal Aviation Administration on the Use of Firearms on Commercial Air Flights," Docket No. FAA-2001-111229, 14 February 2002.
13. M. Janofsky, "Armed Pilots? Many Travelers Are Gun-Shy," *New York Times,* 11 July 2002.
14. Allied Pilots Association, "Debate Over Arming Pilots Is Over," press release, 21 June 2002.
15. R.A. Levy, "Invitation to Terror."

CHAPTER 3

1. Brady Campaign to Prevent Gun Violence, "Sarah Brady: Tighter Gun Laws Needed to Prevent Terrorism and Strengthen National Security," U.S. Newswire press release, 12 October 2001.
2. E. Holder Jr., "Keeping Guns Away from Terrorists," *Washington Post,* 25 October 2001.
3. Brady Center to Prevent Handgun Violence, "Brady Campaign Says Congress' Anti-Terrorism Legislation Should Have Tightened Nation's Gun Laws," press release, 25 October 2001.
4. Editorial, "Gun Shows and Terrorists," *Washington Post,* 16 December 2001.
5. Rep. Conyer's House Web site does not provide a text of his remarks at a press conference to introduce the Gun Show Background Check Act of 2002, held on 20 March 2002, in the Rayburn House Office Building, Room 2141, with members of gun-control groups. However, a recitation of Conyer's remarks is provided in Sam MacDonald's "An Antigun Firefight," Insight on the News, 22 April 2002.
6. T. Eckert, "Advocates Push Gun Control as Anti-Terrorism Measure," Copley News Service, 18 January 2002.
7. KTUV/FOX 2, Bay City News, "Feinstein to Propose New National Gun Law Legislation," 20 December 2001.
8. Print ad released by Americans for Gun Safety (AGS) on 24 October 2001. See also press release issued by AGS, "Ad Links Gun Show Loophole to Homeland Security," 24 October 2001.
9. G. Friddell, "U.S. Gun-Show Loophole Can Be Put to Use by Terrorists," *Virginian-Pilot,* 3 December 2001.

10. Article appeared on a Web site run by Azzam Publications in Britain. Further cited in newspaper article by Bob Port, "Fugitive Linked to Terror Guide/Gun Control Group's Probe," *Daily News* (New York), 22 November 2001.
11. 18 U.S.C. 922(g)(1).
12. Jonathan Cowan, letter to the editor, "Background Checks Invaluable," *USA Today,* 31 December 2001.
13. Gun Show Loophole Closing and Gun Law Enforcement Act of 2001, 107th Cong., 1st Sess., S. 890, introduced in the Senate on 15 May 2001.

CHAPTER 4

1. S.P. Halbrook, "The Arms of People Should Be Taken Away," American Rifleman, March 1989, available at www.nraila.org/Articles.asp?FormMode=Detail&ID=9.
2. R.D. Meade, *Patrick Henry* (Marietta, GA: Lippincott, 1969), p. 34.
3. K.J. Lopez, "Second Amendment Victory," National Review Online, Interrogatory with Nelson Lund, Professor of Law at George Mason University School of Law, 18 October 2001, available at www.nationalreview.com/interrogatory/interrogatory101801.shtml.
4. *U.S. v. Emerson,* No. 99–10331 (Fifth Circuit, 1999).
5. C. Beccaria, An Essay on Crimes and Punishments, 3rd ed. (London: F. Newbery, 1770), pp. 87–88.
6. "Debates and Other Proceedings of the Convention of Virginia convened at Richmond, on Monday the 2d day of June 1788" (Petersburg, VA: printed by Hunter and Prentis, 1788).
7. J. Eliot, *Debates in the Several State Conventions,* vol. 3 (Philadelphia: J.B. Lippincott & Co., 1836–59), p. 45.

CHAPTER 5

1. Sarah Brady speech to the Women's National Democratic Club Luncheon, 21 September 1993.
2. General Accounting Office, "Implementation of the Brady Handgun Violence Prevention Act," GAO/GGD-96-22 Gun Control, January 1996, 8.
3. Ibid.
4. Transactional Records Access Clearinghouse, "Recent Trends in ATF Enforcement," 1998.
5. Ibid.
6. E. Shannon, "Have Gun Will Travel," *Time*, 16 August 1996, p. 30.
7. G. Fields, "Bush Proposal to Combat Gun Violence to Stress Prosecution, Not Limits on Access," *Wall Street Journal,* 11 May 2001.

8. J. Mason and M. Bowes, "Homicide Rate Drops," *Richmond Times-Dispatch,* 2 January 2002, p 81.
9. Colonel Jerry A. Oliver, Chief of Police, Richmond, Va., testimony before the U.S. Senate Subcommittee on Youth Violence, March 22, 1999.
10. K. Caplan, "Gun Cases to Go to U.S. Court; Stiffer Sentences and Quicker Trials Are Program's Goals," *Daily Press,* 23 January 1998.
11. U.S. Attorney General John Ashcroft, "Project Safe Neighborhoods Kickoff Conference," 23 January 2002.

CHAPTER 6

1. D.B. Kopel, P. Gallant, and J. Eisen, "Gun-Packing First Lady," *America's First Freedom* (August 2002): 39–41, 61.
2. E. Roosevelt, *This Is My Story* (New York and London: Harper & Brothers, 1937).
3. D.B. Kopel, P. Gallant, and J. Eisen, "Gun-Packing First Lady."
4. T. Jackson, "Keeping the Battle Alive," *Tampa Tribune,* 21 October 1993.
5. E. Eckholm, "A Little Gun Control, a Lot of Guns," *New York Times,* 15 August 1993.
6. J. Kent, *Commentaries on American Law,* 12th ed., ed. O.W. Holmes Jr. (Boston: Little, Brown & Co., 1873), p. 15.
7. J. Story, *Natural Law* (1836; reprinted in James McClellan, Joseph Story and the American Constitution (Norman: University of Oklahoma Press, 1971), pp. 314–15.
8. The cases are detailed in D.B. Kopel, "The Self-Defense Cases: How the Supreme Court Confronted a Hanging Judge in the Nineteenth Century," *American Journal of Criminal Law,* 27 (2000): 294–327, available at www.davekopel.com/2A/LawRev/SelfDefenseCases.htm.
9. Alfred Lief, ed., *The Brandeis Guide to the Modern World* (Boston: Little, Brown & Co., 1941), p. 212.
10. F. Bastiat, *The Law,* first published as a pamphlet in 1850.
11. J.R. Lott,Jr., *More Guns, Less Crime* (Chicago: University of Chicago Press, 2000), p. 51.
12. G. Kleck and D.J. Bordua, "The Factual Foundation for Certain Key Assumptions of Gun Control," *Law & Public Quarterly,* 3 (1983): 271, 284.
13. R. Waters, *The Best Defense* (Nashville: Cumberland House, 1998). Also a feature in the National Rifle Association magazines (*America's 1st Freedom, American Rifleman, American Hunter*) every month, called "The Armed Citizen," collects such stories from newspapers around the nation.

14. J.R. Snyder, "A Nation of Cowards," *The Public Interest,* no. 113 (Fall 1993): 45—55.
15. L.M. Hamm, "Déjà vu All Over Again in Case of Philandering Ex-Lawyer," Associated Press, 18 October 1996.
16. *Riss v. New York,* 240 N.E.2d 860 (N.Y. 1968).
17. *Hartzler v. City of San Jose,* 46 Cal. App. 3d 6 (1st Dist. 1975).
18. *Warren v. District of Columbia,* 444 A.2d 1, 6 (D.C. App. 1981).
19. For other cases and statutes affirming the doctrine of sovereign immunity as a bar to recovery by crime victims negligently denied government protection, see *Bowers v. DeVito* 686 F.2d 616 (7th Cir. 1982) (no federal Constitutional requirement that police provide protection); *Calogrides v. Mobile,* 475 So. 2d 560 (Ala. 1985); Cal. Govt. Code 845 (no liability for failure to provide police protection) and 846 (no liability for failure to arrest or to retain arrested person in custody); *Davidson v. Westminster,* 649 P.2d 894 (Cal. 1982); *Stone v. State,* 106 Cal. App. 3d 924 (1980); *Morgan v. District of Columbia,* 468 A.2d 1306 (D.C. App. 1983); *Sapp v. Tallahassee,* 348 So.2d 363 (Fla. Dist. Ct. 1977), cert. denied 354 So.2d 985 (Fla. 1977); Ill. Rev. Stat. 4-102; *Keane v. Chicago,* 240 N.E.2d 321 (Ill. App. Ct. 1968); *Jamison v. Chicago,* 363 N.E.2d 87 (Ill. App. Ct. 1977); *Simpson's Food Fair v. Evansville,* 272 N.E.2d 871 (Ind. App. 1971); *Silver v. Minneapolis,* 170 N.W.2d 206 (Minn. 1969); *Wuethrich v. Delia,* 382 A.2d 929, 930, (N.J. Super. 1978) cert. denied, 391 A.2d 500 (1978); *Chapman v. Philadelphia,* 434 A.2d 753 (Pa. Super. Ct. 1981); *Morris v. Musser,* 478 A.2d 937 (Pa. Commw. Ct. 1984).
20. Press release issued by Patrick Henry Center for Individual Liberty, "Patrick Henry Center and Second Amendment Sisters: 'Pro-Choice' with Women's Self-Defense," April 2002.
21. A.E. Roosevelt, *This Is My Story* (New York and London: Harper and Brothers, 1937).

CHAPTER 7

1. J. Russi, Testimony before the Michigan House of Representatives Judiciary Committee, 5 December 1995.
2. J.T. Moore, Florida Department of Law Enforcement, Memo to Governor Regarding Florida's Concealed Weapons Program, 15 March 1995.
3. H. Sterling Burnett, *American Rifleman,* August 2000, pp. 40–41, 79.
4. D. Rudge, "Karkur Bomb Attack Averted," *Jerusalem Post,* 9 March 2002.
5. A. Shadid, "As Attacks Spiral, Gun Sales Soar," *Boston Globe,* 6 April 2002.

6. M. Dudkevitch, "3 Teens Killed at Itamar Yeshiva," *Jerusalem Post,* 29 May 2002.
7. Itim + Ha'aretz Service, "Palestinian Killed After Opening Fire in W. Bank Settlement," *Ha'aretz Daily,* 12 August 2002.
8. J.R. Lott Jr., *American Rifleman,* January 1997, p. 26.
9. N. Lund, "A Primer on the Constitutional Right to Keep and Bear Arms," press release, Virginia Institute for Public Policy, 28 June 2002.

CHAPTER 8

1. J. Jacoby, "The Media's Anti-Gun Animus," *Boston Globe,* 17 January 2000. A book version of Brian Patrick's research will be published in a book titled *The National Rifle Association and the Media: The Mobilizing Effect of Negative Coverage,* by Peter Lang Publishing.
2. Media Research Center, "Outgunned: How the Network News Media Are Spinning the Gun Control Debate," 5 January 2000, available at www.mediaresearch.org/specialreports/news/sr20000105.html.
3. D. Kopel, "Stockton Shootings Disprove Case for Gun Control," *Rocky Mountain News,* 3 February 1989.
4. UPI, "Gunman's Assault Weapon Ordered Through the Mail," *Charlestown (WV) Sunday Gazette Mail,* 17 September 1989, p. 5A.
5. C.E. Cramer, "Ethical Problems of Mass Murder Coverage in the Mass Media," *Journal of Mass Media Ethics,* 9, no.1 (Winter 1993–94) 26–42. This can also be found at www.claytoncramer.com/JMME2.htm.
6. F. Fessenden, "They Threaten, Seethe and Unhinge, The Kill in Quantity," *New York Times,* 9 April 2002.
7. J. Lott Jr., "Rampage Killing Facts and Fantasies," *Washington Times,* 26 April 2000, available at www.tsra.com/Lott20.htm.
8. F. Fessenden, "They Threaten, Seethe and Unhinge, The Kill in Quantity."
9. J. Lott Jr., "Rampage Killing Facts and Fantasies."
10. F. Fessenden, "They Threaten, Seethe and Unhinge, The Kill in Quantity."
11. J. Lott Jr., "Rampage Killing Facts and Fantasies."
12. F. Butterfield, "The Mentally Ill Often Skirt a Landmark Federal Gun Control Law," *New York Times,* 11 April 2000, available at www.nytimes.com/library/national/041100rampage-killers.html.
13. J.R. Lott Jr. and W.M. Landes, "Multiple Victim Public Shootings, Bombings, and Right-to-Carry Concealed Handgun Laws: Contrasting Private and Public Law Enforcement," J.M. Olin Law

and Economics Working Paper No. 73 (2nd Series), The University of Chicago, Law School, 1999, available at http://papers.ssrn.com/sol3/delivery.cfm/99042103.pdf?abstractid=161637; J.R. Lott Jr., "Rampage Killing Facts and Fantasies."

14. J.A. Roth and C.S. Koper, "Impacts of the 1994 Assault Weapons Ban: 1994—96," NCJ 173405 (Washington: National Institute of Justice, 1999), p. 1. Available at www.ncjrs.org/pdffiles1/173405.pdf.
15. Roth and Koper, "Impacts of the 1994 Assault Weapons Ban," p. 9.
16. J. Oliphant, "A Tragedy Compounded: A Triple Murder Draws Unlikely Attention From Pro-Gun Activists and Nigerian Immigrants," *Legal Times,* 17 June 2002; see CNN and ABC news stories on this available at www.cnn.com/2002/US/01/16/law.school.shooting; abcnews.go.com/sections/us/DailyNews/lawschoolshooting020116.html;nandotimes.com/front/v-text/story/220567p-2130518c.html.
17. B.L. Smith, "Bad Guy, Good Guy . . . ," *America's First Freedom,* April 2002, pp. 28–31.
18. D. Kopel, "Dailies Shoot from Hip, Miss," *Rocky Mountain News,* 27 January 2002.

CHAPTER 9

1. Clayton E. Cramer, conversation with author, 9 March 2002.
2. Overwhelmingly positive reviews include the following: Fred Anderson, "Guns, Rights, and People," *Los Angeles Times,* 17 September 2000, Calendar; Edmund S. Morgan, "In Love with Guns," *New York Review of Books,* 19 October 2000; Paul Rosenberg, "Historian Explodes Myth: Gun Culture Firing Blanks," *Memphis Commercial Appeal,* 24 September 2000; Philip Seib, "'Arming' Takes Aim at America's Gun 'Mythology,'" *Milwaukee Journal Sentinel,* 24 September 2000; Philip Seib, "Shooting Holes in Myth of Gun-Toting Forebears," *Dallas Morning News,* 8 October 2000; Richard Slotkin, "The Fall Into Guns," *Atlantic Monthly,* November 2000, p. 114–18; Editorial, "Take Another Look at Gun Rights History," *San Francisco Chronicle,* September 25, 2000, A22; Gary Wills, "Spiking the Gun Myth," *New York Times,* 10 September 2000.
3. There was only one negative review in any of the mainstream media: John Whiteclay Chambers II, "Lock and Load," *Washington Post,* 29 October 2000, p. X2.
4. M.A. Bellesiles, *Arming America: The Origins of a National Gun Culture* (New York: Alfred A. Knopf, 2000), p. 230.

5. M.A. Bellesiles to Professor Eugene Volokh, 10 November 2000, distributed on firearmsconlawprof@listserv.ucla.edu, 13 November 2000.
6. M.A. Bellesiles, "Disarming the Critics," Organization of American Historians Newsletter, November 2001, available at www.oah.org/pubs/nl/2001nov/bellesiles.html?etmnnl04.
7. Bellesiles, *Arming America,* p. 63.
8. N.B. Shurtleft, ed., *Records of the Governor and Company of the Massachusetts Bay in New England* (5 vol., 1853–54, repr. 1968), 1: 25–26.
9. Most of the early work on this has been done by Clayton Cramer. Available at www.claytoncramer.com/ArmingAmericaLong.PDF for a very detailed examination of the problems with Arming America.
10. Bellesiles, *Arming America,* p. 73.
11. U.S. v. Emerson, 270 F.3d 203, 217, fn. 9 (5th Cir., 2001); *U.S. v. Spruill,* 61 F. Supp. 587, 590 (W.D. Tex. 1999); *State v. Hirsch,* 2001 WL 133835 (Or. App.).
12. K. Samples, "Book Aims to Debunk Gun Culture," *Cincinnati Enquirer,* 16 October 2000, available at http://enquirer.com/editions/2000/10/16/loc_samples_book_aims_to.html.
13. Clayton Cramer, conversation with author, 9 March 2002; Karen Samples, "Scholars Squabble Over Guns," *Cincinnati Enquirer,* 2 November 2000, available at http://enquirer.com/editions/2000/11/02/loc_samples_scholars.html.
14. M. Seckora, "Disarming America," *National Review,* 15 October 2001; M. Seckora, "Disarming America, Part II," National Review Online, 26 November 2001; M. Seckora, "Disarming America, Part III," National Review Online, 29 January 2002.
15. D. Skinner, "The Historian Who Couldn't Shoot Straight," *Weekly Standard,* 25 February 2002.
16. D. Mehegan, "New Doubts About Gun Historian," *Boston Globe,* 11 September 2001; D. Mehegan, "University Asks Historian to Defend His Research on Gun Ownership Book," *Boston Globe,* 3 October 2001; D. Mehegan, "Bellesiles Responds to Critics of His Book," *Boston Globe,* 13 November 2001; D. Mehegan, "Historians Criticize Author's Gun Research," *Boston Globe,* 29 January 2002; D. Mehegan, "Emory Opens Its Inquiry into Historian," *Boston Globe,* 8 February 2002.
17. R. Grossman, "Wormy Apples from the Groves of Academe," *Chicago Tribune,* 23 January 2002.
18. D. Mehegan, "New Doubts About Gun Historian."
19. R.F. Worth, "Historian's Prizewinning Book on Guns Is Embroiled in a Scandal," *New York Times,* 8 December 2001.

20. "National Briefing South: Georgia: Professor Faces Inquiry," *New York Times,* 9 February 2002.
21. D.J. Schemo, "Many on Campus Disdain Historian's Practice," *New York Times,* 15 January 2002; E. Eakin, "THINK TANK; Stop, Historians! Don't Copy That Passage! Computers Are Watching," 26 January 2002; J. Wilgoren, "School Cheating Scandal Tests a Town's Values," *New York Times,* 14 February 2002; D. Ahles, "Satire, Unlimited," *New York Times,* 3 February 2002; T. McNichol, "Can It Be Deja Vu All Over Again?" *New York Times,* 10 March 2002; M. Arnold, "History Is an Art, Not a Toaster," *New York Times,* 28 February 2002.
22. K. Ringle, "Plagiarism, or a Case of Something Less Duplicitous?" *Washington Post,* 4 February 2002, p. C1; Associated Press, "Twice-Told Tales: Goodwin Admits Improper Credits," *Washington Post,* 23 January 2002, C4; K. Ringle, "Stephen Ambrose and the Rights of Passage," *Washington Post,* 11 January 2002, p. C1; H. Italie, "New Allegations Against Historian," *Washington Post,* 10 January 2002, p. C4; Associated Press, "Accused of Plagiarism, Ambrose Admits 'Mistake,'" *Washington Post,* 8 January 2002, p. C4; Associated Press, "Historian Ambrose Accused of Plagiarism," *Washington Post,* 6 January 2002, p. A2.
23. A. Cockburn, "The Year of the Yellow Notepad," *Counterpunch,* 23 March 2002.
24. M. Korda, "Loaded Words," *Brill's Content,* February 2001.
25. Ibid.

CHAPTER 10

1. J. Somerville, "Gun Control as Immunization," *American Medical News,* 3 January 1994, p. 9.
2. A.L. Kellermann and D.T. Reay, "Protection or Peril? An Analysis of Firearm-Related Deaths in the Home," *New England Journal of Medicine,* 314, no. 24 (12 June 1986): 1557–60.
3. L. Adelson, "The Gun and the Sanctity of Human Life; or the Bullet as Pathogen," *Archives of Surgery,* 127 (June 1992): 659–64.
4. D. Prothrow-Stith with M. Weissman, *Deadly Consequences: How Violence Is Destroying Our Teenage Population and a Plan to Begin Solving the Problem* (New York: HarperCollins, July 1991).
5. P.W. O'Carroll, Acting Section Head of Division of Injury Control, CDC. Quoted in M.F. Goldsmith, "Epidemiologists Aim at New Target: Health Risk of Handgun Proliferation," *Journal of the American Medical Association* (1989), pp. 675–76.

6. J. Mercy et al., "Public Health Policy for Preventing Violence," *Health Affairs* 12 (1993): 7–29.
7. M.L. Rosenberg, P.W. O'Carroll, and K.E. Powell, "Let's Be Clear: Violence Is a Public Health Problem," *Journal of the American Medical Association,* 267 (1992): 3071–72.
8. Centers for Disease Control and Prevention, Injury Prevention Network Newsletter (Spring 1995), p. 14.
9. D. Satcher, "Gunning for Research; In the NRA Attack on Firearms Studies, Scientific Truth Is the Most Important Casualty," *Washington Post,* 5 November 1995, p. C2.
10. Editorial, "NRA Firing Blanks at CDC," *Atlanta Journal,* 4 June 1995, p. 6B.
11. Departments of Labor, Health and Human Services, and Education, and Related Agencies Appropriation Bill, 1997 [to accompany H.R. 3855], 104th Cong., 2nd Sess. (8 July 1996).
12. G. Kleck and M. Gertz, "Armed Resistance to Crime: The Prevalence and Nature of Self-Defense with a Gun," Northwestern University School of Law, *Journal of Criminal Law & Criminology,* 86, issue 1 (1995).
13. J.R. Lott Jr. and D. B. Mustard, "Crime, Deterrence, and Right-to-Carry Concealed Handguns," *Journal of Legal Studies* (January 1997), p. 16.
14. J. Kassirer, "Effects of Restrictive Handgun Laws," *New England Journal of Medicine,* 326, no. 17 (23 April 1992): 1097–65.
15. W.J. Guglielmo, "How Many Doctors Own Guns?" *Medical Economics,* 9 October 2000, available at www.memag.com.
16. American Academy of Pediatrics, "Suicide and Suicide Attempts in Adolescents (RE9928)," *Pediatrics 105,* no. 4 (April 2000): 871–74.
17. American College of Physicians, Position Paper, "Firearm Injury Prevention," *Annals of Internal Medicine,* 128 (1 February 1998): 236–41.
18. American College of Surgeons, "[ST-12] Statement on Firearm Injuries," *Bulletin of the American College of Surgeons,* 85, no. 4 (April 2000): 24.
19. American Medical Association, *Physician Firearm Safety Guide* (Chicago: American Medical Association, 1998).
20. Doctors Against Handgun Injury Web site, main page, "news & resources," available at www.doctorsagainsthandguninjury.org.
21. J. Benson, "Medical Marchers Ask: Should Guns Be Part of Patient Profile?" *New York Observer,* 19 March 2001, p. 1.
22. J. Barondness, editorial, "Handguns and Assault Weapons in the

Hands of the Civilian Population Serve Little Purpose," *Journal of the American Medical Association,* 24 April 1994.

23. D.B. Kates, "Guns and Public Health: Epidemic of Violence or Pandemic of Propaganda?" *Tennessee Law Review,* 62, no. 3 (1995).
24. T.W. Wheeler, "The AMA's Epidemic of Deceit," posted on Doctors for Responsible Gun Ownership Web site, available at www.claremont.org/projects/doctors/010628wheeler.html, 28 June 2001.
25. American College of Physicians, "Internists' and Surgeons' Attitude toward Guns and Firearm Injury Prevention," *Annals of Internal Medicine,* 128 (1 February 1998): 224–30.
26. Inaugural speech of Richard F. Corlin, MD, AMA president, 19 June 2001, available at www.ama-assn.org/ama/pub/article/2542-4940.html.
27. American Academy of Pediatrics, web-posted Hot Topics brief, "Preventing Firearm Injury: Protecting Our Children," 2001, available at www.aap.org/mrt/firearms.htm.

CHAPTER 11

1. Associated Press Newswires, "Alleged Anonymous Activists Claim Restaurant Arson," 12 September 2001.
2. Statement of James F. Jarboe, FBI Domestic Terrorism Section Chief, Counterterrorism Division, before the U.S. House Resources Committee Subcommittee on Forests and Forest Health, 107th Cong., 2nd Sess. (12 February 2002).
3. Rush Limbaugh's concepts are further discussed in *The Way Things Ought to Be* (New York: Pocket Star Books 1993), pp. 102–6.
4. The Associated Press, 17 May 2002, Friday, BC cycle.
5. "Germany Adds Animal Rights to Constitution," *Miami Herald,* 18 May 2002.
6. League Against Cruel Sports, at ø.league.uk.com.
7. "31st July 2002 Scottish Hunt Ban Adds to Pressure on Government," League Against Cruel Sports, available at www.league.uk.com.
8. Americans for Medical Progress Educational Foundation, "Inside the Humane Society of the United States," 1996.
9. Valerie Richardson details national and international ecoterror in her article "Law Catches Up to Ecoterror," *Washington Times,* 24 March 2002, p. A1.
10. Ibid.
11. Animal Liberation Front, "The ALF Primer: A Guide to Direct

Action and the Animal Liberation Front," 3rd (1998), available at www.animalliberationfront.com/ALFront/ALFPrime.htm.

12. WildAid, available at www.wildaid.org/resources/pdf_files/WildAidPressKitEdited.pdf.
13. Environmental Investigation Agency, available at www.eia-international.org.
14. WildAid, available at www.wildaid.org, see "Methodologies" link; EIA press release, "Environmental Investigative Agency Receives United Nations Environmental Award," 5 June 2001; see also WhaleNet Web site hosted by Wheelock University at www.whale.wheelock.com, which details the activities by EIA, Greenpeace, and IFAW to halt international whaling activities.
15. "Use of Animals in Biomedical Research: The Challenge and Response" (Chicago: American Medical Association White Paper, March 1988).
16. PETA Action Alert, "Documents Reveal Death and Suffering at HLS (U.K.), undated (from PETA's Web site at www.peta.org).
17. ALF, ELF, and PETA tactics detailed in numerous newspaper articles, including E. Journo, "Homegrown Terrorism," editorial produced by the Ayn Rand Institute's MediaLink department at www.aynrand.org/medialink, 16 April 2002; also D. Martosko, "Animal-Rights Fanatics: Dr. Doolittle Gone Bad," guest editorial in the *Seattle Times,* 15 July 2002; "Why Are We Disregarding the Growing Danger of Eco-terrorists?" *Tulsa World,* 21 April 2002.
18. D.R. Sands, "Animal Activist Held in Fortuyn's Killing," *Washington Times,* 8 May 2002.
19. D.G. McNeil Jr., "Not Only in America: Gun Killings Shake the Europeans," *New York Times,* 11 May 2002.
20. P. Wilson, "The Assassin Who Loved Animals," *Weekend Australian,* 11 May 2002.
21. S. G. Stolberg, "Debate Over Whether to Defend Animal Tests," *New York Times,* 23 July 2002, p. 1.
22. Ibid.
23. Ibid.
24. Ibid.
25. S.C. Friedman, "The PETA-ELF Connection," *New York Post,* 7 March 2002.
26. E. Leiberman, "Animal Magnetism; a PETA Party Attracts Pamela Anderson Lee and VIPs," *In Style,* November 1999.
27. B. Sizemore, "Zeal and Guts: PETA Has Made Itself the Most Effective, Most Recognized Animal-Rights Group. When It Comes

to People, Though, Some Disenchanted Members Say, 'They're Brutal,'" *Gazette* (Montreal), 7 January 2001.

28. G. White, "Confronting Animal Rights Activism; Cosmetics: Advocates Have Racked Up Major Victories Against Industry Giants," *Los Angeles Times,* 3 December 1989.
29. A. Hudson, "A Smear Campaign Against Milk?" *Washington Times,* 4 February 2002.
30. S.C. Friedman, "The PETA-ELF Connection," *New York Post,* 7 March 2002.
31. R. Hartzler, "Rights of Fish Now Supercede Rights of People," *University Wire,* 24 July 2001.
32. "Beef Sales Strong Despite Panic in Europe," *Northwest Arkansas Business Journal,* 30 April 2001.
33. B. Wilson, "Experts Wary of Terrorist Plot to Spread FMD," *Western Producer,* 12 April 2001, available at www.producer.com/articles/20010412/news/20010412news07.html.
34. Wayne Pacelle currently serves as senior vice president of the Humane Society, according to a HSUS press release, "Animal Cruelty Initiative Cleared for Ballot," 5 August 2002.
35. Americans for Medical Progress Educational Foundation, "Inside the Humane Society of the United States," 1996.
36. D.T. Oliver, "The Humane Society of the U.S.: It's Not About Animal Shelters," *Alternatives in Philanthropy,* October 1997.
37. P. Carlson, "The Great Silver Spring Monkey Debate," *Washington Post,* 24 February 1991.
38. T. Platt, "Careers in the Conflict Industry: HSUS and the Making of a Conflict Industrialist," Fur Commission USA Commentary, 12 August 2001.
39. Southern Poverty Law Center, "From Push to Shove," Intelligence Report, Fall 2002.

CHAPTER 12

1. *Morial v. Smith & Wesson et al.,* No. 98-18578 (New Orleans Parish Ct).
2. *Chicago v. Beretta U.S.A. Corp. et al.,* No. 98-CH-015596 (Cook County Circuit Court, Chancery Div.).
3. The suit by Bridgeport, Connecticut, added a claim that gun manufacturers have violated federally protected civil rights because shootings take place in "predominantly minority neighborhoods." Eighty percent of homicide victims in Bridgeport are in fact members of "minority groups." Bridgeport does not mention that 90 percent of homicide defendants are also minority group members.

4. Quoted in U.S. Senate Republican Policy Committee, press release, 24 January 2000.
5. For other cases, see, e.g., *Perkins v. F.I.E.Corp.*, 762 F.2d 1250 (5th Cir. 1985); *Burkett v. Freedom Arms, Inc.*, 704 P.2d 118 (Oreg. 1985); *Rhodes v. R.G. Industries,* 325 S.E. 2d 469 (Ga. 1985); *Moore v. R.G. Industries,* 789 F.2d 1326 (9th Cir. 1986); *Martin v. Harrington and Richardson,* 11 743 F.2d 1200 (7th Cir. 1984).
6. *Forni v. Ferguson,* No. 132994/94, Slip. Op. (N.Y. Sup.Ct., New York County, 2 August 1995), aff'd 232 A.2d 176, 648 N.Y.S.2d 73 (1st Dept 1996).
7. *Delahanty v. Hinkley,* 564 A. 2d 758 (D.C. Ct. App. 1989).
8. 935 F.Supp. 1307 (E.D.N.Y. 1996).
9. Law-abiding Chicagoans may buy handguns in Illinois since they are residents of that state. But Chicago has outlawed possession of handguns not registered before a certain date, so Chicagoans cannot legally bring lawfully purchased weapons back into their city.
10. F. Butterfield, "Suit Against Gun Makers Gains Ground in Illinois," *New York Times,* 3 January 2002.
11. M.D. Shear and B.A. Masters, "2 Counties: A Dangerous Difference; While Montgomery's Crime Rate has Risen, Fairfax's Is Down," *Washington Post,* 6 April 1998.
12. W. Olson, "Big Guns," *Reason,* 1 October 1999.
13. R.A. Levy, "Pistol Whipped: Baseless Lawsuits, Foolish Laws," Cato Institute Policy Analysis No. 400, 9 May 2002.
14. The San Francisco suit alleges that some guns used in San Francisco crimes were purchased in Nevada and Arizona, which are oversupplied because they have "weak gun-control laws." In essence, the San Francisco attorney is asking that corporations be held liable because they abided by other states' valid legislation.
15. In an interesting parallel situation, health care companies have been settling what they consider to be typically bogus Medicare suits, because of the potential for bankruptcy (or its equivalent, exclusion from the Medicare program) if they are found liable. The Secretary of Health and Human Services and the Department of Justice recently issued guidelines limiting False Claims Act suits, because of industry claims that they were brought merely to coerce settlements. See, e.g., Peter Aronson, "Health Law Boom: DOJ's Fraud Crusade Has Boosted Health Care Lawyer Numbers," *National Law Journal,* 17 May 1999, A1.

CHAPTER 13

1. *Los Angeles Times* editorial, "Gun Makers in a Vise," 9 December 1999.
2. S. Skolnik, "DOJ Reined in Cuomo on Gun Litigation," *Legal Times,* 13 December 1999.
3. I. Welfeld, "Policies or Programs; Legislative Origins of PHA Problems," *Journal of Housing,* July/August 1985, p. 140.
4. M. Norman, "Newark Ponders Plight of Its Housing Projects," *New York Times,* 22 September 1982.
5. U.S. Department of Housing and Urban Development, Crime in Public Housing: A Review of Major Issues and Selected Crime Reduction Strategies, Volume 1 (Washington, D.C.: Government Printing Office, 1979) p. i.
6. Ibid.
7. M. Plotkin, "Cracking the D.C. Crime Nut," *Legal Times,* 13 January 1992.
8. J. Reh, "The Smith & Wesson Settlement and the 'Code of Conduct'—Why We Have Not Signed," NRA-ILA Research & Information, 5 September 2000.
9. E. Lichtblau and R. Alonso-Zaldivar, "Smith & Wesson Agrees to Key Safety Reforms," *Los Angeles Times,* 18 March 2000.
10. "Press Conference with Secretary Andrew Cuomo, Department of Housing and Urban Development, Senator Charles Schumer (D-NY), Representative Carolyn McCarthy (D-NY) and others; Subject: Gun Agreement with Smith & Wesson," Federal News Service, 22 March 2000.
11. "Agreement Between Smith & Wesson and the Departments of the Treasury and Housing and Urban Development, Local Governments and States; Summary of Terms," HUD, U.S. Dept. of Housing & Development, 17 March 2000.
12. W. Kip Viscusi, "The Lulling Effect: The Impact of Child-Resistant Packaging on Aspiring and Analgesic Injections," AEA Papers and Proceedings, vol. 74, no. 2.
13. J. Reh, "The Smith & Wesson Settlement and the 'Code of Conduct.'"
14. Press release, U.S. Senate Republican Policy Committee, 24 January 2000.
15. J.J. Goldman, "N.Y. Takes Aim at Gun Makers with Public Nuisance Lawsuit," *Los Angeles Times,* 27 June 2000.
16. Ibid.

17. Ibid.
18. J.R. Labbe, "Uncle Sam Blackmailed Smith & Wesson," *Dayton Daily News,* 30 March 2000.
19. Press release, "Statement of Sturm, Ruger & Co., Inc. Regarding New York Attorney General's Lawsuit," Southport, Conn., 26 June 2000.
20. Press release, The National Shooting Sports Foundation, 26 June 2000.
21. Press release, "New York State Suit Against Sturm, Ruger Dismissed," Sturm, Ruger & Company, Inc., 15 August 2001.

CHAPTER 14

1. J. Brazil and S. Berry, "Australia's Answer to Carnage: A Strict Law," *Los Angeles Times,* 27 August 1997, p. A1.
2. The Australian Firearms Buyback, in the archive of the 1997–1998 federal government web site, available at www.gun.law.gov.au/Guns/intromain.htm.
3. C. Sutton, H. Gilmore, and Simon Kent, "He Could Have Been Stopped: Bungling Let the World's Worst Killer Go Free," *Sydney (Australia) Sun-Herald,* 5 May 1996, p. 1.
4. Tasmania Frequently Asked Questions, Tasmanian History, The Port Arthur Massacre, available at www.tased.edu.au/tasfaq/history/portarthur.html.
5. Gun Control Australia, "A Beginners Guide to Australian Gun Laws," 15 April 2000 available at www.guncontrol.org.au/ top5.html.
6. The Great Australian Gun Law Con, What's the Hurry? available at http://members.ozemail.com.au/_/~confiles/hurry.html.
7. National Coalition for Gun Control, available at http://health.su.oz.au/cgc/index.html
8. Dr. James B. Lawson, New National Gun Laws—Are They Cost Effective? Institute of Public Affairs, "Review," vol. 51, no. 4, December 1999.
9. J. Brazil and S. Berry, "Australia's Answer to Carnage: A Strict Law."
10. CNN, "Australian gunman Laughs as He Admits Killing 35," November 7, 1996, available at http://asia.cnn.com/WORLD/9611/07/australia/
11. S. Horsburgh, "A Disarming Conclusion," *Time South Pacific,* 150, no. 10, (September 1997): 8.
12. G. Chan and D. Shanahan, "Howard Praises Minister's Decision," *Weekend Australian,* 11 May 1996, p. 1.
13. K. Sullivan, "Turning Against Guns in Wake of Slaughter: Australia's New Laws," *Washington Post,* 7 November 1997.

14. R. A. Wilmoth, "The Great Australian Gun Law Con," available at http://members.ozemail.com.au/~confiles/quotes.html.
15. V. Joshi, "Australians Demolish Guns to Prevent Another Massacre," *Fort Worth Star Telegram,* 25 May 1997.
16. Reuters News, Canberra, "Australia PM Pledges Tougher Handgun Controls," 17 April 2002.
17. Gun Control Australia Web site document "The Task Ahead," found under the "Who Are We?" link available at www.guncontrol.org.au/.
18. Australian Associated Press, "Call to Clamp Down on Handgun Ownership on the Rise," 18 October 2001.
19. S. Lee and R. Peters, "Handguns, Deadly Loophole in Control," *Newcastle Herald* (Australia), 30 April 2001, p. 9.
20. J. Mozingo, "The Reality of Weapons Buybacks," *Los Angeles Times* (Home Edition), 13 August 1999, p. A—27.
21. P. Mickelburough, "UP IN ARMS, Victoria's Gun Arsenal Grows: Shooters Win Back Support," *Herald-Sun,* Victoria, 2 July 2002.
22. "Firearms Seizure Prompts Warning," 14 August 2002, available at www.news.com.au.

CHAPTER 15

1. J.N. Kesteren, P. Mayhew, and P. Nieuwbeerta, Criminal Victimisation in Seventeen Industrialised Countries: Key Findings from the 2000 International Crime, Victims Survey, the Hague, Ministry of Justice, WODC, Onderzoek en beleid, nr. 187 (2000), available at www.unicri.it/icvs/publications/index_pub.htm.
2. A. Travis, "England and Wales Top Crime League," *Guardian,* 23 February 2001.
3. B. Brady and S. Fraser, "Prompted by the Shootings in Germany, Tony Blair Orders Crackdown on Convertible Airguns," *Scotsman on Sunday,* 28 April 2002.
4. The Home Office (United Kingdom), "The Firearms Compensation Scheme," available at www.homeoffice-gov.uk/ppd/oppu/compsch.htm, June 1997.
5. The Home Office (United Kingdom) press release, "Government Keeps Its Promise As Handgun Surrender Is Completed," 27 February 1998.
6. Ibid.
7. J. Steele, "Police Fear Crime Explosion as School-age Muggers Graduate to Guns," *Daily Telegraph* (London), 3 January 2002.
8. J. Davenport, "Massive Rise in Gun Murders," *Evening Standard* (London), 19 December 2001, p. 2.

9. J.N. Kesteren, P. Mayhew, and P. Nieuwbeerta, Criminal Victimisation in Seventeen Industrialised Countries. www.unicri.it/icvs/publications/index_pub.htm.
10. Criminal Justice System Web site, Justice For All, CJS White Paper, CJS online July 2002, available at www.cjsonline.org/library/pdf/CJS_whitepaper.pdf.
11. Gun Control Network, "He Who Pays the Piper Calls the Tune," Illegal Firearms in the UK, press release, 14 July 2001.
12. D. Sapsted, "Shot Buy Raider Had Appeared in Court 18 Times," electronic Telegraph (Telegraph Group Limited), 12 April 2000, available at www.telegraph.co.uk.
13. S. Wright, "Burglar's Legal Aid to Sue Tony Martin," *London Daily Mail,* 6 July 2002.
14. G. Kleck, *Targeting Guns* (New York: Aldine de Gruyter, 1991), p. 187.

CHAPTER 16

1. S.P. Halbrook, *Target Switzerland: Swiss Armed Neutrality in World War II* (Rockville Centre, NY: Sarpedon, 1998), p. 56.
2. "Firearm Form 101: Application for a Firearm Certificate," FIR101 (9/98), Thames Valley Police.
3. S. Goodchild, "Britain Is Now the Crime Capital of the West," London, *Independent,* 14 July 2002,
4. Canadian Firearms Centre, "History of Firearms Control in Canada," 23 December 1998, available at www.cfcccaf.gc.ca/en/historical/firearms/firearms_control.asp.
5. D.B. Kates Jr., *Restricting Handguns: The Liberal Skeptics Speak Out* (Croton-on-Hudson, N.Y.: North River Press, 1979).
6. Ibid.
7. J. Weller, "The Sullivan Act," *American Rifleman,* April 1962, p. 33–36.
8. J.V. Lindsay, "The Case for Federal Firearms Control," (pamphlet published by N.Y. City), (Also reprinted in Firearms Legislation Hearings Before the Subcommittee to Investigate Juvenile Delinquency of the Senate Committee on the Judiciary, 94th Congress, 1st Session, v.II) November 1973.

CHAPTER 17

1. G. Kleck, *Targeting Guns: Firearms and Their Control* (New York: Aldine de Gruyter, 1997), p. 94.
2. Sen. Zell Miller, press release, "Miller Legislation Calls for Objective Study of 'Ballistic Fingerprinting,'" 21 October 2002.

3. David Kopel and Paul H. Blackman, "Not So Fast," *National Review,* 23 October 2002 available at http: www.nationalreview.com.
4. Robert E. Andrews, Dear Colleague Letter, "Law Enforcement Officials Need a Database of Gun Ballistics," 15 October 2002
5. Kopel and Blackman, ibid.
6. Frederic A. Tullemers, "Technical Evaluation: Feasibility of a Ballistic Imaging Database for All New Handgun Sales."
7. Dr. Jan De Kinder, "Ballistic Fingerprinting Databases," Nationaal Intituut voor Criminalistiek en Criminologie, Department of Justice, Brussels.
8. Grand Lodge Fraternal Order of Police, "F.O.P. Viewpoint: Ballistics Imaging and Comparison Technology," October 2002
9. John R. Lott, Jr., "Bullets and Bunkum," *National Review,* 11 November 2002, p. 28

CHAPTER 18

1. P.K. Howard, "An Overview of a Few Well-known National Children's Gun Safety Programs and ENA's Newly Developed Program," *Journal of Emergency Nursing,* 27, no. 5 (1 October 2001); 0485–88.
2. P.C. Roberts, "Guns and Violence," *Washington Times,* 29 July 2002, p. A14.
3. Violence Policy Center, "Eddie Eagle Grants Made by the NRA Foundation, 1994 and 1995," 1998, available at www.vpc.org/fact_sht/eddiests.htm.
4. National Center for Injury and Prevention Control, "1999 United States Unintentional Firearm Deaths, All Races, Both Sexes, Ages 0 to 14," available at http://webapp.cdc.gov/sasweb/ncipc/mortrate10.html.
5. National Center for Injury and Prevention Control, "1999 United States Unintentional Drowning Deaths, All Races, Both Sexes, Ages 0 to 5," available at http://webapp.cdc.gov/sasweb/ncipc/mortrate10.html.
6. Senate Judiciary Committee, "U.S. Senate Holds Fourth Day of Confirmation Hearing for Attorney General-Designee John Ashcroft," FDCH Political Transcripts, 19 January 2001.
7. In 1999, according to the Centers for Disease Control, there were 3,385 firearms deaths of persons under age 20—or 9.3 per day. Eighty-six percent were persons ages 15–19. Fifty-nine percent were homicides; most of the rest were suicides. Centers for Disease Control, "Table 17. Number of Deaths From Injury By Firearms By

Age, Race, and Sex: United States, 1999," National Vital Statistics Report, vol. 49, no. 8, 21 September 2001.

8. Ibid.
9. J.F. Sheley, Z.T. McGee, and J.D. Wright, "Gun-related Violence in and Around Inner City Schools," *American Journal of Diseases of Children,* 1991, vol. 146, pp. 677—82. See also J.L. Lauritsen, R.J. Sampson, and J.H. Loub, "The Link Between Offending and Victimization Among Adolescents," Criminology, 29 (1991); 265–92.
10. "Around the Nation," Law Enforcement News, 31 October 1994.
11. H.R. Hudson et al., "Adolescents and Children Injured or Killed in Drive-By Shootings in Los Angeles," *New England Journal of Medicine,* 330 (3 February 1994): 324–27.
12. S.I. Singer, "Victims at a Birth Cohort," in *From Boy to Man, From Delinquency to Crime,* ed. Marvin E. Wolfgang et al. (Chicago: University of Chicago Press 1987), pp. 169, 171–79.
13. A. Morales, "A Clinical Model for the Prevention of Gang Violence and Homicide," in *Substance Abuse and Gang Violence,* ed. P.C. Cervantes (Newbury Park, Calif.; Sage Publications, 1992), p. 173.
14. S.H. Decker and B. Van Winkle, *Life in the Gang: Family, Friends, and Violence* (Cambridge, England; New York: Cambridge University Press 1996), p. 173.
15. D.M Kennedy and A.A. Braga, "Homicide in Minneapolis: Research for Problem Solving," Homicide Studies, 2, no. 3 (August 1998): 282–83.
16. A.B. Loper and D.G. Cornell, "Homicide by Juvenile Girls," *Journal of Child & Family Studies,* 5 (1996): 323–36.
17. D. Dahl, "NRA Too Strong? So Was Big Tobacco," Join Together Online, 15 March 2002, available at www.jointogether.org/gv/news/features/reader/0,2061,549149,00.html.
18. Thomas Jefferson's First Inaugural Address, 4 March 1801, available at www.yale.edu/lawweb/avalon/presiden/inaug/jefinau1.htm.
19. D. Kopel, P. Gallant, J. Eisen of the Independence Institute, "Zero Good Sense," *National Review,* 6 June 2001.
20. R.J. Skiba, Zero Tolerance, Zero Evidence (Indiana Education Policy Center, August 2000), available at www.indiana.edu/%7Esafeschl/ztze.pdf. An excellent source of information about "zero tolerance" incidents is Walter Olson's "Overlawyered" Web site, available at www.overlawyered.org/topics/guns.html.
21. "Boy Suspended for Pointing Chicken Finger," Associated Press, 31 January 2001.

22. "Student Suspected for Drawing a Picture," Associated Press, 24 March 2001.
23. Ibid.
24. "Third-Grader Suspended for Bringing Gun-Shaped Medallion to School," Associated Press, 12 January 2001.
25. C. Santos, "NRA T-shirt Incident Produces Lawsuit," *Richmond Times-Dispatch,* 18 September, 2002.
26. R.J. Skiba, Zero Tolerance, Zero Evidence.
27. F. Morgan, "Deadly Consequences," *Salon,* 9 March 2001 available at www.salon.com/news/feature/2001/03/09/shooting/index.html.
28. A.C. Allen, "Brooklyn High School Readmits Boy with 'Dangerous' Ruler," *New York Post,* 12 January 2001.
29. "York Officials Want More Say in What a 'Dangerous Object' Is in School," Associated Press, 21 January 2000.
30. "New Zealand School Tightens Rules on Toy Guns," AP Worldstream, 4 September 2000.
31. "Children's Game Nothing to Kid About; Kindergarten Students Suspended for Playing 'Cops and Robbers,'" *Atlanta Journal-Constitution,* 6 April 2000.
32. Jennifer Harper, "Robbers Suspended from N.J. School; 'Cops' Too," *Washington Times,* 7 April 2000.

CHAPTER 19

1. R.T. Nelson, "Politicos Use Polls at Every Step Now—Results Have Played a Major Role Already in 2000 Campaigns," *Seattle Times,* 23 May 1999.
2. Report of Governor Bill Owens' Columbine Review Commission, May 2001, p. 12.
3. Testimony of Darrell Scott before the U.S. House of Representatives Judiciary Committee's Subcommittee on Crime, 27 May 1999.
4. M. Sager, "Schools Safety Talks' Target," *Tampa Tribune,* 10 August 2002.
5. B. Fox, "Teen Pleads Guilty to Santee Shooting," *Contra Costa Times,* 21 June 2002.
6. J.R. Lott Jr., "The Missing Gun," *New York Post,* 25 January 2002.
7. *The Jefferson Cyclopedia,* vol. 1 (1900; reprint, John Foley, ed., New York: Atheneum House Inc., 1967), p. 318.
8. Discussion of various results of the study, and of related topics, can be found in A.J. Lizotte, M.D. Krohn, J.C. Howell, K. Tobin, and G.J. Howard, "Factors Influencing Gun Carrying Among Urban Males over the Adolescent-Young Adult Life Course," *Criminology,* 38

(2000): 811–34; A.J. Lizotte, G.J. Howard, M.D. Krohn, and T.P. Thornberry, "Patterns of Carrying Firearms Among Juveniles," *Valparaiso Univ. Law Review,* 31 (1997): 375–93; B. Bjerregaard and A.J. Lizotte, "Gun Ownership and Gang Membership," *Journal of Criminal Law & Criminology,* 86 (1995): 37–58; A.J. Lizotte, J.M. Tesoriero, T.P. Thornberry, and M.D. Krohn, "Patterns of Adolescent Firearms Ownership and Use," *Justice Quarterly,* 11 (1994): 51–74.

9. B. Owens, "A Year After Columbine: How Do We Heal a Wounded Culture?" The Heritage Foundation, Heritage Lectures no. 662, 24 April 2000, p. 6.

CHAPTER 20

1. R.D. Novak, "The Great GOP Gun Rout," *New York Post,* 24 May 1999.
2. S.F. Hayes, "Hostile Learning Environment," *Washington Times,* 12 April 2002, available at www.washingtontimes.com/op-ed/20020412-2457844.htm.
3. N. Carter, "Linking of 'Basketball Diaries,' Columbine Shootings Upsets Author," *Milwaukee Journal-Sentinel,* 6 May 1999, available at www.jsonline.com/Enter/gen/may99/0506jim.asp.
4. J.R. Lott, Jr., "Small Arms Save Lives," *Wall Street Journal,* 30 July 2001, available at www.frontpagemag.com/guestcolumnists/lott073101.htm.
5. "Spielberg Removes Guns from ET," International Action Network on Small Arms newsletter, 10 January 2002, available at www.iansa.org/news/2002/Jan2002/spielberg_et01202.htm; "Alien resurrection," *Sydney Morning-Herald,* 5 March 2002, available at http://old.smh.com.au/news/0203/05/text/entertain3.html.
6. S. Hunter, "Strafing 'Private Ryan,'" *Washington Post,* 9 August 1998, p. G1.
7. L.B. Bozell III, "Hollywood's Holiday Fireworks: All Duds," *Creator's Syndicate,* 30 June 1998.
8. "Stallone's Miami Mansion Sold for $16.2 million," *South Florida Business Journal,* 23 December 1999, available at http://southflorida.bizjournals.com/southflorida/stories/1999/12/20/daily16.html.
9. A. Saxe, "Opinions," 23 August 2001, available at www.abc-texas.com/saxe08232001.html.

INDEX